North Shields.
WARD.
L. D. S.

The Family Records Centre

A User's Guide

The Family Records Centre

A User's Guide

Stella Colwell

CLOSED – 15 March 2008.

PUBLIC RECORD OFFICE

Public Record Office Readers' Guide No. 17

First published in 1997 as *Never Been Here Before?*
by Jane Cox and Stella Colwell

Second edition published in 2002 by

Public Record Office
Kew
Richmond
Surrey
TW9 4DU

www.pro.gov.uk

NORTH TYNESIDE LIBRARIES

011990877

Cypher	26.04.02
929.3	£7.99
CEN	S.H

Withdrawn

First edition © Crown Copyright 1997
Second edition © Stella Colwell 2002

ISBN 1 903365 36 8

The right of Stella Colwell to be identified as the Author of this Work has been asserted by her in accordance with the Copyright, Designs and Patents Act 1988

A catalogue record for this book is available from the British Library

Photograph credits

Front cover: Exterior of the Family Records Centre (photograph © Hugh Alexander 2002). Several generations of the Mackereth family pose for a golden wedding photo at Cornhow, Cockermouth, in Cumberland; photograph by Faith Bell, registered by her for copyright on 23 August 1902 (COPY 1/456).

Back cover: Census return for 45 Grosvenor Place, Westminster, 1881 (RG 11/98). Grant of letters of administration for the personal estate of John Constable, 1 June 1837 (PROB 6/213).

Pages 14 and 16: Photographs of the ground floor of the FRC © Hugh Alexander 2002

Printed in the United Kingdom by Antony Rowe, Chippenham, Wiltshire

Contents

Illustrations

About this book

This guide is intended to provide an informal introduction to the Family Records Centre (FRC), in Myddelton Street, London. Run jointly by the General Register Office (GRO) – which is part of the Office for National Statistics – and the Public Record Office (PRO), the FRC brings together under one roof some of the key sources and indexes used by family historians. Illustrated with examples of many of these documents, this book offers you detailed practical advice on how to find them, what they contain, and how the system works in both parts of the Centre. It explains how to begin your research, and suggests some research strategies. The two case studies lead you step by step through the most popular sources, to the stage where you are able to set out your evidence in a pictorial way.

The PRO's *Pocket Guides to Family History* series will introduce you to the wealth of genealogical sources housed in the Public Record Office, Kew. For a more in-depth survey, read the new edition of *Tracing Your Ancestors in the Public Record Office* by Amanda Bevan.

Acknowledgements

The author would like to thank the staff of the Family Records Centre for their help, in particular Pauline Mason, Laura Urwin and Mike Saunders of the GRO and Dave Annal, Steve Cable, John Crawford, Keith Mitchell, Lee Oliver and Mona Singh of the PRO. Thanks also to Amanda Bevan, Margaret Brennand, Suzanne Carroll, Chris Durban, Steve Hirschorn, Karen Horn, David Thomas, David Priest and his team, and others at the PRO, Kew; to John Mackay of the General Register Office for Scotland; to Peter Leek for editing the book and preparing it for press; to Hugh Alexander, Brian Carter and Lee Oliver for their photography; to John Cox for reading the proofs; to Lisa Kenwright of Indexing Specialists for compiling the index; to Deborah Pownall for suggesting the golden-wedding group for the front cover; and to Norah Conrad for permission to use her family tree.

The birth, marriage and death certificates featured in this book were provided by the Certificate Services Section and Overseas Section of the General Register Office, Office for National Statistics, whose help has been greatly appreciated. The design of the certificates is Crown Copyright, and is reproduced with the permission of the Controller of HMSO. The marriage register entry reproduced on p. 148 is included by courtesy of the London Metropolitan Archives and the Rector and Churchwardens of Christ Church, Chelsea.

Preface

'The FRC is great! We loved every minute we spent here . . . I think the FRC is the best thing since sliced bread.' – from a 'Your views matter to us' form

When the previous edition of this book appeared in 1997, under the title *Never Been Here Before?*, less than 100,000 people had passed through the doors of the Family Records Centre. It had opened in March of that year as a pioneering example of joined-up government, bringing together the resources of the Public Record Office and the Office for National Statistics. Now the figure is fast approaching a million visitors, many of whom return again and again to take advantage of its growing range of services, designed to facilitate the study of family, social, local and other branches of history.

Looking back, we frequent users often forget that there wasn't a single computer to be seen in the public search areas, equipment we take for granted today. Now there is an internet café, 16 networked servers offer a choice of various online databases, 48 PC terminals grant access to the digitized images of the 1901 census returns for England and Wales, with the promise of more census years to come, and there are automated indexes to Scottish and Northern Irish vital records. Who can say what direction the Centre's services will next take, because technological innovations are occurring at breakneck speed? Users have embraced this revolutionary way of searching with enthusiasm, as a means of getting results easily and quickly.

There still remain earlier census returns and other popular genealogical sources to trawl through on microfilm and microfiche, many of which can also be examined at the Public Record Office, Kew. What the FRC increasingly offers, though, is a one-stop shop for family historians, where you will be in the company of like-minded people from all over the world, who have come to trace their roots, aided by the expertise and guidance of the staff.

In 1997, at the FRC, you still couldn't search the deposited non-parochial registers for England and Wales on microfilm, nor the five important series of miscellaneous overseas non-statutory returns lodged with the Registrar General running up to 1965, or the indexes to English and Welsh divorces between 1858 and 1958, or the National Probate Indexes from 1858 until 1943. For each of these (except the last, which relate to records held elsewhere) you would have had to go to the PRO. Now, you can access computerized indexes to Northern Irish births, too; and a string of online Family History Databases have even replaced the packs of CD-ROMs many of us were once familiar with.

The FRC is rightly recognized as a Centre of Excellence for family history services, but it doesn't rest on its laurels. Nor does it stand still. It is an evolving entity, so be prepared for lots of new treasures, as additional resources are being introduced all the time.

I hope you will find this updated guide a useful introduction to the core materials for your research, and be bold enough to explore some of the new items that will no doubt have arrived even since the publication of this edition.

Happy hunting!

Stella Colwell
February 2002

Where to find the Family Records Centre

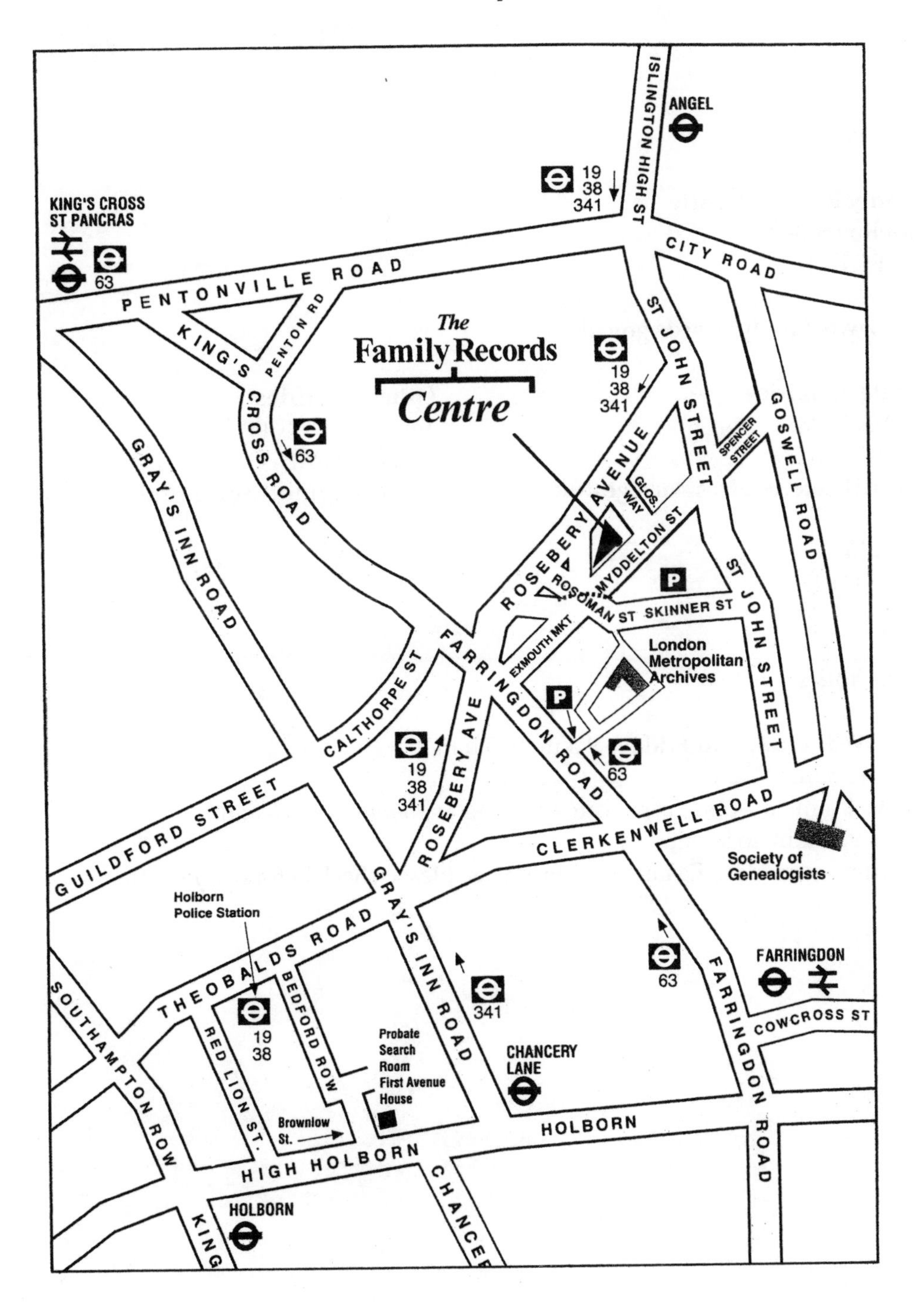

FRC contact details and opening hours

Contact details

The Family Records Centre
1 Myddelton Street
London EC1R 1UW

Website: **www.familyrecords.gov.uk**

Certificate enquiries
Tel: 0870 243 7788
Fax: 01704 550013
Email: **certificate.services@ons.gov.uk**

Other enquiries
Tel: 020 8392 5300
Fax: 020 8392 5307
Email: **enquiry@pro.gov.uk**

Scottish Link
Tel: 020 7533 6438

Opening hours

Monday, Wednesday and Friday: 9 a.m. to 5 p.m.
Tuesday: 10 a.m. to 7 p.m.
Thursday: 9 a.m. to 7 p.m. (certificate ordering available from 10 a.m.)
Saturday: 9.30 a.m. to 5 p.m.
(for Saturdays preceding Easter and Christmas, please check before you visit)

1 Introduction to the Family Records Centre

Researching your family history – the perfect hobby

Family history is one of the most popular global hobbies. You are in for hours, if not days, weeks or years, of endless fun tracking down your ancestors. It really is endless, because every stage throws up new challenges and surprises, as you progress.

In the last three decades this pursuit of ancestry or pedigrees – what was once called 'genealogy' – has developed into 'family history'. Millions of us are driven by a desire to find out who exactly our ancestors were, where they came from, and what they got up to.

Why were people in the past interested in their forebears? Proving your descent from an ancient gentry or noble family confirmed or conferred legal and social status. A knowledge of your place in the family tree protected any future rights of inheritance or land ownership, and might affect your choice of marriage partner. The paternal line was generally the one selected, as the surname tended to stay the same. But a family tree can extend both vertically and laterally, reaching out to its remoter branches. You can dig deep into people's lives and preoccupations, in search of answers to the 'whats' and 'whys' of their actions. This adds an extra dimension as the searcher carves out his or her own personal slice of history. What makes this hobby so exciting and enthralling is the constant element of surprise, the challenge of working out where to look next, the knotty puzzles it throws up, and the sense of achievement when you crack a particular problem. Moreover, you can proceed at your own pace, spending as much or as little time and money as you choose.

Not so long ago, genealogy involved a good deal of trekking around the country, hunting for old documents in local record offices, libraries, church vestries or private houses. Churchyards were scoured for family gravestone inscriptions. These days it can be very different. Since March 1997, the Family Records Centre has helped make genealogical research much more straightforward, bringing together under one roof access to the prime sources for England and Wales (and some for Scotland and Northern Ireland, too) spanning several hundred years. The advent of the internet as a family history resource has led to a further explosion of interest, and there are countless websites devoted to the subject.

Armed with nothing more than your own date and place of birth (if it was in England, Wales or Scotland), you may be able to trace your family back as far as the eighteenth century or even to Tudor times without having to visit any other archive or library. You will be following in the footsteps of hundreds of thousands of other visitors to the FRC, many of whom return again and again to pursue their ancestors.

No specialist knowledge is required to start. You will acquire skills in reading old handwriting as you go along, and feel inspired to broaden your horizons by learning about how things were in the past, and about the places where your family lived. You will almost certainly want to share your discoveries with others in your family, and to link up with missing living relatives you may not have known about before you started. You will hopefully want to preserve your findings for future generations.

The more careful you are in planning and conducting your research, the more likely you are to be successful and not miss vital clues. Before you begin, here are a few things to consider . . .

Before you begin

What can your family tell you?

First, as every family history guidebook should tell you, ask your family. Elderly relations can save you a lot of unnecessary delving around (there is often at least one living storehouse of family lore); but, conversely, they may mislead you with half-remembered facts and anecdotes, or even deliberately misinform you in order to withhold unsavoury details about individuals in your family. Try not to be judgmental as you collect such information, and don't insist on their collaboration – know when to quit. If you can locate a family Bible in which the births, marriages and deaths of a generation or two have been written up, your luck will be in. Make sure you confirm such entries with official sources, since dates may have been recalled wrongly (especially if recorded a long time after the event) or deliberately altered.

Has anyone traced your family's history before?

It's worth checking the following sources:

- The *Genealogical Research Directory, National and International*, edited by Keith A. Johnson and Malcolm R. Sainty, has been published annually since 1981. Each edition lists a completely new set of names and addresses of people throughout the world who are currently tracing the ancestry of named families. Most of these annual editions are to be found on the shelves of the library in the General Reference area on the first floor of the Family Records Centre, and there is a consolidated index to more than 600,000 entries between 1990 and 1999 on CD-ROM. You can also consult the directory in good reference libraries and at the Family History Centres (*see* p. 4) run by the Church of Jesus Christ of Latter-day Saints (LDS).

- The *Ancestral File* and *Pedigree Resource File* are both accessible on the LDS website (**www.familysearch.org**). These are family trees deposited by patrons of the Church's library and made available for others to search. They have not been authenticated by checking against the original sources from which the information was derived – so be sure to do this yourself if you find a pedigree which might relate to your own family. You can consult these two databases online at the FRC.

- The *BIGR* (*British Isles Genealogical Register*) is a consolidated index of family names in this country that are currently being investigated, together with the names and addresses of contributors worldwide. With more than 200,000 entries per edition, this is a useful tool for finding out who else might be tracing your family's history. Microfiche copies of the second (1997) and third (2000) editions are kept at the FRC. County sections are held by appropriate local family history societies (*see below*), and the 2000 edition is also available on CD-ROM.

- The library of the Society of Genealogists (*see* p. 4) has thousands of manuscript and printed family trees and family histories. You can request a free catalogue search for your family name by sending details and a stamped self-addressed envelope (or three international reply coupons from overseas) to the Society, or by email to **library@sog.org.uk** or fax to 020 7250 1800. You can also consult the online catalogue in the Society's library (if you are not a member of the Society, you will have to pay a fee to use it).

Organizations you should know about

Your local family history society

Ask about this at your local library or record office. Founded in 1974, the Federation of Family History Societies (FFHS) is the umbrella organization for about 200 local and one-name family history societies, and it has member societies overseas as well. These are listed, with contact details, on its website (**www.ffhs.org.uk**) and in the half-yearly *Family History News and Digest*, which the Federation publishes. You can buy current issues at the FRC bookshop; and back numbers are available in the library in the General Reference area on the first floor of the FRC. The Federation Administrator can be contacted at PO Box 2425, Coventry CV5 6YX (email **info@ffhs.org.uk**). Remember to enclose an SAE. Many of the family history societies host their own websites. These can be accessed directly or via the Federation's website.

Family history societies meet regularly for support, talks and exchange of information, and to work on projects. Some have their own premises, and most have a reference library for members. Group research trips to the FRC are often organized by local societies and are generally advertised in their journals.

The Federation and individual family history societies publish a large range of inexpensive guides and indexes. You will find references to some of these throughout this book. Many can be bought at the FRC bookshop, or ordered from the PRO via the internet (on **www.pro.gov.uk/bookshop/shop**).

Your local Family History Centre

The Church of Jesus Christ of Latter-day Saints (LDS) has an ongoing programme of microfilming crucial family history sources all over the world. You can consult millions of these microfilms, microfiches and books at their Family History Centres (FHCs) throughout this country and abroad. Because many of them have to be ordered from the LDS headquarters in Salt Lake City, Utah, a small monthly fee is charged for their hire at the FHCs. You can discover about these and their whereabouts in three ways: by searching the Salt Lake City *Family History Library Catalog* on the LDS website, **www.familysearch.org**; online at the FRC, using the Family History Database *FamilySearch*; or on CD-ROM. All Family History Centres have a copy of at least one edition of the LDS's regularly updated index to birth, baptism and marriage entries extracted from parish registers, vital records and other sources, known as the *International Genealogical Index (IGI)*, and of the 1881 census indexes for England, Wales, Channel Islands, Isle of Man and Scotland. These are explained in more detail on pp. 73–6 and 78–80.

For those who cannot spend time and money making the journey to London or around the country, the LDS centres offer an excellent local service. Always telephone before a visit. Each operates its own hours of opening, as they are manned by willing volunteers, and you may also need to book a seat.

For details of your local centre, either write with an SAE to British Isles Family History Service Centre, The Genealogical Society of Utah, 185 Penns Lane, Sutton Coldfield, West Midlands B76 8JU, or phone 0121 384 2028 or visit the LDS website (**www.familysearch.org**).

The Society of Genealogists

The Society of Genealogists was founded in London in 1911. Situated at 14 Charterhouse Buildings, Goswell Road, London EC1M 7BA (telephone 020 7251 8799, website **www.sog.org.uk**), its premises are about 15 minutes' walk from the FRC (*see* map on p. xv). The SoG's outstanding genealogical library contains published and unpublished material of great value to family historians, including transcripts of thousands of parish registers of baptisms, marriages and burials. These are listed, county by county, in *Parish Register Copies in the Library of the Society of Genealogists* (11th edn 1995), which you can purchase at the FRC bookshop. A copy is available in the General Reference area on the first floor of the FRC.

The library is open on Tuesdays, Wednesdays, Fridays and Saturdays from 10 a.m. until 6 p.m., and on Thursdays between 10 a.m. and 8 p.m. There is a well-stocked bookshop, and books can also be ordered from the SoG online via the website. The Society publishes research guides and two quarterlies, *Genealogists' Magazine* and *Computers in Genealogy.* It also runs regular courses and lectures, both for beginners and for more experienced researchers. You can apply to join the Society and pay an annual subscription; non-members are able to use the library, paying an hourly, four-hourly or daily fee. There is a printed guide, *Using the Library of the Society of Genealogists.*

Growing numbers of the Society's collections of record abstracts and personal-name indexes are being made available on the internet at **www.englishorigins.com**. Access costs £6, payable by debit or credit card, which permits up to 150 records to be retrieved over 48 hours. Using the free surname searcher, you can get an idea of how many records of interest there may be or read more about the datasets. At present, these include the indexes to marriage allegations made prior to the issue of marriage licences by the Vicar-General and the Faculty Office of the Archbishop of London, 1694–1850; part of Boyd's Marriage Index (for counties in East Anglia, 1538–1837); the Bank of England will extracts index, 1717–1845; the Archdeaconry Court of London wills index, 1700–1857; the London Consistory Court depositions index, 1700–13; and London apprenticeship abstracts, 1568–1850.

Always read the accompanying text to find out exactly what such indexes and abstracts include, especially the covering dates and geographical spread. For instance, Boyd's Marriage Index consists only of summarized entries extracted from parish registers already in print at the time it was compiled.

Getting started

How do you start doing your own research?

Let's suppose you have checked out what research has already been done and found nothing, so you have to start more or less from scratch. The Family Records Centre is the place to begin.

In the General Register Office (GRO) search area, on the ground floor, you can search the relevant indexes and then order your own birth certificate – or that of your mother or father, or perhaps of a grandparent of whichever line you fancy tracing. Tracking your family back in time through a sequence of birth, marriage and death certificates, you can then supplement your discoveries by poring over copies of census returns, wills and other records held in the PRO's Census and Wills Reading Room on the first floor. Remember, though, that each certificate costs money.

This book will help you find your way round the Family Records Centre, and tell you how all this is done. The case studies on pp. 141–56 will demonstrate how to use the certificates, census returns and other sources to extract information for constructing a family tree, and offer clues about where to look next.

How far back will you get?

This is the great unknown. Everyone has ancestors stretching back into the mists of time; how visible they are, if at all, is a different matter. Generally speaking, it is the traces left by individuals at the extremes of society that are most easily picked up – either because they were prominent nationally or locally or because they attracted the attention of those in authority. Family history thus tests your ingenuity in identifying which records are most likely to contain references that will help you on your way.

If your family did not stray from England, Wales or Scotland, you have a fair chance of locating eighteenth-century ancestors – and even Stuart or Tudor antecedents, if you are really lucky. However, on the whole, families tended not to linger in one place for long, often not even for a single lifetime (think of your own life). Even if they stayed put, a person's origins might be difficult to detect because there were others with identical names and ages living in the same community at the same time. This happened because of the widespread practice in the past of drawing from only a small pool of forenames when baptizing children. In rural areas, there may be the added problem of many families bearing the same surname but not connected by recent blood ties. Sometimes, people just seem to have vanished off the face of the earth.

How do you untangle it all, and avoid ending up ensnared in someone else's family tree? Working back carefully from the known to the unknown, rather than employing a scattergun approach, will stand you in good stead. If you draw up a research plan, take accurate referenced notes, critically assess your sources, and review your findings at every stage, you will quickly spot any gaps or discrepancies and be able to question the relevance and validity of your 'evidence' before things veer too far off-course.

Which line should you trace?

Any one you like. If you come unstuck trying to locate your father's father, try your mother's family, the maternal line, instead. Most family historians these days branch out into as many lines as they can – four grandparents with four different surnames to research, eight great-grandparents with a choice of eight different surnames to pursue, and so on along the branches of your family tree until you have hundreds of them! Remember, everyone of the same generation is related to you equally.

What's in a name?

Obviously, common names present more difficulties than unusual ones. Attempting to identify the 'right' John Smith can prove a nightmare. The more specific you can be about *your* John Smith (for example, names of parents, date and/or place of birth, or where he lived), the simpler it will be to eliminate the other options.

Most surnames did not become fixed or hereditary until the fifteenth century, just before the Tudors began to rule. Studies have suggested that the number of surnames then declined, and began to fan out within restricted neighbourhoods as the population expanded during the sixteenth and seventeenth centuries. Each part of Britain has its own characteristic set of surnames, offering clues to where they originated. For examples of local surname clusters and surname distributions, look at H. B. Guppy, *Homes of Family Names in Great Britain* (London, 1890; reprinted 1968), the 1881 census index *(see* pp. 78–80) and the *International Genealogical Index (see* p. 74–6).

Before literacy became widespread, names were transmitted orally rather than written down and there were no standard spellings. Even within the last 100 years, Owlett and Howlett may be variations of the same surname. Mishearing, dialect pronunciation and unfamiliar names of newcomers all helped to determine the way people's names were spelt. Foreign names are also likely to have been mangled or misconstrued by immigration, customs, census or registration officers, or whoever first wrote them down. Aliases were fairly common until the eighteenth century, perhaps indicating adoption or illegitimacy.

Welsh genealogy is made more complex by the use of patronymics (in the depths of the countryside, as late as the nineteenth century) and the vast numbers of individuals carrying the same forename and surname. A Welsh person was a walking genealogy, identified by a string of names such as Evan Ap Thomas Ap Richard – meaning Evan, son of Thomas, son of Richard. When Evan himself had a son, the son might be called Thomas Ap Evan Ap Thomas, Richard being dropped from the genealogical string. Welsh people were often distinguished by the property they lived in, or by a nickname associated with their occupation or characteristics.

There are a number of books suggesting the possible origins of English and Welsh surnames. A few of these are listed in the Bibliography at the end of this book (pp. 169–71). Copies of them are available in the library in the General Reference area on the first floor of the FRC.

Look in the *Genealogical Research Directory, National and International* for listed one-name researchers and societies, many of which are registered members of the Guild of One-Name Studies. To find out if there is a one-name study of your surname, visit their website (**www.one-name.org**). Alternatively, you can write for this information to the Secretary, Guild of One-Name Studies (GOONS), Box G, Society of Genealogists, 14 Charterhouse Buildings, Goswell Road, London EC1M 7BA, enclosing a self-addressed envelope (or two international reply coupons if writing from abroad); or email **guild@one-name.org**.

Rather than constructing pedigrees, one-name researchers extract every entry of a particular surname and its variants from prime family history indexes and databases in order to build up a picture of its frequency, geographical spread, and changing local densities over time.

Far fewer forenames were available in the past than today. John, Edward, Henry, Thomas, William, Mary, Elizabeth and Ann can be found everywhere. The tradition of naming the eldest son after the father and the eldest daughter after the mother, then subsequent children after their grandparents, can provide vital clues in forging generation links. Sons, especially second sons, might be given the mother's maiden name as their first or second forename. There were also fashions for forenames reflecting the names of famous people or heroes of the day.

Very occasionally you may come across two or more surviving children of the same parents with identical names – but later-born children given the same names as older siblings are usually an indication of the latter's earlier deaths and a desire to commemorate them or to use the name again.

Victorian families – some facts relevant to your research

Much of your research at the FRC is probably going to focus on nineteenth-century ancestors, so it's worth considering the following points.

- Families could be very large – your great-great-grandmother may have been producing babies regularly over 20 years or more. (Some of the illustrations in this book relate to the ancestry of Her Majesty Queen Elizabeth the Queen Mother, who was one of 10 children. Her parents were married in 1881, but she was not born until 1900 and had a younger brother.)

- Infant mortality was high. In 1841, life expectancy at birth was 40 for males and 42 for females. As many as one child in six died before its first birthday. If it survived the first year, expected duration of life increased.
- Throughout the nineteenth century there was a continuing drift from the countryside to towns and cities. At the start of the century more than half of the population worked on the land; by the end, the bulk of the workforce was urban. Moreover, a population of just over 8 million in 1801 had mushroomed to more than 32 million in 1901. People not only moved about, their numbers drastically multiplied.
- Working-class parents did not always go through the formalities of a wedding ceremony. If they did, it might be after or very shortly before the birth of their first child.
- Marriages between people of different religious persuasions were more likely to take place in a register office or chapel than under the auspices of the established Church of England.
- For some, weddings in register offices (which began on 1 July 1837) carried the stigma of the Poor Law.
- In an era when divorce was an extremely difficult and costly process, couples might separate or one desert. They might then start another family. That second family of children, though registered under the father's surname, was illegitimate in the eyes of the law. Often, it is only when the hapless searcher fails to find a marriage registration for the parents that the truth comes to light.
- Don't assume that your great-great-grandparents married only once. In the past, life was shorter and more precarious, and second and third marriages were common. Frequently, half-brothers and half-sisters, step-brothers and step-sisters were brought up together and adopted the surname of their new father.
- Orphaned children might be adopted by married females of the family, or godparents, neighbours or friends, or other kinsfolk, and change their surnames accordingly. There were no formalities needed for adoption until legislation was passed in 1926.
- Don't assume that your family remained in one place. People went in search of work wherever it could be found; the railways made travel easier, and the expanding towns and cities beckoned workers to factories and municipal jobs. However, a rural family might not go far afield, especially in areas where transport was mostly on foot or horseback.
- In the nineteenth century the majority of the population did not own their own houses. It was easy to up sticks and move somewhere cheaper, or to rent a larger or grander property without any sense of permanence. If there's no sign of them at the expected address, your family might only be round the corner or down the road, rather than hundreds of miles away.
- As in other epochs, Victorian people disappeared. Their eventual deaths might then be registered under an assumed identity. A number of the 'vanished' resurfaced in British colonies or North America, having taken advantage of the emigration fever that spread through the United Kingdom in the nineteenth century.

Using the internet for family history research

Throughout this book you will come across references to websites, reflecting the ever increasing use by genealogists of the internet to tap into the vast electronic storehouse of information that now exists. The internet is like a huge reference library that you can search at any time, from any place. You do not need to own a computer yourself. The FRC has four networked computer terminals in its internet café, and computers are available in many public libraries, usually on a timed basis for a small fee. At the FRC, the charge is 50p for every quarter of an hour's use.

The computer brings together data from throughout the world in a single memory bank, but there is no catalogue to the billion or more websites in which this information is kept. Because this information is not organized in a systematic way, it can prove difficult to find your way around and get to what you want. There is no right or wrong way of surfing the internet, but there are some powerful search engines to help you reach your destination. Try **www.google.com**, for example. Key in your chosen name or subject, and see how quickly it will retrieve and list websites containing the words you've keyed in. However, many of these sites may be totally irrelevant to your needs, so you will probably have to be more selective in making your search request.

A search engine may yield entries under a rare surname that enable you to contact long-lost relatives, and it may come up with websites you might never otherwise have visited. It is also an easy way of keeping up with new websites, since one of the problems with the internet is that websites come and go all the time, or are superseded by new addresses. It is a fast-moving environment, and by the time you read this book it is likely that some websites will have been replaced or more data will have been loaded onto them.

Also of help are the subject-based gateways linking you to relevant websites. For family historians, the chief of these are **www.genuki.org.uk** – which focuses on research in the United Kingdom and Ireland and includes a brief introduction for beginners – and **www.cyndislist.com**, which is particularly strong on North America and provides a wealth of links to websites worldwide, arranged under subject. Government portals such as **www.familyrecords.gov.uk** will save you time by providing links, at the click of a mouse, to family history resources in UK national archives and other major public institutions.

But not all of what you find on the internet will be reliable. A lot of it needs careful evaluation and interpretation – which is something the internet does not provide – and some of it may turn out to be misleading or completely wrong. You should therefore regard information gleaned from internet compilations as no more than a signpost to the original records, and always inspect the sources from which it is derived to be sure of its accuracy and completeness. Also, always read the introduction on the home page of each website, so you are aware of the site's scope and its aims and limitations.

The internet and email have made it much easier to make contact with other people with similar research interests. You can list yours at sites such as **www.genuki.org.uk/indexes/SurnamesList.html**, and you can email contributors using their cited addresses.

If you need help with your research or want answers to queries or advice on interpretation of sources, you can join a specialist mailing list, such as those operated by **www.Ancestry.com** and **http://rootsweb.com**, or post your enquiry on one of their notice boards.

It isn't necessary to use the internet to trace your family's history – but increasingly record offices, libraries, genealogical societies and other organizations and thousands of individuals are using it as a means of sharing their resources with a global audience. For instance, by visiting **www.pro.gov.uk** you can conduct searches of the PRO catalogues, place an order for document copies, order material in advance of your visit, purchase PRO publications online, consult a range of information leaflets and (using the charged service) access some of the original census returns, all without leaving home. You can also save yourself a lot of time by using the internet to help you plan research trips before you set off. Regularly update the websites you have 'bookmarked' for easy and regular access, since they may change addresses or sometimes even disappear.

Some databases make accessible a resource that was once only available by postal enquiry. From **www.cwgc.org**, the Commonwealth War Graves Commission's website, you can now download, save or print out details from the Debt of Honour Register of casualties for both World Wars, without having to spend time and money on a letter.

You can use many of the websites free of charge. For example, **www.familysearch.org**, which includes a number of databases (especially the *International Genealogical Index* of births, baptisms and marriages worldwide); and **http://freebmd.rootsweb.com**, an ever growing index drawn from the English and Welsh centralized indexes of births, marriages and deaths since 1837. However, you have to pay to use others, such as **www.englishorigins.com** and **www.scotsorigins.com**, which grant access to some prime English compilations and Scottish indexes and original official records. Nevertheless, this is likely to be cheaper than having to make a journey to where the records themselves are kept, although the odds are that eventually you will have to visit an archive to check the veracity of your findings and to look at sources not yet loaded onto the internet.

For storage and speedy retrieval of widely scattered sources, the internet has revolutionized the way family historians tackle their research. It has facilitated the discovery of raw materials and their whereabouts, the sharing of personal-name indexes and findings, and quick and easy communication with researchers throughout the world. But it is not an original source in itself, and you shouldn't rely on it to conduct all your researches.

To learn more about the internet, read P. Christian, *The Genealogist's Internet* (PRO, 2001) or S. A. Raymond, *Family History on the Web, An Internet Directory for England and Wales* (FFHS, 2000) and *Irish Family History on the Web, A Directory* (FFHS, 2001).

The Family Records Centre

The Family Records Centre combines the public searchrooms of the General Register Office (part of the Office for National Statistics), once situated in St Catherine's House, in the Strand, with the central-London Census and Wills Reading Room of the Public Record Office, formerly in Chancery Lane. It was opened in March 1997, and has won a number of awards as a Centre of Excellence for family history services.

The FRC is easily accessible by public transport and there are public car parks close at hand (*see* map on p. xv). Metered parking is available nearby, too. On site there is limited disabled car parking, which should be reserved at least a day in advance by phoning 020 7533 6436.

The Centre is open to all. You don't need to make an appointment to visit it, nor do you need a reader's ticket. It is open six days a week, with two late evenings, on Tuesdays and Thursdays (*see* p. xvi). Smoking is prohibited in the building, including the entrance area, and on the steps and ramp outside. To avoid disturbing other researchers, mobile phones and pagers must be switched off or in silent mode in the public search areas and in the lobby on the first floor. We also ask that children under 16 be accompanied by an adult at all times.

At the FRC, you can use pens (which are not permitted in record offices where original documents are kept) as well as pencils. All the index volumes, microforms – both microfilm and microfiche – and computerized indexes and databases are self-service. Portable computers and audio dictation are allowed in some areas of the Centre. Ask the staff which these are.

Groups are welcome, and organizers are encouraged to let staff know when they plan to come and how many there will be in the party. Guided tours and talks for up to 16 people can be arranged on request. These should be booked at least six weeks ahead; and are available on Mondays, Tuesdays and Saturdays at 10.30 a.m. and on

Tuesdays at 3.30 p.m. (phone 020 8392 5300 to make a booking). The tours last about 40 minutes. There is also a Meetings Room on the first floor, which can be hired at certain times.

The FRC publishes a quarterly newsletter, *The Family Record*, which is displayed in the search areas and at the PRO, Kew. It is also available online at **www.familyrecords.gov.uk**. To subscribe to the electronic version, email **FRC-Newsletter@pro.gov.uk** with the word 'Subscribe' as the subject heading. This will keep you abreast of the latest news and developments.

What's where at the FRC

As you enter, you will see the bookshop (on the left of the entrance lobby). This sells a wide range of family history guides, including PRO publications, family history magazines, maps, magnifying sheets, and birth, marriage and death certificate binders. Turning right and going through the doors, you will see two public telephones.

Downstairs, on the lower ground floor, there are three more public telephones, one of which has email facilities. All of them take coins and cards. On this lower level there are vending machines, selling snacks and hot and cold drinks, a drinking-water fountain, and plenty of tables and chairs where you can sit and relax. You are welcome to bring your own sandwiches to eat here (in the searchrooms eating is not allowed). A staffed food service is being introduced, too.

On each of the three floors there are public toilets, including disabled facilities. A lift serves all three floors as an alternative to the stairs. On the lower ground floor, you will find a baby changing room, a First Aid Room, and a cloakroom area where you can secure your coat. You will need a £1 coin, which is refundable, to stow your belongings in one of the lockers (also downstairs).

The GRO searchroom is situated on the ground floor of the FRC, beyond the reception and bookshop area. The indexes are self-service, but you will need to spend money if you want to order a certified copy of any of the registrations you find. Certified copies (or certificates, as they are often called) cost £6.50 each. You can collect them in person on the fourth working day after handing in your application form with your payment at one of the tills, or have them sent to you by first-class post on the fourth working day. If you need advice, go to the Customer Services Desk in the middle of the GRO search area.

The 'St Catherine's indexes', in the GRO search area, cover registrations of births, marriages and deaths in England and Wales since 1 July 1837, adoptions since 1927,

Figure 1 Part of the GRO search area. The birth indexes are in the background. All the index shelves are clearly labelled with the dates and events to which they relate.

and registrations of similar vital events, relating to Britons, at sea, abroad or in the Armed Services. These overseas registrations may overlap with the miscellaneous non-statutory returns held by the PRO (*see* pp. 138–40), which are available on microfilm on the first floor of the FRC.

If you are trying to trace Scottish ancestors, you can book one of the two Scottish Link computer terminals (*see* p. xvi) on the ground floor and pay for up to two consecutive hours' research of the computerized indexes to key Scottish records. The second terminal operates on a 'first come, first served' basis. When you have found what you are looking for, complete one of the application forms displayed nearby with the extracted information and post your order and payment for a certified copy direct to the General Register Office in Edinburgh (*see* p. 64). There are no printing facilities, so you will have to write down any information you find.

You can search the computerized index to birth registrations in Northern Ireland since 1 January 1922 free of charge, without booking; this computer terminal is also in the Scottish Link area. You can then order and pay for a certified copy of a specific registration direct from the General Register Office in Belfast (*see* p. 25). Again, there are no printing facilities.

If you go up to the first floor, you will pass the Meetings Room and a small exhibition of popular family history sources. There is also a changing themed display. You can check the Surname Interest Registers for references to your own, and are welcome to add your contact address and details about your research. In this area is a set of four networked computers which you can use to surf the internet. The cost is 50p for each 15 minutes' use.

You then enter the PRO search area. Any research here should take you a stage or two further. There are no original documents. You can inspect copies on microfilm of some of the main national archives of use to family historians, such as the 10-yearly census returns of England and Wales from 1841 until 1891, nonconformist registers, miscellaneous non-statutory returns of births, marriages and deaths of British subjects overseas, and administration grants and wills proved in the chief church court that served England and Wales before 1858. All the microfilms except the microfilmed census returns up to 1891 can also be searched at the PRO, Kew. The 1901 census returns of England and Wales are available online, as a charged service.

Whilst the indexes to births, marriages and deaths on the ground floor are organized by personal name, the 10-yearly census returns from 1841 to 1901 are arranged by place (city, town, village or hamlet). There are, however, complete online personal-name indexes and transcripts for the 1881 and 1901 returns. The 1881 database includes Scotland and is freely accessible on 16 terminals. Once you go beyond the personal-name index to the 1901 census, you have to pay to view the transcripts and digitized images of the actual returns.

Genealogical compilations belonging to the LDS's *FamilySearch* program (*see* p. 21) can be viewed on the first floor, as can a number of other personal-name indexes. Some of these form part of the Family History Databases network (*see* pp. 73–80), while others are on CD-ROM or microfiche or in books. There are printing facilities for the online databases and copying facilities for microfiches and books (subject to copyright restrictions).

On the first floor, everything apart from booking the 1901 servers is entirely self-service, including copying. There are two help desks – one for 'New Customers' and the Research Enquiries Desk. Alongside these you will find a Copy Service Desk, where you can buy and recharge Copycards at £5 apiece or obtain loose change for use at the self-service copiers dotted around the search and reference areas. If you do the photocopying yourself, it will cost you 25p each for microfilm and microfiche copies or 20p for photocopies from books and online databases. For each film or fiche frame copied for you by the staff, the charge is 35p. The Copycards can also be used at the Public Record Office, Kew.

What should I take to the FRC?

To get the most out of your visit to the Family Records Centre, take some or all of the following items with you:

Figure 2 Cabinets containing microfilm copies of the census returns for England and Wales from 1841 to 1891, in the PRO Census and Wills Reading Room. The Research Enquiries Desk is in the background.

- A plan of action, as little baggage as possible, pens, pencils and plenty of paper to write on. Make sure your name and address are written inside notebooks. Any mislaid or forgotten belongings find their way to the security staff (telephone 020 7533 6436) each day.
- A gazetteer or atlas is a good idea. You are going to find your ancestors in places you have never heard of, and will need to check their exact whereabouts to make sure you have found the right people. The FRC has some maps.
- Wear comfortable shoes and clothes. If you are going to be searching the GRO indexes you will be on your feet a good deal. It can get very hot.
- To buy certificates and pay for photocopies, you will need either cash or a credit card or your cheque book and cheque card.
- Don't leave your belongings lying around unattended. They clutter up your work space, and may disappear. Bring a £1 coin (*see* p. 13) and lock them up safely.

The surrounding area

Although the FRC occupies a modern building, it is in a part of London redolent of the past. Clerkenwell is one of the oldest and most rumbustious of the City's suburbs, a red-light district in Shakespeare's day, and traditionally associated with Huguenot watchmakers and Italian immigrants. It is a vibrant area, with a market, and offers a good choice of cafés, restaurants and pubs.

The Society of Genealogists (*see* map on p. xv) is within walking distance. You can become a member of the Society or buy up to a day's worth of research (*see* pp. 4–5) in its well-equipped library and delve amongst its unrivalled collection of parish register transcripts, manuscript pedigrees and printed family histories and books.

If your ancestors were Londoners, you may want to stroll over to the London Metropolitan Archives (*see* map on p. xv) – formerly called the Greater London Record Office – at 40 Northampton Road, London EC1R 0HB (telephone 020 7332 3820, email **ask.lma@corpoflondon.gov.uk**, website **www.cityoflondon.gov.uk**). On the LMA website you will find microfilms of many London parish registers, the Middlesex deeds registry, some wills of Londoners proved before 1858, a terrific map and photograph collection, an excellent library, advice on London ancestry, and much else besides.

The London Metropolitan Archives are open from 9.30 a.m. to 4.45 p.m. Monday, Wednesday and Friday; and from 9.30 a.m. to 7.30 p.m. on Tuesdays and Thursdays. You can also visit the LMA on the second and fourth Saturdays in each month, public holidays permitting.

Sources in the Family Records Centre

The General Register Office (Office for National Statistics)

You can search the following volumes of **GRO personal-name indexes**.

England and Wales

- Births, marriages and deaths registered since 1 July 1837:
  - Online access (via the Scottish Link, if preferred) to birth and death indexes, 1984–92, and to marriage indexes, 1984–93
  - Microfiche copies of indexes to births, marriages and deaths, 1837–1984, available to searchers with special needs or as a substitute when an index is being repaired
- Adoptions since January 1927

Overseas

- Births and deaths at sea (Marine returns) registered between 1837 and 1965
- Civil aviation births, deaths and missing (presumed dead), from 1947 to 1965
- Consular returns of births, marriages and deaths of British subjects abroad, from July 1849 until 1965

- United Kingdom and British High Commission returns of births up to 1966 and deaths and marriages up to 1965, from the date of independence of the Commonwealth country

Armed services

- A typed list of Army regiments provides details of deposited registers of births, baptisms, marriages and deaths. At the front of it, there is an index of regiments; this includes regular and territorial regiments, garrisons, volunteers and militia.
- Regimental registers of births and baptisms, 1761–1924. These include Army personnel in Britain and Ireland, as well as abroad.
- Army chaplains' station returns (Army returns) of births and marriages (1796–1955) and deaths (1796–1950) of officers, soldiers and their families outside the United Kingdom
- Military, civil and chaplains' registers of births, marriages and deaths in the Ionian Islands, 1818–64
- Royal Air Force returns of births, marriages and deaths from 1920, indexed with the Army returns (*see above*)
- Service Departments' registers of births and marriages, 1956–65, and deaths, 1951–65 (including Royal Air Force and, from 1959, Royal Navy personnel and their families)

Births, deaths and marriages at sea, in the air and overseas, from 1966 onwards

- Annual union indexes for each event

War deaths

- Natal and South African Field Forces, 1899–1902 (Boer War)
- Army officers, 1914–21 (First World War), including Royal Flying Corps and, from 1 April 1918, Royal Air Force commissioned officers
- Army other ranks, 1914–21 (*as above*)
- Royal Navy officers and ratings, 1914–21, including submariners, Royal Marines and Royal Naval Air Service
- Indian Services, officers and men, 1914–21
- Army officers, from 3 September 1939 to 30 June 1948 (Second World War), including those dying later of wounds
- Army other ranks, 1939–48 (*as above*)
- Royal Navy officers, 1939–48 (*as above*)
- Royal Navy ratings, 1939–48 (*as above*)
- Royal Air Force, all ranks, 1939–48 (*as above*)
- Indian Services, all ranks, 1939–48 (*as above*)

In order to obtain a certified copy of any registration, you will need to make a note of the full index details. For English and Welsh registrations, don't forget to note down the year and quarter when the event was registered, as appropriate.

The Scottish Link (part of the GRO)

There are **computerized indexes** to the following.

Scotland

(access is based on a fee of £4 per half hour, up to a maximum of 2 hours' continuous use)

- Birth, marriage and death registrations from 1 January 1855 to date, including adoptions since 1930
- Divorces since 1984
- Old Parochial Registers of marriages and births or baptisms from 1553 to 1854 (also available as one of the online Family History Databases on the first floor of the FRC). It is planned to make images of the registers themselves available via the charged service offered on **www.scotsorigins.com**.
- 1881 census returns (also available as one of the online Family History Databases on the first floor of the FRC, with transcripts of the entries)
- 1891 and 1901 census returns (using the Internet Access Point computers on the first floor of the FRC, you can view images of the census pages via the charged service offered on **www.scotsorigins.com**)

Northern Ireland

- Births, registered from 1 January 1922 to date

England and Wales

- Registered births and deaths, 1984–92, and marriages, 1984–93. Online indexes to overseas registrations are planned, but not yet available.
  - There are microfiche copies of quarterly indexes to births, marriages and deaths from 1 July 1837 until 31 December 1983; and to overseas registrations of births, baptisms, marriages and deaths of British subjects up to 1994.
- Marriage indexes, March 1969 to 2000

You can also read about registration of births, deaths and marriages in Northern Ireland, the Republic of Ireland, Channel Islands and Isle of Man, and how to order certificates.

The Public Record Office

England and Wales, Channel Islands and Isle of Man

- Microfilm copies of census returns, 1841, 1851, 1861, 1871, 1881 (online personal-name index and transcripts for 1881, including Scotland; microfiche national and

Figure 3 Using one of the 48 computer terminals that give access to personal-name indexes, transcriptions and digital images of the 1901 census returns for England and Wales.

county by county personal-name indexes and transcripts for 1881, excluding Scotland) and 1891. There are Place Name Indexes and many Street Indexes for these years on the open shelves. You can also consult a number of personal-name indexes, listed by place in Surname Index volumes for each census year.

- Online personal-name index, transcripts and images of 1901 census returns (charged service after initial index search). Images of the 1891 and 1881 returns are forthcoming.
- Microfilm copies of registered wills and administration grants filed in the Prerogative Court of Canterbury (PCC), from 1384 to 9 January 1858. Published indexes of wills up to 1800 and administration grants for 1559–1661 (A–Sweetinge only), 1663–4 and 1701–49; thereafter (from 1750), yearly initial indexes to names until 1852 and 1858; and a printed consolidated index for 1853–7. Online indexes and images of wills proved in the PCC, 1850–8 (charged service to view the images). Images of 1830–49 wills are imminent.
- Microfilm copies of Death Duty registers, 1796–1857, and indexes 1796–1903.
- Microfiche copies of yearly National Probate Indexes of wills and administration grants, from 12 January 1858 to 31 December 1943.
- Microfilms of Divorce indexes relating to England and Wales, 1858–1958.
- Microfilms of deposited non-parochial registers, 1567–1970, including births of dissenters registered at Dr Williams's Library, 1717–1837, and Wesleyan Methodist Metropolitan Registry, 1818–40; various registers from dissenters' burial grounds; Religious Society of Friends (Quaker) births, marriages, deaths and burials;

clandestine and irregular marriages, from 1667 until 24 March 1754; births, baptisms, marriages and burials of foreign Protestant congregations in England, and of the Russian Orthodox Church in London.

- Maps indicating registration district, sub-district and census enumerators' district boundaries: 1870 and 1891 (incomplete series covering England and Wales, excluding London); 1848–50 and 1891 (incomplete series for London, used for the 1861 and 1891 censuses respectively). All except the 1891 map of London were Ordnance Survey maps, to which there is an index map that will help you find the one(s) you want.
- Bound copies of London directories of names of residents, professional and tradespeople and street by street lists of heads of household, published round about each census year.
- Microfiche and bound copies of county and urban directories of names of residents and tradespeople around census years. There is a typed index to these. A number of them are being digitized and made available on the Family History Databases terminals.

Overseas

- Microfilm copies of the Registrar General's miscellaneous non-statutory returns of births, baptisms, marriages, deaths and burials of British subjects and of nationals of British colonies, the Commonwealth and countries under British jurisdiction, 1627–1965, with personal-name indexes for 1627–1960. These include references to marriages on board Royal Naval ships, 1842–79, marriages of servicemen abroad, British military deaths in France and Belgium during the First World War, Second World War notifications of death of Armed Service personnel, prisoners of war and civilian internees and of deaths from enemy action in the Far East, and deaths on aircraft lost in flight. There are also some Channel Islands and Lundy Island entries.

The Family History Databases

- The *FamilySearch* database. No living people are included. You can search the *Ancestral File* (pedigrees deposited by patrons at the LDS Library, Salt Lake City, up to 5 January 1998); the *International Genealogical Index* (March 1993 edition) and *Addendum* (as of January 2000) of millions of births, baptisms and marriages, taken from a variety of sources including parish registers and information submitted by relatives; the *American Social Security Death Index*, 1937–99; the *American Military Death Index, covering Korean and Vietnam Wars*, 1950–75; the *Index to Scottish Old Parochial Registers*, 1553–1854; and the *Family History Library Catalog* of items in the LDS Library, Salt Lake City (which is updated periodically, the online edition being as of 31 March 1997 and the version on **www.familysearch.org** being as of August 2001).
- The *British Isles Vital Records Index*, 1998 (currently as of 1998, though a new edition is due early in 2002). This comprises births, baptisms and marriages extracted from vital records and parish registers. No living people are included.

- The *National Burial Index* (April 2001), covering many counties in England and Wales. It contains about 5½ million entries extracted from 4,440 parish and cemetery registers, 1538–2000.
- 1881 census indexes and transcripts for England, Wales, Channel Islands and Isle of Man and for Scotland.
- Trade directories of various dates, relating to England and Wales.
- PRO Online Resources, featuring Advance Document Ordering, Electronic Records, Other Useful Websites and the main PRO website (**www.pro.gov.uk**). As well as the Public Record Office's online catalogues (the main one being PROCAT), Family History menu and indexed information leaflets, the PRO website offers access to the PCC wills database and digital images of other PRO records (via **www.pro-online.pro.gov.uk**) and to **www.familyrecords.gov.uk**, the portal site that provides links to all of the UK's national archive repositories.
- There is a set of miscellaneous indexes on CD-ROM (*see* p. 82).

Miscellaneous

- Microfiche copies of the March 1992 edition of the *International Genealogical Index* (British Isles only, including Ireland), plus the *Vital Records Listing* of places, events and periods covered (July 1993).
- The *British Isles Genealogical Register* of families and places currently being researched, with cross-references to names and contact details of contributors worldwide (1997 and 2000 editions on microfiche).

The library in the General Reference area on the first floor of the FRC contains a wealth of useful books to help you in your researches, both at the FRC and elsewhere. There are also bound back numbers of genealogical periodicals such as *Family Tree Magazine*, *Practical Family History* and *Family History Monthly*.

Access to the records is free, except for the charged services relating to the 1901 census and to PCC wills online. You can make copies of any of the material, except for the *FamilySearch* databases.

Important sources not in the Family Records Centre

Parish registers for pre-1837 births, marriages and deaths in England and Wales, and pre-1854 for Scotland

Parish church registers of baptism, marriage and burial are your main stepping stones back through the centuries before civil registration of births, marriages and deaths began in 1837. Since the sixteenth century, Church of England parishes have kept records of baptisms, marriages and burials – a pattern repeated in Scotland, where details of births as well as baptisms were written down. Scottish burial registers tend not to be as thorough as those in England or Wales.

Most English and Welsh parish registers are now in record offices, rather than the churches where they were originally stored. To find their present whereabouts, and those of Scottish Old Parochial Registers, consult *The Phillimore Atlas and Index of Parish Registers*, edited by C. R. Humphery-Smith (Chichester, 2nd edn 1995), in the library in the General Reference area on the first floor of the FRC or at the Customer Services Desk in the GRO searchroom on the ground floor. *The Atlas* contains useful county and regional maps, and the index at the back indicates whether there are any register copies. Look also in *Parish Register Copies in the Library of the Society of Genealogists* (11th edn 1995) for more detailed information. *Record Offices: How to Find Them*, by J. Gibson and P. Peskett (FFHS, 9th edn 2002), also in the library in the General Reference area at the FRC, includes town maps, contact addresses and phone numbers. Many record offices have their own websites supplying such information; you can use the PRO's website (**www.pro.gov.uk**) as a gateway to these, or access them via **www.hmc.gov.uk/archon**. Always phone before visiting a record office, to check the opening hours and regulations for searchers, and whether you have to book a seat.

Details from parish registers accessible at the FRC

You won't find any parish registers at the Family Records Centre – but, as mentioned earlier, the *International Genealogical Index* (*see* pp. 21 and 74–5) is based on hundreds of millions of baptism and marriage registers throughout the world, microfilmed and indexed by the Church of Jesus Christ of Latter-day Saints. Use it as a signpost, not as a complete source in itself. Always check the original sources.

Since the first version appeared in the 1960s, the *IGI* has been updated regularly, with new entries added. The *Vital Records Index* serves as a key to what places, dates and events are in each new edition. The March 1992 edition of the *IGI* for the British Isles, including Ireland, is available on microfiche at the FRC, with the *Vital Records Index* (July 1993). In addition, you can search the *IGI* for the whole world (March 1993 edition) online, together with the January 2000 *Addendum* and *British Isles Vital Records Index* (1998), as part of the Family History Databases on the first floor of the FRC. The *IGI* is also available on the internet, at **www.familysearch.org**.

Indexes to Scottish births, baptisms and marriages in Church of Scotland parishes between 1553 and 1854 (*Scottish Old Parochial Registers*), can be accessed (for a fee) via the Scottish Link on the ground floor of the FRC, using the computerized indexes; or (free) online as part of *FamilySearch*, using one of the Family History Databases terminals on the first floor.

Check these indexes before looking elsewhere.

Some notes about marriages

Marriages tend to be more difficult to locate. They generally took place in the bride's church; but this was not necessarily in her native parish. The couple might then move to the husband's place of residence or somewhere else entirely, so their children's baptisms may be scattered around the country. A single marriage might generate a large number of progeny.

The *IGI* (*see above*) consists of marriages as well as births and baptisms. Marriage entries extracted from English parish registers prior to 1837 and published by W. P. W. Phillimore and E. A. Fry are gradually being released county by county on CD-ROM. Look at S. A. Raymond, *British Family History on CD* (FFHS, 2001) for details. Marriage indexes compiled by P. Boyd from printed registers and other sources are being made available by the Society of Genealogists as part of a charged service offered on **www.englishorigins.com**. Scan *A List of Parishes in Boyd's Marriage Index* (Society of Genealogists, 1994) for details of parishes and periods covered. If you are looking for a London marriage between 1780 and 1837, it is worth tracking down the CD-ROM of Pallot's Marriage Index. This has entries from all except two City of London parishes. Look in *The Phillimore Atlas and Index of Parish Registers* for more information. Even if you don't home in on your ancestor's marriage, you may find someone of the same surname whose place of marriage will provide the key to your ancestor's parish of origin, because they were brother and sister or close kin.

Examine J. Gibson and E. Hampson, *Marriage and Census Indexes for Family Historians* (FFHS, 8th edn 2000) to see if there is a relevant county index. This covers the entire British Isles. Often, marriage indexes in private hands can be searched for you for a small fee – which may be a lot cheaper and quicker than having to plough speculatively through volumes of wedding entries.

Especially if it took place before 1754, consider the possibility that the missing marriage might have been clandestine or irregular (*see* pp. 136–7).

Many marriages were conducted by licence, rather than after the public reading of banns. Known indexes of marriage licence allegations and bonds (the necessary preliminaries to the issue of the licence itself) and a list of their known whereabouts can be traced in J. Gibson, *Bishops' Transcripts and Marriage Licences: A Guide to their Location and Indexes* (FFHS, 4th edn 1997). Indexes to marriage allegations made before the Vicar-General and Faculty Office of the Archbishop of Canterbury, 1694–1850, can be accessed on the internet, using the charged service offered on **www.englishorigins.com**, and there are printed copies in the library in the General Reference area on the first floor of the FRC.

Records of Irish ancestors

Many of the records needed to trace Irish ancestry are in Ireland. For details of these, buy one of the guides to Irish genealogical research at the FRC bookshop. It's also worth looking at the *IGI*, because extracts of birth registrations from 1 January 1864 to 31 December 1875 and non-Catholic marriages from 1 April 1845 to 31 December 1863 are included.

For birth, marriage and death records for the whole of Ireland from 1864 until 1921 (including non-Catholic marriages from 1845) and for the Republic of Ireland to date, apply to the General Register Office of Ireland, 8–11 Lombard Street East, Dublin 2, Ireland (telephone 003531 6354000, website **www.groireland.ie**). Microfilm copies of the indexes can be searched at LDS Family History Centres, too. Computerized indexes to births registered in Northern Ireland since 1 January 1922 can be searched in the Scottish Link area (*see* p. 65) of the GRO searchroom at the FRC, but you will need to apply to the Registrar General, General Register Office (Northern Ireland), Oxford House, 49–55 Chichester Street, Belfast BT1 4HL (telephone 028 9025 2000) for certified copies of registrations. Indexes to marriages and deaths in Northern Ireland are held at the GRO in Belfast, too. Look at the website **www.groni.gov.uk** for more information about the service.

Census returns and other records are held in the National Archives of Ireland, Bishop Street, Dublin 8 (telephone 003531 4072300). Also, look at its website **www.nationalarchives.ie**. The 1901 and 1911 censuses have been microfilmed, and copies may be ordered to read at LDS Family History Centres. Only fragments of earlier census returns from 1841 now survive, and there are none at all for 1881. For a county by county inventory, consult J. Gibson and M. Medlycott, *Local Census Listings, 1522–1930, Holdings in the British Isles* (FFHS, 3rd edn 1997).

Abstracts of the service records held at the PRO, Kew, of members of the Royal Irish Constabulary have been published alphabetically by name in J. Herlihy's *The Royal Irish Constabulary: A Complete Alphabetical List of Officers and Men, 1816–1922* (Dublin, 1999), enabling you to identify the PRO document in which each man will be found. The Army, Navy, Royal Marines, Royal Air Force and Merchant Navy records of service at Kew contain lots of references to Irishmen. To find out more, look at the information leaflets on **www.pro.gov.uk**.

The Society of Genealogists holds some useful material on Irish families, summarized in A. J. Camp's *Sources for Irish Genealogy in the Library of the Society of Genealogists* (SoG, 2nd edn 1998). For useful websites, see S. A. Raymond, *Irish Family History on the Web, A Directory* (FFHS, 2001).

Records of ancestors in India

Indexed ecclesiastical returns of births, baptisms, marriages, deaths and burials of Britons, Europeans and Eurasian Christians in India, Burma and territories controlled from India, from the late seventeenth century to 1947, and a few between 1948 and 1952, are kept among the India Office Collections, along with registered wills and administration grants, East India Company military, merchant and civil service records, railway-company appointments, printed almanacs listing pre-1947 British residents, and a variety of other biographical sources and official publications. There is also a growing biographical card index. These form part of the British Library Oriental and India Office Collections, 96 Euston Road, St Pancras, London NW1 2DB (telephone 020 7412 7873, email **oic-enquiries@bl.uk**, website **www.bl.uk/collections**). You will need a reader's ticket to gain entry. This can be issued when you visit, on production of identification such as a valid UK driving licence or credit card (see the website for more information). It is planned to make the catalogues available on the internet, and details of the holdings can be found in I. A. Baxter, *India Office Library and Records: A Brief Guide to Biographical Sources* (London, 2nd edn 1990), a copy of which is in the library in the General Reference area on the first floor of the FRC.

Divorce records

You can search microfilmed copies of indexes to divorces granted in England and Wales, 1858–1958, at the FRC and at the PRO, Kew; some files of divorce papers, up to 1954, have been preserved at Kew, too. However, you cannot inspect later indexes at either the FRC or the PRO. These are kept by the Principal Registry of the Family Division, Decree Absolute Search Section, First Avenue House, 42–49 High Holborn, London WC1V 6NP (telephone 020 7947 7017). There is a fee of £20 per 10-year search, which includes a copy of the decree absolute (or decree nisi, if applicable), which will be posted to you within 10 working days. Crossed cheques or postal orders should be made payable to HM Paymaster General. Make sure you write your name and address on the back, plus the name of the divorce case. There is no refund if a particular divorce is not found. If the divorce was granted in another court, you will be given its name and the case number, and that court will be instructed to send you a copy of the decree. If you already have the case number and title from the above indexes or elsewhere, you can purchase a copy of the relevant decree for £1 from the Principal Registry of the Family Division (*address above*).

Wills and administration grants, 1858 onwards (England and Wales)

Although there are microfiche copies of the annual National Probate Indexes from 12 January 1858 until 1943 on the first floor of the FRC, the actual wills and administrations can be read, as faxed copies, in the Probate Searchroom of the Principal

Registry of the Family Division (telephone 020 7947 7022, website **www.courtservice.gov.uk/wills_probate/probate_famhist.htm**) at the address given in the section on divorce (*see* p. 26). Help yourself to a leaflet and map from the Research Enquiries Desk at the FRC. Alternatively, you can search copies in any of the District Probate Registries, whose addresses are available on the same website. Microfiche copies of the indexes are also kept in the Microfilm Reading Room at the PRO, Kew, and in many local record offices, reference libraries and district probate registries. For details of locally held indexes and registered wills since 1858, consult J. Gibson, *Probate Jurisdictions: Where to Look for Wills* (FFHS, 4th edn 1997), which covers the whole of the British Isles.

A complete set of indexes from 1858 onwards is available on the open shelves in the Probate Searchroom (opening hours Monday to Friday, from 10 a.m. to 4.30 p.m.). When you have located the will or grant you want, you can order a copy to be faxed to you in the searchroom. This may take up to an hour, so you need to get there well before 3 p.m., when the last orders are dispatched. The service costs £5 per request. You can arrange for the copy to be posted to you, if you prefer. Ask about free facilities for reading copies of wills over 100 years old. Unless you specifically want a copy, usually the index entries relating to administration grants will reveal as much information as you will ever get.

If you are not able to visit the Probate Searchroom at First Avenue House, you can order copies of wills and administrations by post. The address to write to is Postal Searches and Copies Department, York Probate Sub-Registry, Duncombe Place, York YO1 7EA. If you do not know the exact date of death, probate or grant, quote the full name and last known address of the deceased and request a search of the indexes for up to four years around the year you think that person may have died. This costs £5, including a copy of the will or grant, if found; further four-year searches cost £3 apiece. As with divorce searches, crossed cheques and postal orders should be made payable to HM Paymaster General. Allow 21 working days for a reply.

Wills proved in courts other than the Prerogative Court of Canterbury before 1858

Although registered copies of wills and grants of administration from the PCC up to 9 January 1858 may be read on microfilm at the FRC and at Kew, there was a multitude of local church courts, and other courts, with authority to prove wills and make grants of letters of administration. For a complete list of these, plus their dates, whereabouts, and finding aids to them, consult the guide by J. Gibson mentioned above.

Other PCC probate material up to 1858

Original wills bearing the signatures or marks of testators and witnesses are kept at the PRO, Kew, along with thousands of indexed inventories of personal estates, probate act books, and records of contested wills. These are described in M. Scott's

Prerogative Court of Canterbury Wills and Other Probate Records (PRO, 1997), of which there is a copy in the library in the General Reference area on the first floor of the FRC. Copies of some of the probate inventory indexes are kept in this area, too.

Death Duty registers, 1858–1903

At the FRC you can search microfilm copies, from 1796 to 1903, of the yearly indexes to wills and administration grants that attracted Death Duty, not only in the Prerogative Court of Canterbury but in all the country courts (*see* pp. 117–19), too. However, at present, the microfilmed Death Duty registers themselves only extend up to 1857, so later registers have to be ordered as original documents at Kew. Because some volumes are held off-site, you will need to give a minimum of three days' notice of your request.

Records about men and women in the Armed Forces

Personnel records relating to millions of British soldiers, sailors, airmen, merchant seamen and women in the Armed Services are held at the PRO, Kew. If you take 1921 as the cut-off date for discharged soldiers and airmen, and 1928 for date of entry of Royal Naval ratings, you will have a good idea of what you can search there. *Tracing Your Ancestors in the Public Record Office* describes the records in more detail, and there are information leaflets covering each Service on **www.pro.gov.uk** and at the PRO itself. There is a small stock of these leaflets at the FRC, and you can either print out a copy yourself or request a copy of a leaflet to be printed for you from the internet.

The PRO publishes a series of handbooks about each of the Services, which are updated regularly as more records become available to the public to search; details are included in the Bibliography on pp. 169–71. Copies of these handbooks are available in the library in the General Reference area on the first floor of the FRC and in the library at Kew.

And you won't find the following at the FRC

- Apprenticeship records
- Cemetery and cremation records
- Changes of name*
- Civil litigation records*
- Criminal court records*
- Electoral registers
- Naturalization certificates (but the FRC does have indexes for 1509–1936)*
- Occupational records (for example, those of coastguards, customs and excise officers, dockyard workers, nurses, policemen, railway staff, and teachers)*

- Old newspapers (national or local)
- Ships' passenger lists (outgoing or incoming)*
- Tax lists*
- Tithe maps*
- Valuation Office maps*
- Transportation registers of convicts*

However, many of these (*) are to be found at the PRO, Kew. To find out more, see *Tracing Your Ancestors in the Public Record Office*, or visit **www.pro.gov.uk** and click on the index to the online leaflets.

Search etiquette

Here are 12 tips to becoming a model family history researcher:

- Be prepared! Have a good idea of who and what you are looking for, and where. A little forward planning will go a long way towards making your trip a success, and helps the staff when you seek advice.
- Don't bring too much clobber. A summary of the stage you have reached and a checklist of things to do are invaluable – but quite sufficient.
- Leave your bags, drinks and coat in the lockers and cloakroom. Otherwise they'll impede your progress and take up space, may trip you or other searchers up, and may even get lost.
- Only use your mobile phone in the ground floor lobby or on the lower ground floor. Better still, leave it at home.
- Read any leaflets on display, They are designed for you, to make searching easier and steer you through the system.
- Always read the introduction to any index, to find out how it works and what each reference means. Each index tends to be unique.
- Try to avoid sharing your success or frustration with everyone around you or chatting too loudly with companions. It's easy to get carried away by enthusiasm, but distracting for those still trying to track down that elusive ancestor.
- Only remove one microfilm or microfiche at a time, please – and don't forget to put a marker box or microfiche card in its place when you remove the film or fiche from its drawer.
- Don't take the marker box or microfiche card out of the searchroom. They are security tagged and will set off the alarm!
- As soon as you have finished with it, make sure you return the marker box or microfiche card to where you first found it. This will give someone else a turn.
- Don't hog the photocopiers. Find the page(s) or folio(s) you want to copy at one of the microfilm or microfiche readers and write them down, then use the copier.
- Leave the place as you found it – tidy!

2 The General Register Office search area

Indexes of births, marriages and deaths in England and Wales

The General Register Office (GRO) holds **indexes only** to:

- **Registers of births, marriages and deaths in England and Wales from 1 July 1837 onwards**
- **Registers of adoptions since 1927 in England and Wales**
- **Regimental registers of births and baptisms, 1761–1824, including soldiers and their families stationed in the British Isles**

You can search the indexes during FRC opening hours (*see* p. xvi). However, to permit staff training, on Thursdays the tills are not open until 10 a.m. The registers themselves are kept in the General Register Office, part of the Office for National Statistics, in Southport.

The GRO holds registrations of stillbirths that have occurred since 1927. These, and the indexes to them, are not open to the public. Details about stillbirths will be revealed only with the consent of the Registrar General to the parents, or to siblings when both parents are dead.

Having found a likely reference in the indexes, you will need to purchase a certified copy of the original entry in the registers for full information. Each of these certified copies – generally referred to as certificates – costs £6.50, payable in advance. Certificates can be paid for by cash, credit or debit card, or by cheque (with a valid guarantee card) made payable to ONS. They are available for collection at the FRC in four working days, or can be sent to you by first-class post on the fourth working day. Some family history societies and individuals offer a courier service; for details, look at their websites or the family history press. There is a priority service for people needing certificates urgently. Such certificates are available one working day after your application, if you apply before 4 p.m. The fee for this service is £22.50.

If you asked for your certificate to be posted to you and it hasn't arrived within the specified time, write to the General Register Office, PO Box 2, Southport, Merseyside PR8 2JD, or phone 0870 243 7788. If you are collecting your certificate and it isn't ready, the staff at the Customer Services Desk on the ground floor of the FRC should be able to assist you.

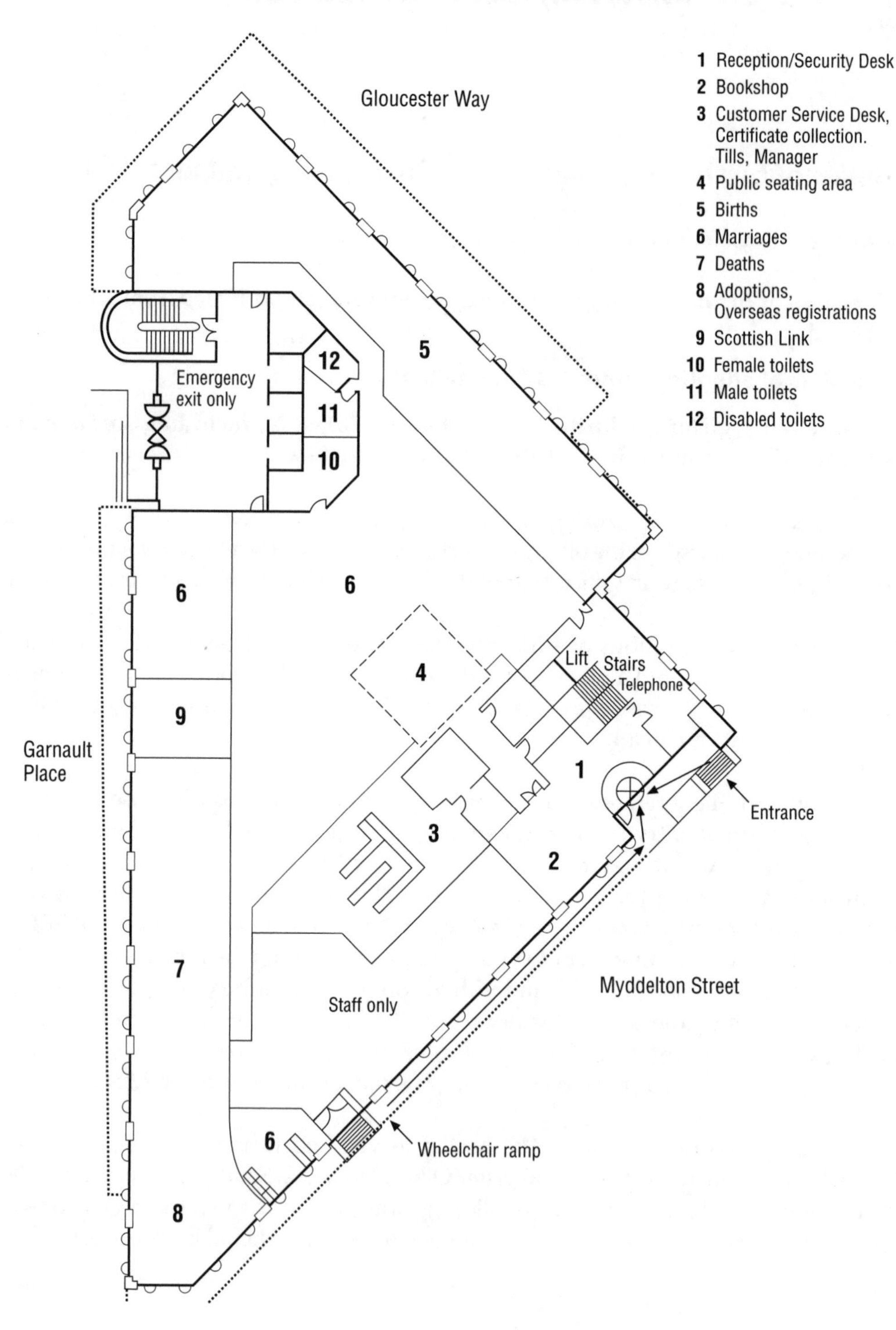
GROUND FLOOR OF THE FAMILY RECORDS CENTRE
1 Reception/Security Desk
2 Bookshop
3 Customer Service Desk, Certificate collection. Tills, Manager
4 Public seating area
5 Births
6 Marriages
7 Deaths
8 Adoptions, Overseas registrations
9 Scottish Link
10 Female toilets
11 Male toilets
12 Disabled toilets
Gloucester Way
Garnault Place
Myddelton Street
Emergency exit only
Lift
Stairs
Telephone
Entrance
Staff only
Wheelchair ramp

The GRO indexes for births, marriages and deaths in England and Wales from 1837

Births, marriages and deaths have been centrally registered since 1 July 1837. There are separate series of indexes to births, marriages and deaths. These are colour-coded (red books for births, green for marriages, and black for deaths). The indexes are arranged, in strict alphabetical order by surname and forename, in quarterly volumes up to the end of 1983. Thereafter, they are arranged alphabetically under each year of registration. The spine of each volume tells you what period it covers.

The quarterly indexes start with the September quarter 1837 and relate to births, marriages and deaths registered between 1 July and 30 September. The next set of indexes, for the December quarter 1837, include registrations from 1 October to 31 December. Indexes for the March quarter of 1838 record registrations from 1 January until 31 March 1838, while those for the June quarter of 1838 refer to registrations from 1 April up to 30 June 1838. And so on, until the last day of the December quarter of 1983. The annual indexes, from 1984 onwards, include birth, marriage and death registrations from the beginning of January to the end of December each year.

Against each person's name you will find the registration-district name, volume and page numbers of the registered entry (*see* p. 37 for an example). It is essential to write all this down, plus the year and quarter, which are stamped on the spine of the index book and usually typed at the top of each page. It is a good idea to transfer this information directly onto one of the application forms. You can collect these near the tills, from the Customer Services Desk, or in the appropriate search area. The forms are pink for births, green for marriages, and mauve for deaths.

Using indexes nearer home

If you live out of London, there is no need to visit the FRC to consult these indexes. Microfiche and microfilm copies are widely available in local libraries and LDS Family History Centres. Visit **www.familia.org.uk** for information about local library copies, and **www.familysearch.org** for addresses and contact numbers of Family History Centres. To order a copy of the certificate you want, you can download the online application form at **www.statistics.gov.uk**, then complete it, quoting your credit card details, and send it to the given address. It is planned to introduce direct online ordering. If you do not have access to the internet, post the index details to General Register Office, PO Box 2, Southport, Merseyside PR8 2JD, citing the exact index reference and enclosing credit or debit card details or a cheque or postal order made payable to ONS for £8. Payments from abroad should be made in sterling, either by cheque or international draft, in favour of ONS and bear the name and address of a

London clearing bank. You can also order a certificate by phone on 0870 243 7788 (Monday to Thursday 8 a.m. to 6 p.m., Friday 8 a.m. to 5 p.m., Saturday 10 a.m. to 4 p.m.) or by fax on 01704 560958. Results are dispatched within five working days. In the event of a reference or references being quoted incorrectly, you will be charged a fee of £4.50 for the first reference checked and £3 for each subsequent reference checked on the same application.

If you do not have access to the GRO indexes, you can request a search of any specified three-year period. This costs £11 per three-year search, including the cost of the resulting certificate. The results of these applications will be dispatched to you within 20 working days of receipt. Financially, it is probably not a good idea to follow this route if you have a lot of research to do.

A priority service is also available. If you are applying by post, mark the outside of your envelope 'Priority', and enclose payment of £24 for each full certificate, quoting the GRO index reference, or £27 if you require an index search. Certificates are posted out on the next working day following receipt of the application. Adoption certificates cost £11 by post (there are no local copies of indexes to adoptions).

If you have any general enquiries, either phone the above number or fax 01704 550013, or email **certificate.services@ons.gov.uk**.

Figure 4 Some of the quarterly index volumes listing births registered in England and Wales. Full details from these indexes are required before you can order certified copies of the registrations.

If you live overseas, find out if your genealogical societies and libraries have copies of the indexes to English and Welsh registrations. For instance, the Genealogical Society of Victoria operates a search service of the GRO indexes between 1837 and 1910, and you can order a copy of the appropriate certificate online on **www.gsv.org.au**, using Australian currency, or do the search yourself in the Society's library.

You can consult some of the GRO's English and Welsh birth, marriage and death indexes before 1901 online at **http://freebmd.rootsweb.com**, although these are as yet incomplete. If you find the entry you want, there is a direct link to **www.statistics.gov.uk**, where you can download an application form. The Family History Society of Cheshire and the South Cheshire Family History Society are gradually creating online indexes to the births, marriages and deaths registered throughout the county between 1837 and 1950 (**www.cheshirebmd.org.uk**), drawing on local registration-district indexes. Having found the entry you want, fill in the appropriate online application form and send it with your payment to the relevant local register office (*see* p. 44). Remember, though, that the local district registrars' index details will not be the same as the Registrar General's centralized indexes, which cover the whole of England and Wales. If you apply to the local district office where the event was registered, the fee is £6.50. For district office addresses, see under 'Registrations of births, deaths and marriages' in the phone book; or consult R. Blatchford, *The Family and Local History Handbook* (York, 6th edn 2002).

Searching the GRO indexes

The indexes are in large volumes. If you have difficulty handling the books, there is a microfiche set of birth, marriage and death indexes from 1837 to 1983 and a computerized index of births and deaths, 1984–92, and marriages, 1984–93. Ask at the Customer Services Desk if you want to use these.

Remove only one index from the shelves at a time. Go through it looking for your 'vital event'. All the index entry will reveal is the **registration district** of the birth, marriage or death – and not the name of the place where the event happened.

Marriages are registered at the time they take place, but births may be registered some time later, since parents are given up to six weeks within which to register the event. Deaths are normally registered within five days; if there was any delay, that might be because there was a coroner's inquest.

Birth indexes (red)

These are handwritten before 1860. From the September quarter of 1911, they give the child's mother's maiden surname. Between 1984 and 1992, the yearly indexes record registration details slightly differently: you will find the name and number of the registration district as well as the volume and page on which the entry can be found. From 1993, the registration-district name and number, register and entry numbers are followed by the month and year of registration. To order a birth certificate, you will need to transfer all this information onto the pink application form.

Marriage indexes (green)

Almost all the indexes are handwritten up to the December quarter of 1865. There are two index entries per marriage – one for the bride, the other for the groom – and the details against their names match each other exactly. Cross-references in each index entry to the surname of the spouse have been made since 1912.

Women are listed under the name they were using at the time of marriage. For previously unmarried women, this will be their maiden surname. However, if a woman had been married before and continued to use that name (for example, if she was a widow), she would be indexed under her former married surname.

From 1984 until 1993, the indexes give the registration-district name and number as well as the volume and page numbers of the registered entry. Indexes from 1994 onwards record the registration-district name and number, month, page and entry numbers, and a source code, all of which must be included on the green application form for a marriage certificate.

Death indexes (black)

The indexes are mostly handwritten up to the December quarter of 1865. Up to then, the indexes do not record given ages at decease. On the application form for a pre-1866 death, it is always a good idea to write the minimum age you would have expected that person to be, or add other facts about which you are certain. You will then receive a partial refund of £3.50 if the information doesn't tally.

Starting with the March quarter of 1866, alleged ages are included in the death indexes. From 1 April 1969, dates of birth are given (commencing with the index for April–June, 1969). Between 1984 and 1992, the yearly indexes supply the registration-district name and number, volume and page numbers against each entry; and from 1993 onwards, the registration-district name and number, register and entry numbers, and the month and year of registration. You need to copy all this information onto the mauve application form for a death certificate.

Supposing you know that your grandfather died in 1950, you can look up his name in the indexes and discover that he was apparently 70 years of age. You can then search for his birth registration in the birth indexes for 1880. If you don't find it there, search the indexes for the years around 1880, starting with 1881 and 1879, because his age at death might have been guesswork on the part of the informant.

How do I know if I have got the correct entry?

There will often be a number of people with the same name whose births, marriages and deaths were registered in the same quarter of the year. Here is an example of a list of birth registrations:

Name	Registration District	Volume Number	Page Number
PEARCE Edward	Bourn	7a	289
PEARCE Edward	Mile End	1c	491
PEARCE Edward	Halifax	9a	475
PEARCE Edward	Mile End	1c	580
PEARCE Edward	Kensington	1a	147
PEARCE Edward Richard	Pembroke	11a	697
PEARCE James Edward	Melksham	5a	101
PEARCE Male	Camelford	5c	12
PEARCE Male	Marylebone	1a	392

You will need to know the **registration district** where the event occurred. There are two maps on the walls of the GRO search area showing registration districts from 1837 to 1851 and from 1852 to 1946 (*see* pp. 162–3 for a list of the districts and their numbers). You can buy copies of these maps at the Customer Services Desk or in the FRC bookshop. Registration districts correspond roughly to a medium-sized town. Originally they were based on the Poor Law unions (the civil administrative districts set up in 1834 to supervise relief of local paupers). If you are looking for a village birth, you may find that it is in a registration district bearing the name of the nearest market town. Some names are purely artificial.

If you have a query about a particular place and the registration district it might be in, ask at the Customer Services Desk, where a copy of the current issue of *The Official List* will tell you the answer. *The List* gives a complete directory of addresses, opening hours and phone numbers of English and Welsh district registrars' offices, together with an index of abolished or renamed districts, indicating dates of closure and successor districts.

In the Census and Wills Reading Room, on the first floor of the FRC, there is a copy of *An Index to Civil Registration Districts of England and Wales, 1837 to date*, compiled and published by J. A. Newport in 1989, which lists every district change since registration began. Ask about this at the Research Enquiries Desk. You can also find addresses of English and Welsh registration districts between 1837 and 1930 on **www.genuki.org.uk/big/eng/RegOffice** (use the alphabetical place-name index if you're not sure in which county or district they belong). If you find two or more events for your name in the same registration district, in the same quarter, like the two Mile End Edward Pearces above, then you can do a reference check (*see below*).

Applying for a certificate

When you have located the birth, marriage or death you want, complete one of the application forms, taking down the details from the index. If you want a birth certificate, make sure you order a full certificate on one of the pink forms (not a peach form, which is for a short certificate). If the birth you are after took place within the last 50 years, you will need to supply details of the child's parents' names on the application form, or produce some kind of personal identification for yourself. Similarly, if the deceased was a child aged 16 or under, the full names of the father and mother are required on the mauve death application form.

Take the completed form to one of the windows in the tills area, together with your payment (£6.50, or £22.50 if it is a priority order). Cash, credit and debit cards, or a cheque with a valid guarantee card are accepted. Remember that on Thursdays you can search the indexes from 9 a.m. but cannot order a certificate before 10 a.m., when the tills open. You will be given a receipt which tells you when the certificate will be ready for you to collect on the fourth working day (or after 24 hours if it is a priority order). If you have indicated on the application form that you want the certificate to be posted to you, you will be handed an envelope on which to write your name and address. The certificate will be dispatched to you by first-class post on the fourth working day after your application. Applications handed in on a Saturday will be ready for collection, or dispatched to you, on the following Friday.

Reference checking

If there is only one index entry but you are not sure if it is the one you want, complete an application form as usual but fill in the back of the form with any additional identifying details. The GRO staff will then check the registration and only issue a certificate if the information ties up. If it does not, no certificate will be issued and you will receive a refund of £3.50.

If there are several entries that might be the right one, you can request a reference-checking sheet. First of all, fill in an application form with the first reference you would like to have checked. You must complete the back of the form with some extra details, which the GRO staff can use to identify the entry you want. For instance, you might know the exact date of birth, or the parents' forenames, or mother's maiden surname. Then insert on the reference-checking sheet the other entries you want checked, placing them in order of likelihood of being correct. You will have to pay

CERTIFIED COPY OF AN ENTRY OF MARRIAGE

GIVEN AT THE GENERAL REGISTER OFFICE

Application Number PSR 2002

1881. Marriage solemnized at the Parish Church in the Parish of Petersham in the County of Surrey

No.	When Married.	Name and Surname.	Age.	Condition.	Rank or Profession.	Residence at the time of Marriage.	Father's Name and Surname.	Rank or Profession of Father.
266	July 16 1881	Claude George Bowes Lyon (Lord Glamis)	full	Bachelor	Earl's Son & Lieut. in 2nd Life Guards	Hyde Park Barracks	Claude Bowes Lyon	Earl of Strathmore Kinghorn
		Cecilia Nina Cavendish Bentinck	minor	Spinster		Forbes House Ham	Charles Cavendish Bentinck	Priest in holy orders

Married in the above Church according to the Rites and Ceremonies of the Established Church, by Special Licence or after by me, Robert Liddell, Vicar of

This Marriage was solemnized between us, Claude George Bowes Lyon, Cecilia Nina Cavendish Bentinck

in the Presence of us, Strathmore, Portland, F. W. Strathmore, E. Burnaby, M. Genl., A. W. Scott, C. Louisa Scott, Claude Wilson

CERTIFIED to be a true copy of an entry in the certified copy of a register of Marriages in the Registration District of Richmond, Surrey

Given at the GENERAL REGISTER OFFICE, under the Seal of the said Office, the 21st day of January 2002

MXA967935

This certificate is issued in pursuance of section 65 of the Marriage Act 1949. Sub-section 3 of that section provides that any certified copy of an entry purporting to be sealed or stamped with the seal of the General Register Office shall be received as evidence of the marriage to which it relates without any further or other proof of the entry, and no certified copy purporting to have been given in the said Office shall be of any force or effect unless it is sealed or stamped as aforesaid.

CAUTION: THERE ARE OFFENCES RELATING TO FALSIFYING OR ALTERING A CERTIFICATE AND USING OR POSSESSING A FALSE CERTIFICATE. ©CROWN COPYRIGHT

WARNING: A CERTIFICATE IS NOT EVIDENCE OF IDENTITY.

GENERAL REGISTER OFFICE ENGLAND

Figure 5 Marriage certificate of Lord Glamis and Cecilia Nina Cavendish Bentinck, grandparents of HM Queen Elizabeth II, July 1881. The witnesses include the groom's parents, the bride's uncle, Major General Burnaby, her mother and stepfather, and her kinsman the Duke of Portland.

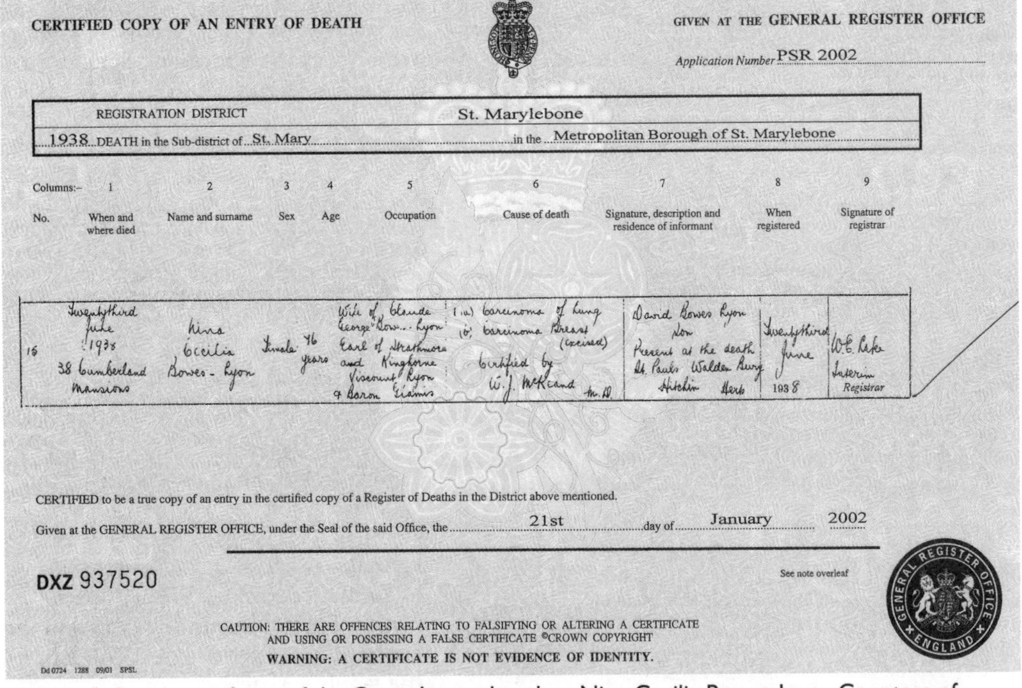
CERTIFIED COPY OF AN ENTRY OF DEATH

GIVEN AT THE GENERAL REGISTER OFFICE

Application Number PSR 2002

REGISTRATION DISTRICT St. Marylebone

1938 DEATH in the Sub-district of St. Mary in the Metropolitan Borough of St. Marylebone

No.	1 When and where died	2 Name and surname	3 Sex	4 Age	5 Occupation	6 Cause of death	7 Signature, description and residence of informant	8 When registered	9 Signature of registrar
15	Twentythird June 1938 38 Cumberland Mansions	Nina Cecilia Bowes-Lyon	Female	76 years	Wife of Claude George Bowes-Lyon Earl of Strathmore and Kinghorne Viscount Lyon & Baron Glamis	1 (a) Carcinoma of Lung (b) Carcinoma Breast (excised) Certified by W. J. McKeand M.D.	David Bowes Lyon Son Present at the death St. Pauls Walden Bury Hitchin Herts	Twentythird June 1938	W. E. Leke Interim Registrar

CERTIFIED to be a true copy of an entry in the certified copy of a Register of Deaths in the District above mentioned.

Given at the GENERAL REGISTER OFFICE, under the Seal of the said Office, the 21st day of January 2002

DXZ 937520

See note overleaf

CAUTION: THERE ARE OFFENCES RELATING TO FALSIFYING OR ALTERING A CERTIFICATE AND USING OR POSSESSING A FALSE CERTIFICATE ©CROWN COPYRIGHT

WARNING: A CERTIFICATE IS NOT EVIDENCE OF IDENTITY.

GENERAL REGISTER OFFICE ENGLAND

Figure 6 Death certificate of the Queen's grandmother, Nina Cecilia Bowes-Lyon, Countess of Strathmore and Kinghorne, 1938. She died a year after seeing her daughter crowned Queen Consort of King George VI. Her youngest son, David Bowes-Lyon, was the informant.

CERTIFIED COPY OF AN ENTRY OF BIRTH

GIVEN AT THE GENERAL REGISTER OFFICE

Application Number PSR 2002

REGISTRATION DISTRICT Hitchin

1900 BIRTH in the Sub-district of Hitchin in the County of Hertford

Columns:- No.	1 When and where born	2 Name, if any	3 Sex	4 Name and surname of father	5 Name, surname and maiden surname of mother	6 Occupation of father	7 Signature, description and residence of informant	8 When registered	9 Signature of registrar	10 Name entered after registration
269	Fourth August 1900 St. Pauls Walden Bury Parish Paulswalden	Elizabeth Angela Marguerite	Girl	Claude George Bowes Lyon	Cecilia Nina Bowes Lyon formerly Cavendish Bentinck	Peer's Eldest Son	Glamis Father St. Pauls Walden Bury Saint Paulswalden	Twenty first September 1900	H. Bayliss Registrar	

CERTIFIED to be a true copy of an entry in the certified copy of a Register of Births in the District above mentioned.

Given at the GENERAL REGISTER OFFICE, under the Seal of the said Office, the 21st day of January 2002

BXBZ 418028

CAUTION: THERE ARE OFFENCES RELATING TO FALSIFYING OR ALTERING A CERTIFICATE AND USING OR POSSESSING A FALSE CERTIFICATE ©CROWN COPYRIGHT

WARNING: A CERTIFICATE IS NOT EVIDENCE OF IDENTITY.

GENERAL REGISTER OFFICE ENGLAND

BXBZ Series Dd 0723 1285 09/01 SPSL

Figure 7 *(above)* Birth certificate of the Queen's mother, Elizabeth Angela Marguerite Bowes-Lyon, 1900. She was registered as being born at home in St Paul's Walden Bury, Hertfordshire. Lord Glamis, her father, was the informant, almost seven weeks later.

QBDX 134843

Application Number PSR 2002

CERTIFIED COPY OF AN ENTRY

BIRTH

NHS Number SBSS 115 — Entry No. 115

Registration district: Westminster — Administrative area

Sub-district: Westminster — City of Westminster

CHILD

1. Date and place of birth: Twenty first June 1982 St Mary's Hospital Praed Street Westminster
2. Name and surname: His Royal Highness Prince William Arthur Philip Louis — 3. Sex: Male

FATHER

4. Name and surname: His Royal Highness Prince Charles Philip Arthur George Prince of Wales
5. Place of birth: Westminster
6. Occupation: Prince of the United Kingdom

MOTHER

7. Name and surname: Her Royal Highness The Princess of Wales
8. Place of birth: Sandringham Norfolk
9. (a) Maiden surname: SPENCER — (b) Surname at marriage if different from maiden surname: —
10. Usual address (if different from place of child's birth): Highgrove Near Tetbury Gloucestershire

INFORMANT

11. Name and surname (if not the mother or father): — 12. Qualification: Father
13. Usual address (if different from that in 10 above): —
14. I certify that the particulars entered above are true to the best of my knowledge and belief: Charles — Signature of informant
15. Date of registration: Nineteenth July 1982 — 16. Signature of registrar: [illegible] Registrar
17. Name given after registration, and surname

*See notes overleaf

QBDX Series

CERTIFIED to be a true copy of an entry in the certified copy of a register of Births or Deaths in the District above mentioned. Given at the GENERAL REGISTER OFFICE, under the Seal of the said Office on 25th January 2002

CAUTION: THERE ARE OFFENCES RELATING TO FALSIFYING OR ALTERING A CERTIFICATE AND USING OR POSSESSING A FALSE CERTIFICATE ©CROWN COPYRIGHT

WARNING: A CERTIFICATE IS NOT EVIDENCE OF IDENTITY.

GENERAL REGISTER OFFICE ENGLAND

Figure 8 *(left)* Birth certificate of the Queen's grandson, Prince William Arthur Philip Louis, 1982. Parents' birthplaces and usual address have been recorded since 1 April 1969. Prince William's birth is indexed in the September quarter, under Windsor, the family surname.

£6.50 for the first reference, and £3 for each of the other ones. This fee covers the cost of any resulting certificate.

On the bottom of the reference sheet there are two options: either a check of all the references, or for the check to stop at the first reference that agrees. If you opt for the first, all the references will be checked and a certificate produced of the first corresponding entry (if one is found). If you choose the second option, the references will be checked one by one, until an entry is found that matches your information – in which case, you will receive a refund of £3.50 for each reference that remains unchecked. The searches are specific, so only include information about which you are certain and don't be tempted to make guesses, or you may not get the certificate you want. Also, be careful when using 'father's occupation' as a checking point, since people's jobs may change over time.

As mentioned above, you might know from some other source the exact date of birth or the name of the parent. In the case of the two Edward Pearces born in the Mile End area, let's suppose 'your' Edward Pearce's mother's first name was Lucy. Insert her name on the back of the application form, and the certificate will only be produced if one of the Edward Pearces in the index had a mother called Lucy.

Information on the certificates

Look at the certificate of HM the Queen Mother's birth in 1900 (*opposite*), her parents' marriage certificate in 1881 and her mother's death certificate in 1938 (both on p. 39), or at the certificates reproduced in the case studies on pp. 142, 143 and 156.

The given information varies slightly according to the date of the registration. All full birth certificates, from 1837 onwards, include the child's registered name(s) – or the child's sex if no names had been chosen – and the precise date and place of birth. They disclose the father's name, surname and occupation, the mother's name and maiden surname and any former surnames, the informant's name and address and relationship to the child, the date of registration and the name of the registrar. The informant is usually one of the parents, so check whether his or her address is the same as that of the birth.

Birth and death certificates changed format on 1 April 1969. Thereafter, birth certificates include the child's surname and National Health Service number. Look at the certificate of Prince William's birth in 1982 (on p. 40), and compare it with the information on his great-grandmother's birth certificate (on the same page).

Prior to 1 April 1969, you will see that no surname was given for the child. It was assumed from the surname of the parents, and indexed accordingly. In addition, a post-1969 certificate will include details of the places of birth of both parents and, where relevant, both the mother's maiden name and, if she had been married more than once, the most recent name she was using when she married the father. The mother's usual address, if the baby was not born there, is also recorded. So are the name and surname of the informant, if not one of the parents, plus that person's usual address and qualification to be the informant.

Every birth certificate contains a final column for any name given to the child after registration.

In 1947, short birth certificates, with no details of parentage, were introduced as an option for those applicants wanting copies mainly for administrative purposes. These are of no use for family history, because they merely feature the child's name, surname, sex and date of birth, plus the registration district and sub-district of birth.

The content of marriage certificates has remained unchanged since 1 July 1837. They specify the date and place (church, chapel or register office) and whether the ceremony was by licence or after the reading of banns or by registrar's certificate. You can find the current names of both parties, their marital status at the time of the wedding, occupation (if any), age (sometimes given as 'over 21' or 'of full age', which means the same) and present address, plus the name and occupation of their fathers. The names of witnesses who signed the register and the name of the officiating minister and/or registrar are inserted at the bottom.

From 1837 up to 31 March 1969, the informant for a death registration was obliged to supply the date, place and cause of death, the person's name, sex, age and occupation, and his or her own name, description and address. The date of registration and the registrar's name were also recorded. The death certificate of a married or widowed woman will also mention the name and occupation of her husband. Before 1874, the cause of death might be pure conjecture; subsequently it is more likely to be reliable, because a medical certificate had to be produced. In addition to these details, since 1 April 1969 death certificates record the date and place of birth and usual address of the deceased, plus maiden surname if the deceased was a married woman.

Be wary of accepting all the information at face value. People lie about their age for a variety of reasons, and in the past they would not necessarily have been sure how old they really were. Ages given on marriage certificates should be treated with caution, because a minor might add on a few years to avoid having to prove parental consent to an unpopular union, or one of the parties might have wanted to conceal the fact that he or she was much older than the other. Ages on death certificates can be misleading, since the informant may not have known the deceased's true age. Addresses on marriage certificates are notoriously unreliable, because couples often 'establish residence' somewhere in order to get married in a certain church. The stated occupations of grooms and fathers may have been embellishments or fabrications to impress the relatives of the other party; and a father's name could be an invention, designed to avoid an embarrassing gap if one of the couple was illegitimate or did not know the father's identity. Before 1875, a mother or other relative registering an illegitimate birth might name anyone as the father with impunity. Although the law was then tightened up (*see* p. 44), there are known cases of much more recent illegitimate births away from home being registered by a grandparent as their own legitimate issue.

'Missing' births, marriages and deaths

Most experienced family historians will tell you they have at least one ancestor whose birth, marriage or death has for years eluded them. Some examples of the most common reasons why you can't locate an event that should be there are set out below.

- You are looking under Coom but the event is registered as Combe. Check alternative spellings.
- You haven't searched both columns of entries written on each typed page, or have missed out a quarterly index volume.
- The event happened in a different year from the one you have searched. Widen the period.
- The child was originally registered under different forenames – which were altered at baptism and notified to the Registrar General, but not altered in the index.
- Without realizing it, you are searching under a nickname. Pet names pose terrible hazards for the unwary.
- You haven't looked for forenames arranged in different configurations (for example, Maurice Albert, Albert Maurice, Albert M., etc.), or have overlooked an additional forename that was later dropped.
- The child was registered simply as 'male' or 'female', because no names had yet been chosen.
- The child's birth was registered in a different area to the expected.
- The birth was registered under the mother's maiden or previous married name. Since the Legitimacy Act 1926, it has been possible to register a child's birth a second time, under the married name of the mother, if she subsequently married the child's father.
- There may be a clerical error. The Registrar General's clerks in London may have failed to copy an entry registered locally, or may have misread it. If you know where the event took place, contact the local district registrar and request a search of his/her indexes (*see* p. 35), or search the original marriage registers (*see* pp. 22–3). Each such certificate will cost you £6.50 (cheques should be made payable to 'The Superintendent Registrar'). Enclose a stamped self-addressed envelope, or add 50p for postage if applying from outside the UK.

- Some births were never registered. There were many omissions before 1875, because until then the onus was on the district registrar to collect the information from parents. Thereafter responsibility lay with the parents; and if they failed to notify the registrar within six weeks of the birth, they faced a penalty. In the early years of civil registration, some parents chose between having their children baptized and registering their births, in the mistaken belief that they had a choice. You could try looking in local parish registers to see if this was the case with your family, or try the *IGI* or *BIVRI* (*see* p. 23). Registration-dodging went on until 1940, when evidence of registration became necessary for the issue of ration books. If you cannot find a registration, school admission registers can be culled for details of a pupil's name, date of birth, father's name, address and occupation. These records, starting around 1868, are now generally in county record offices or still held by the school itself. For addresses and information about record offices in your area, visit **www.hmc.gov.uk/archon** or consult *Record Repositories in Great Britain* (PRO, 11th edn 1999).
- A change of identity. This will foil even the most diligent of searchers, because your ancestor's birth and death will be registered under different names – and he or she may have married, or remarried, under the assumed identity.
- You can't find the marriage of a couple you know had children. Keep on looking – you may come across it after the birth of one or more of them.
- Your ancestors may not have married at all. The woman might simply have adopted the surname of her partner, which was used when registering their children's births. Or perhaps she might have been married before and set up home with a new man, by whom she had a new family.
- Your female ancestor remarried under a previous married name, but the birth registrations of her children merely give her maiden surname.
- Perhaps your forebear's birth was registered under a completely different name and then changed at adoption (*see* pp. 45–9).
- The event you are seeking took place in Scotland or Ireland, or abroad. If abroad, you can search the overseas indexes (*see* p. 49–55). If in Scotland, try the FRC's Scottish Link (*see* pp. 63–5); if in Ireland, *see* p. 25. If you are trying to trace a birth registered in Northern Ireland after 1 January 1922, you can search the computerized indexes in the Scottish Link.

Births outside marriage

Births outside marriage are usually registered by the mother, and a blank left where the father's name should be. If the parents were living as man and wife, then the father's name will probably appear. Until 1874, the mother could give any name she chose as the father of her child. After that date, the father's name was only inserted if he went with the mother to register his child's birth and signed the register with her, or if a statutory declaration could be produced acknowledging his paternity. In both cases, the father's name was added only with his consent.

If there is no hint in family lore as to who the father might be, you face problems – and are probably best advised to pursue the mother's line. You may perhaps find a reference to the father's name in parish, Poor Law union or quarter sessions records. Most of these are now deposited in local record offices. Catalogues to holdings of this kind are increasingly being made available via the internet; to find out what there is for your county, visit **www.a2a.pro.gov.uk**. J. Gibson and C. Rogers, *Poor Law Union Records* (see Bibliography for details) lists known records and their whereabouts; copies can be consulted in the library in the General Reference area on the first floor of the FRC. The boards of guardians of the Poor Law unions were the enforcement agency of the past. It was their job to ensure children were financially supported by their fathers, if they could be identified – and so save them from falling on the parish rates, or a worse fate in the workhouse.

If family tradition suggests that a child was sired by the local landowner or some famous person, then it may be worth checking the will of that individual and also the Death Duty registers for references to any provision made for such offspring (*see* pp. 117–24). The latter have a 'consanguinity' column, which explains the exact nature of the relationship between the beneficiary and the deceased.

Adoption (England and Wales)

Before January 1927 there was no central registration of adoption in this country.

Since time immemorial, childless couples have brought up other people's progeny and the informal fostering of illegitimate babies within the family circle or local community was commonplace. Masters might adopt orphaned apprentices to give them a better start in life; and godparents and family friends might take in orphaned children or those belonging to large families. The children generally assumed the surname of the family that gave them a home.

There was usually no formal record of such arrangements, but a mention might be made in the adopter's will or in correspondence. Church records include details of parish adoptions when children were boarded out and regular contributions made from the rates towards their upkeep; and those of private charities may shed light. Records of this kind are likely to be found either in local record offices or in the archives of the parish or charity. Again, the boards of guardians of Poor Law unions might arrange for boarding out or emigration. Evidence of this can be found among Poor Law material in county record offices and at the PRO, Kew. Visit **www.archives.ca** to search the database of over 100,000 names of such children sent to Canada between 1869 and the 1930s which is being created by members of the British Isles Family History Society of Greater Ottawa, using ships' passenger lists in the National Archives of Canada.

In the nineteenth century the numbers of poor orphan children escalated and orphanages were set up to house them, many under the auspices of religious bodies. The best-known organizations running orphanages are Barnardo's, the Church of England Children's Society (originally called the Waifs and Strays Society) and the National Children's Homes (Methodist). The Catholic Children's Society also ran a number of orphanages. Specific searches may be undertaken by these organizations for a fee – but before 1984 adoption agencies were only required to keep their records for 25 years, so you may be disappointed.

By 1900 there were in the region of 20 adoption agencies, but informal adoption of poor children by middle-class couples seems to have become popular during and after the First World War, when a baby boom coincided with a drop in the birth rate among the middle and upper classes. In 1926 legislation was introduced for the control of adoption by court order, and a registry was established. However, private arrangements still continued to be made, perhaps using the agency of a doctor, solicitor or friend. Some children are adopted by their grandparents or other relatives, and many are adopted by a step-parent.

Adoption indexes and certificates from 1927

In the GRO search area of the FRC, on the ground floor, you can search the Adopted Children's Register indexes from 1927 to date. These are red or buff books, with a buff or red spine on which are written the years covered by each volume. They contain information under the child's adopted name only, and there is no way you can cross-check with registered birth names. Between 1927 and 1965 the indexes record the adopted name, year of birth, date of adoption entry, and entry and volume numbers. From 1966 until 1992 the indexes give adopted name, year of birth, and entry and volume numbers; and from 1993 onwards, the adopted name and the Adopted Children's Register entry and volume numbers. Indexes for several years are often bound in one volume, so make sure you look at each of the yearly indexes within it.

You can order an adoption certificate in the same way as a birth certificate, by completing one of the yellow application forms nearby with information extracted from the index. A full certificate will cost £6.50 (or £22.50 if you choose the priority service), and collection or posting follows the same pattern as for birth certificates (*see* p. 31). You can also order an index search and certificate by post (*see* p. 34), by sending your application to Adoptions Section, General Register Office, Smedley Hydro, Southport, Merseyside PR8 2HH (telephone 0151 471 4830). Your cheque, postal order, international money order, or draft payable through a London clearing bank, for £11 (or £27 if you select the priority service) should be made out to ONS. If no trace is found, you will be refunded £3.50.

Adoption certificates refer to the adoptive parents and the child's adopted name only; there is no reference to the child's natural parents or original name. The certificates state the child's precise date of birth, the date of adoption, and the name of the authority making the adoption order. Up to 1949, if you purchase a short certificate (which will cost you £5, or £21 for priority service), rather than a full certificate, the country of birth will be given if it appears in the adoption order. Between 1950 and March 1959, the country of birth is invariably included. From 1 April 1959, the registration district of birth is included if the child was born in England or Wales; the country of birth is given if the child was born elsewhere.

Finding out who the natural parents were

There are two ways of making a link with the child's birth certificate – on which will be recorded the original registered names, the name of the mother (and father, if entered) and an address. Under the Adoption Act 1976, adopted adults, on reaching the age of 18, can apply to the Registrar General for access to their original birth record.

1. **If you are the adopted person,** you can apply to the Adoptions Section of the General Register Office under Section 51 of the Adoption Act 1976. If you were adopted before 12 November 1975, the law requires you to see a counsellor before you are given sufficient information to enable you to obtain your original birth record. Parents placing children for adoption were generally told such offspring would never have access to their birth records, making the break total. Because these arrangements were made in good faith, the purpose of the counselling is to give you basic information about your adoption and to help you understand some of the possible effects on you and others of any further enquiries you might wish to make about your birth family. The Registrar General will have sent the counsellor most of the information from your adoption order, including your original name, the name of your birth mother and possibly that of your birth father, and the name of the court that made the adoption order. You can then use this information to apply for a copy of your original birth registration at any time you decide you want to (the procedure is exactly the same as if you were searching for your birth certificate from the outset).

   You can ask for an interview with an adoption counsellor at the Family Records Centre, between Monday and Friday; to arrange this, you will need to make an appointment by phoning 0151 471 4831. You may prefer to arrange an interview locally, by contacting your local Social Services Department (whose telephone number will be listed in your local phone book); or if you were adopted under the auspices of a voluntary adoption society, you can elect for its advice, if it is still operating.

Since October 1991, overseas residents who were placed for adoption in England or Wales before 12 November 1975 can receive statutory counselling in the country where they now live. You can obtain an application form from the Adoptions Section of the General Register Office in Southport. The form will ask for details about the body or organization in your country of residence agreeing to conduct the counselling interview. Counselling is not necessary if you were adopted in Scotland, but you can send for an application form to the Registrar General in Edinburgh. For details about birth records in Northern Ireland, contact the Registrar General in Belfast.

If you were adopted on 12 November 1975 or later, you do not have to see a counsellor unless you want to (this applies to both UK and overseas residents). You can apply directly to the Registrar General for information about your birth. You will be furnished with the name of the court that made the adoption order, the number of the adoption application if any, your original registered name, and the name of your natural mother. You can then apply for your birth certificate in the usual way. You will also receive an authorization form to enable you to approach the court for the name of the local authority or adoption society that took part in the adoption arrangements.

You might want to contact the National Organisation for Counselling Adoptees and their Parents (NORCAP), 112 Church Road, Wheatley, Oxfordshire OX33 1LU (telephone 01865 875000, fax 01865 875686, email **enquiries@norcap.org**, website **www.norcap.org.uk**). TALKadoption is a helpline for young people under 26 who have a link with adoption, because they are adopted or have given a child for adoption, or are relatives or friends of adopted people. The freephone number (0808 808 1234) is manned Tuesday to Friday, from 3 p.m. until 9 p.m. You can visit the website at **www.talkadoption.org.uk**.

2. You can apply to the courts for the Registrar General to divulge the link between the adoption and the original birth records, under Section 50(5) of the Adoption Act 1976. Such applications are very rare, and generally only succeed on medical or inheritance grounds.

You can ask for your name and address to be inserted in the Adoption Contact Register. Part I of the Register is for adopted persons; Part II lists birth parents or other relatives of an adopted person who have similarly chosen to register an interest in making contact with the adopted person. The Registrar General will send the adopted person the names of these relatives, together with their given addresses, when a connection is found between entries in Parts I and II. These relatives are then notified that a link has been established. It is then up to the adopted person to make the initial contact. Registration fees (£15 for Part I, £30 for Part II) are payable for placing an entry in the Register. Application forms may be obtained from the Adoptions Section at the address given above (*see* p. 46). It usually takes about two to three weeks to process an application. When you move to another address, remember to inform the Registrar General. If you change your mind about registration, write to the Registrar General, who will then remove your name and address from the Register. Allow 28 days for this to be done.

For people adopted in Scotland, there is a separate voluntary service. Contact Birth Link, Family Care, 21 Castle Street, Edinburgh EH2 3DN, Scotland, for details.

Ask at the Customer Services Desk in the GRO search area of the FRC for the various booklets about access to birth records for people adopted in England and Wales and their birth relatives, the Adoption Contact Register, NORCAP and TALKadoption. There is also a booklet on access to birth records for adopted people living overseas.

Births, marriages and deaths of Britons abroad (Overseas Section)

Details about these events are scattered in many places. Be prepared to dig around. Although the Overseas Section of the GRO, in Southport, receives returns of births, marriages and deaths of British citizens from British registering authorities around the world, registration has never been compulsory.

The main series of records relating to British nationals in foreign countries are held by the GRO, to which there are indexes in the FRC. Microfilmed copies of the Registrar General's miscellaneous non-statutory returns, 1627–1965, and of the indexes, 1627–1960, can be searched in the PRO search area on the first floor of the FRC and in the Microfilm Reading Room of the PRO, Kew, where you can also search the GRO overseas indexes on microfiche. For details of known PRO holdings, refer to A. Bevan, *Tracing Your Ancestors in the Public Record Office* or S. Colwell, *Dictionary of Genealogical Sources in the Public Record Office* (London, 1992); or use the online catalogue on **www.pro.gov.uk**. *See also* pp. 54–5.

Other major collections, incomplete sets, copies and indexes of returns or registrations of overseas births, baptisms, marriages, deaths and burials are to be found at the Society of Genealogists, the Corporation of London Guildhall Library, the Oriental and India Office Collections of the British Library, and elsewhere. *The British Overseas* (Guildhall Research Guide 2, 3rd revised edn 1994) contains an inventory of known sources in the United Kingdom. There may well be more.

If your family lived in a country that was formerly a British colony, then the chances are their 'vital events' will have been recorded locally. You will have to write off to the registry of the state, province or country concerned. The GRO Customer Services

Desk on the ground floor of the FRC and the PRO Research Enquiries Desk on the first floor have an up-to-date list of civil-registration start dates, contact details of general registrars worldwide, and their embassy or consulate addresses in the United Kingdom. Consult T. J. Kemp's *International Vital Records Handbook* (Baltimore, 4th edn 2000), in the library in the General Reference area on the first floor of the FRC, for similar information about official registration authorities throughout the world. There are sample application forms included for each country, and details about certificate costs. This book also indicates whether the LDS has filmed copies of the registers and/or indexes, which you can hire in and search at LDS Family History Centres. The *Family History Library Catalog* (*see* p. 76) will give you microfilm or microfiche call numbers.

Increasingly, overseas birth, marriage and death indexes are being made available on the internet, including indexes for some Australian states and for British Columbia, in Canada. Try a powerful search engine such as **www.google.com** for your chosen country, state or province. These sites generally let you order a certificate online, using your credit card.

The Society of Genealogists holds copies on CD-ROM, microfilm or microfiche of indexes to registrations in all the Australian states and in New Zealand.

Records for India, to at least 1948, should be sought in the Oriental and India Office Collections of the British Library (*see* p. 26). The holdings relate mainly to births, baptisms, marriages, deaths and burials in India, 1698–1948; St Helena, 1767–1835; Sumatra, 1759–1824; Malacca, Penang, and Singapore, 1799–1829; Macao and Canton, 1820–33; Kuwait, 1937–61; and Aden, 1840–8.

The GRO Overseas Section

The Overseas Section in the GRO search area is marked on the plan on p. 32. There you will find an assortment of indexes to returns of births and baptisms (red books), marriages (green books) and deaths (black books). From 1966 there is a consolidated series of indexes covering all returns of births, marriages, and deaths abroad. Before that date, check the spine or title page to make sure you are looking in the right volume, as the books are sometimes misplaced when returned to the shelves.

Be careful to search both columns of entries written on each page of the indexes, as appropriate.

The **GRO overseas indexes** relate to:

- Births and deaths at sea (Marine returns) registered from July 1837 until 1965

- Civil aviation births, deaths and missing (presumed dead), from 1947 until 1965
- Consular returns of births, marriages and deaths of British subjects abroad from July 1849 until 1965
- UK and British High Commission returns of births to 1966 and marriages and deaths to 1965, from the date of independence of the Commonwealth country
- Returns of births and deaths at sea and abroad and marriages overseas, 1966 to date. These include births and deaths on British-registered hovercraft; and deaths on offshore installations, including lifeboats or other emergency survival craft belonging to the installation.
- Regimental registers of births and baptisms, 1761–1924 (including entries in Britain and Ireland)
- Army chaplains' station returns of births and marriages, 1796–1955, and deaths, 1796–1950, of officers, soldiers and their families stationed outside the United Kingdom (including Royal Air Force births, marriages and deaths from 1920)
- Military, civil and chaplains' registers of births, marriages and deaths in the Ionian Islands, 1818–64
- Service Departments' registers of births and marriages, 1956–65, and deaths, 1951–65, of Army, Royal Navy (from 1959) and Royal Air Force personnel and their families

  A list of Army regiments provides details of deposited registers of births, baptisms, marriages and deaths, with an index to them (at the front). For regimental marriages, you will need to write to the Overseas Section, General Register Office, PO Box 2, Southport, Merseyside PR8 2JD (telephone 0151 471 4801). Searches of the marriage registers are free, but you will be charged £6.50 for any resulting certificate.

- War deaths:
  - Natal and South African Field Forces, 1899–1902 (Boer War)
  - Army officers, 1914–21 (First World War), including Royal Flying Corps and, from 1 April 1918, Royal Air Force
  - Army other ranks, 1914–21 (*as above*)
  - Royal Navy, all ranks, 1914–21, including submariners, Royal Marines and Royal Naval Air Service
  - Indian Services, all ranks, 1914–21
  - Army officers, from 3 September 1939 to 30 June 1948 (Second World War)

- Army other ranks, from 3 September 1939 to 30 June 1948
- Royal Navy officers, from 3 September 1939 to 30 June 1948
- Royal Navy ratings, from 3 September 1939 to 30 June 1948
- Royal Air Force, all ranks, from 3 September 1939 to 30 June 1948
- Indian Services, all ranks, from 3 September 1939 to 30 June 1948

These indexes include deaths after the war which resulted from wounds.

If you find your 'event', fill in the relevant overseas application form (overwritten in red on blue for a full birth certificate application, in dark blue on blue for a short birth certificate, in dark green on green for a marriage certificate application, and in black on blue for a death certificate) and pay £6.50 (£5 for a short birth certificate, or £22.50 for the priority service) at one of the tills. You can then collect the certificate after four working days, or opt for it to be sent to you by first-class post on the fourth working day after your application. Applications made on a Saturday are available for collection or sent out on the following Friday. If there are any problems, phone the number given on p. 31. If you are applying by post, make your cheque or postal order payable to ONS for the sum of £8 (or £11 if you have no index reference – consisting of £4.50 for the search and £6.50 for the certificate – or £27 for the priority service) and send your application to the Overseas Section at the address given on p. 51. Alternatively, you can order the certificate, using a credit or debit card, by phoning 0151 471 4801 or emailing your request to **overseas.gro@ons.gov.uk**.

Records of births and deaths at sea from 1 July 1837

Births and deaths on board British registered ships and of British residents on certain foreign registered vessels are notified to the Registrar General of Shipping and Seamen (RSS), in Cardiff, who forwards monthly returns of these to the Overseas Section of the GRO, in Southport. There are no GRO registrations of marriages at sea. The indexes are not strictly alphabetical for returns of births until 1875, nor for deaths before 1876. Between 1837 and these dates, surnames are indexed by initial letter and according to where the first vowel appears and then listed chronologically within each alphabetical grouping. So you may find the surnames of **A**d**a**m, **A**ll**a**n, **A**ll**a**n, **A**d**a**ms, **A**ll**a**n are listed chronologically under **A–a**; followed by **A**sl**e**tt, **A**ll**e**n, **A**nd**e**rson, **A**l**e**xander, **A**ng**e**l, **A**v**e**ry, **A**nst**e**d, **A**nd**e**rson, **A**ndr**e**w and **A**b**e**rnethy under **A–e**; **A**l**i**ster, **A**shbr**i**dge, **A**tk**i**nson, **A**tk**i**ns and **A**lg**i**r under **A–i**; and so on.

For births and deaths at sea from 1966 onwards, search the annual Births Abroad and Deaths Abroad indexes. You can also search for births and baptisms occurring at sea between 1831 and 1931 in the microfilmed Registrar General's miscellaneous non-statutory returns (RG 32/1–16) in the PRO search area on the first floor of the FRC. There are microfilmed indexes to these in RG 43/2. Marriages on Royal Naval vessels, 1842–89, appear in RG 33/156 (again on microfilm) and are indexed in RG 43/7. You can also search these in the Microfilm Reading Room of the PRO, Kew.

There are more (complementary) series of Marine registers at the PRO, Kew. For details, consult *Tracing Your Ancestors in the Public Record Office* and the leaflet on *Births, Marriages and Deaths at Sea* available from the Research Enquiries Desk on the first floor of the FRC and on **www.pro.gov.uk** or at the PRO.

Births and deaths on board civil aircraft

These registers and indexes commence in 1947 and run to 1965, after which the annual Births Abroad and Deaths Abroad indexes should be consulted. The indexes to air births and deaths provide the name, place, year and page reference in the Overseas

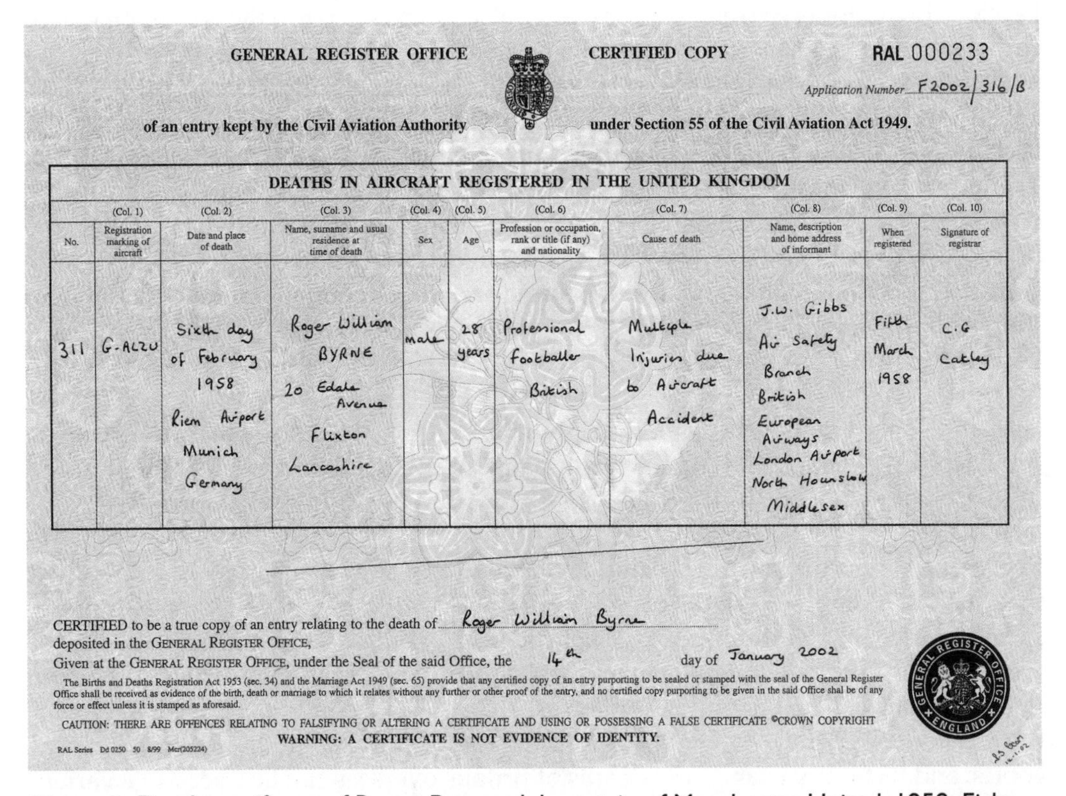

GENERAL REGISTER OFFICE — CERTIFIED COPY — RAL 000233

Application Number F2002/316/B

of an entry kept by the Civil Aviation Authority under Section 55 of the Civil Aviation Act 1949.

DEATHS IN AIRCRAFT REGISTERED IN THE UNITED KINGDOM

	(Col. 1)	(Col. 2)	(Col. 3)	(Col. 4)	(Col. 5)	(Col. 6)	(Col. 7)	(Col. 8)	(Col. 9)	(Col. 10)
No.	Registration marking of aircraft	Date and place of death	Name, surname and usual residence at time of death	Sex	Age	Profession or occupation, rank or title (if any) and nationality	Cause of death	Name, description and home address of informant	When registered	Signature of registrar
311	G-ALZU	Sixth day of February 1958 Riem Airport Munich Germany	Roger William BYRNE 20 Edale Avenue Flixton Lancashire	male	28 years	Professional footballer British	Multiple Injuries due to Aircraft Accident	J.W. Gibbs Air Safety Branch British European Airways London Airport North Hounslow Middlesex	Fifth March 1958	C.G Catley

CERTIFIED to be a true copy of an entry relating to the death of Roger William Byrne
deposited in the General Register Office,
Given at the General Register Office, under the Seal of the said Office, the 14th day of January 2002

The Births and Deaths Registration Act 1953 (sec. 34) and the Marriage Act 1949 (sec. 65) provide that any certified copy of an entry purporting to be sealed or stamped with the seal of the General Register Office shall be received as evidence of the birth, death or marriage to which it relates without any further or other proof of the entry, and no certified copy purporting to be given in the said Office shal be of any force or effect unless it is stamped as aforesaid.

CAUTION: THERE ARE OFFENCES RELATING TO FALSIFYING OR ALTERING A CERTIFICATE AND USING OR POSSESSING A FALSE CERTIFICATE ©CROWN COPYRIGHT

WARNING: A CERTIFICATE IS NOT EVIDENCE OF IDENTITY.

RAL Series Dd 0250 50 8/99 Mcr(205224)

GENERAL REGISTER OFFICE ENGLAND

Figure 9 Death certificate of Roger Byrne, club captain of Manchester United, 1958. Eight of the 'Busby Babes' were killed when their aircraft crashed on take-off at Riem Airport, Munich, Germany, after winning a European Cup quarter-final against Red Star Belgrade.

Section register where the full entry can be located. The air deaths index includes ages, for instance:

Name	Age	Place	Year	Page
Byrne, Roger W.	28	Riem Airport, Munich, Germany	1958	102

There is a separate page at the end of the air deaths index devoted to Missing Persons, 1948–80. This records name, age, place or aircraft missing, the year, and the page reference of the entry. Poignantly, whole families may be found together.

Consular returns of births, marriages and deaths of British subjects abroad

Returns of births, marriages and deaths of British citizens abroad, registered with British consuls in foreign countries worldwide since July 1849, are transmitted each year to the Registrar General, in Southport. You can search the Consular indexes to these up to 1965, and then scan the annual Births Abroad, Marriages Abroad and Deaths Abroad indexes from 1966 onwards. The indexes refer to the consulate where each event was registered, not the actual place where it happened. Up to 1965, the indexes to Consular returns of births record the surname of the parent, the name (if any) or sex of the child, the consul's district, and the volume and page numbers of the book where the registration is to be found, from which your certificate will be copied. The indexes to Consular returns of deaths show the surname, forename(s), consul's district, volume and page numbers of each registered entry, adding the given age of the deceased from 1901 onwards. Consular returns of marriages are indexed by surname, forename, consul's district, volume and page reference to the registrations; from 1906 onwards, the surname of the spouse is written against each entry as a helpful cross-reference.

As before, once you have located the right index entry, in order to obtain a certificate copy down the details onto the relevant overseas application form and take it to the tills with your payment.

Registration of births, marriages and deaths with British consuls is voluntary, so you may have to contact the local official registration authority if you cannot locate a specific record; or try other sources, such as the microfilmed indexes and registers of the Registrar General's miscellaneous non-statutory returns, 1627–1965, on the first floor of the FRC. The microfilmed indexes, 1627–1960, are in PRO series RG 43; and the registers, 1627–1965, are in RG 32–RG 36. The PRO, Kew, holds similar microfilm copies; and births, marriages and deaths of Britons overseas can be traced in a variety of original records there, particularly amongst Colonial Office and Foreign Office series (see *Tracing Your Ancestors in the Public Record Office*, and *Dictionary of*

Genealogical Sources in the Public Record Office for details arranged by country and/or city or town). You can also use the PRO's online catalogue (**www.pro.gov.uk**) for specific references to documents. Look also in *The British Overseas* for possible information elsewhere in the United Kingdom; and at T. J. Kemp's *International Vital Records Handbook*, as you may be able to search filmed copies of indexes and/or registers at an LDS Family History Centre near you.

A list of countries, with civil-registration start dates, contact addresses and those of embassies in the UK, is kept at the Customer Services Desk on the ground floor of the FRC and at the Research Enquiries Desk on the first floor. This list also indicates whether returns will be indexed in the Consular or High Commission volumes.

UK and British High Commission returns of births, marriages and deaths

You can search indexes to UK (up to 1960) and British High Commission (UKHC) returns from 1961 to 1965 of births, marriages and deaths of British subjects made to the Registrar General of Commonwealth countries after their dates of independence. Ask at the Customer Services Desk about which countries are likely to be indexed under Consular returns and which under High Commission returns. There are also some countries for which there is no provision for Consular or High Commission registration (for example, Australia, New Zealand, the Falkland Islands, Canada and Zimbabwe). For these, and for earlier registrations, you will need to contact the civil-registration authority serving that country, state or province. The 'List of General Registrars Worldwide' (*see* p. 50) contains a complete listing of addresses.

The earliest returns seem to begin about 1940, and the indexes run up to 1966 for births and to 1965 for marriages and deaths. Thereafter they form part of the annual union indexes to Births Abroad, Marriages Abroad and Deaths Abroad. Some of the 1966 birth index entries are duplicated in the Births Abroad index for the same year, where the mother's maiden surname is listed too. The birth indexes give the child's registered name, place of birth, year of birth, volume/type of post, and page reference, all of which you will need to write onto the application form. The marriage indexes mention the surname of the other partner, against each entry, plus the place, year and folio reference of the registration. Between 1961 and 1965 the 'place' appears as 'station', and 'folio' as 'page'. The death indexes set out the name, age, place of death, year of death, volume and page numbers.

Regimental registers of births and baptisms

The indexes to regimental registers from 1761 to 1924 concern births and baptisms only. They disclose the surname, forename, place, year, regiment, volume and page numbers of the entry itself. They cover regiments stationed in the British Isles, as well as overseas, as far afield as Australia, India and Canada. To obtain a certificate, complete one of the overseas application forms and take it to the tills with your payment.

Regimental registers of marriages

Regimental registers of marriage between 1786 and 1924 are held by the GRO, in Southport. Application forms have to be completed for searches of the indexes, which are processed in the usual way. On the form, you will need to specify the regiment. A typed list of Army registers is available on the shelves of the GRO Overseas Section at the FRC. At the front is an alphabetical roster of regiment titles, including militia, volunteers, garrisons, Royal Marines, Indian Staff Corps, Royal Armoured Service Corps and Commissariat. From this book you can discover what surviving birth, baptism, marriage and death records have been deposited. There is no charge for the search itself, but a certificate will cost £6.50 if applied for at the FRC, or £8 if applied for by post, email, fax or phone (for address, *see* p. 51). Some of the regimental registers of marriage are arranged in the form of 'family returns', incorporating details about any children of the union (the children's names will be supplied to you, but not all the other information).

Army chaplains' station returns (Army returns) of births, marriages and deaths of officers, soldiers and their families outside the United Kingdom

The indexes to Army chaplains' returns from stations outside the United Kingdom, are labelled as 'Army returns'. They cover the period 1796 to 1955 for births and marriages, and from 1796 to 1950 for deaths. Look at the Service Departments Indexes to later registers up to 1965; and then at the annual indexes to Births Abroad, Marriages Abroad and Deaths Abroad, starting in 1966.

Such events occurring in England or Wales will be registered among those of residents, and indexed accordingly. For War Deaths, during the Boer War and the First and Second World Wars, there are separate registers and indexes (*see* pp. 58–63), although there appears to be a certain amount of overlap with the Army returns, as we shall see later.

The birth, marriage and death indexes to Army returns give surname, forename, station and year, plus the page number of each registered entry. From 1911, the marriage indexes record the surname of the other partner, as well. Starting in 1886, the death indexes supply age at decease.

To obtain a certified copy of a registered entry, complete one of the overseas application forms and take it, with the £6.50 fee, to one of the tills in the usual way.

Military, civil and chaplains' registers of births, deaths and marriages in the Ionian Islands, 1818–64

There is one index book, divided into three sections, covering births, deaths and marriages in the military registers, civil registers and chaplains' registers between 1818 and 1864. The births, deaths and marriages are indexed in that order, separately within each section. Under each person's name, a handwritten entry gives the name of the island, the volume and the page reference in the relevant register – but no year is indicated for any event, which is not very helpful.

Royal Air Force returns of births, marriages and deaths

The RAF was established on 1 April 1918, when the Royal Flying Corps (a branch of the Army) merged with the Royal Naval Air Service (a branch of the Royal Navy). Returns of marriages up to 1955, deaths until 1950 and names of children born to personnel overseas up to 1955 are indexed with the Army returns described above. From then until 1965 they can be found in the indexes relating to the Service Departments; and thereafter in the annual indexes to Births Abroad, Marriages Abroad, and Deaths Abroad. Casualties during the First and Second World Wars are to be found among the indexes to Army, Royal Navy and RAF War Deaths (*see* pp. 61–3).

Once you have found 'your' event, write down full index details on an overseas application form and order a certificate in the usual way.

Service Departments' registers of births, marriages and deaths

The GRO indexes cover births and marriages outside the United Kingdom registered by servicemen and women between 1956 and 1965, and deaths of servicemen and women overseas between 1951 and 1965. Returns of this kind are made twice a year to the Overseas Section of the GRO, in Southport. Late registrations are also sent there, and the indexes annotated accordingly. However, returns relating to Royal Naval personnel date only from 1959. The birth indexes give the surname and forename of the child, the station and year, and the page reference for each registration; the marriage indexes give the surname of the spouse. The death indexes record the age of the deceased, and include deaths at sea, some deaths on mainland Britain, and deaths during the Korean War (1950–3).

Registrations relating to the Armed Services stationed in Northern Ireland are held by the General Register Office (Northern Ireland), Oxford House, 49–55 Chichester Street, Belfast BT1 4HL (telephone 028 9025 2000, **www.groni.gov.uk**).

Births, deaths and marriages at sea, in the air and overseas, from 1966 onwards

Starting in 1966, all the above series of indexes are consolidated into annual volumes of indexes to Births Abroad, Deaths Abroad and Marriages Abroad, including events at sea (among them, those on hovercraft and offshore installations) and in the air. This makes searching easier and quicker. Some index books combine a couple of years or more, but each year is separately indexed, so take care to look in each one. The birth indexes record the child's name and the mother's maiden name, the registration post and the volume and page numbers of the original return, plus the date or year of birth. The annual indexes to marriages give the names of each person, the surname of the new spouse, the name of the registration post, and the volume and page numbers of the entry. The annual death indexes also embrace shipping, civil aircraft and BAOR returns; they state the name of the deceased, age at demise (from 1981 the precise date of birth, instead), the name of the registration post, and the volume and page numbers.

Births and deaths on British-registered hovercraft are reported to the Registrar General of Shipping and Seamen, and each month details are sent to the Overseas Section of the GRO. Entries from 1972 can be found among the annual indexes of Births Abroad and Deaths Abroad.

Deaths on British-owned offshore installations, such as oil rigs, and aboard lifeboats and other emergency survival craft belonging to the installations, are similarly reported by the installation owner to the Registrar General of Shipping and Seamen, who each month forwards the details to the Overseas Section of the GRO. From 1972 onwards, look for these in the annual indexes of Deaths Abroad.

You can order a certificate by completing the relevant overseas application form and taking this, with your payment, to one of the tills, as usual.

War deaths

There may be some overlap with entries indexed in the Army and Marine returns of deaths, so check these indexes too. Among the miscellaneous non-statutory foreign returns of deaths abroad – indexed in the PRO series RG 43 (available on microfilm in the PRO search area on the first floor, *see* pp. 138–40) – are some First and Second World War casualties, including prisoners of war.

- **Natal and South African Field Forces, 1899–1902**
  These relate to the deaths of servicemen who died during the Boer War. The indexes include references to regular units, irregular forces (such as the New Zealand

An Extract from an Entry in the Army War Records of Deaths 1914-1921

CERTIFIED COPY OF AN ENTRY OF DEATH SA 059167

Application Number F2002/316/B

Registration of Births, Deaths and Marriages (Special Provisions) Act 1957

Army Officers Records of War Deaths 1914 - 1921

Name and Rank	Unit	Cause, Date and Place of Death
Hon Fergus BOWES-LYON, Capt	8 Bn R. Highrs	Killed in Action, 27/9/15 France

An Extract from an Entry relating to the death of Fergus Bowes-Lyon

CERTIFIED to be a true copy of ~~the certified copy of~~* an entry made in a Service Departments Register.
Given at the GENERAL REGISTER OFFICE, under the Seal of the said Office, the 14th day of January 2002

*If the certificate is given from the original Register the words "the certified copy of" are struck out.

Section 3(2) of the above mentioned Act provides that "The enactments relating to the registration of births and deaths and marriages in England and Wales, Scotland and Northern Ireland (which contain provisions authorising the admission in evidence of, and of extracts from, certified copies of registers and duplicate registers) shall have effect as if the Service Departments Registers were certified copies or duplicate registers transmitted to the Registrar General in accordance with those enactments."

CAUTION: THERE ARE OFFENCES RELATING TO FALSIFYING OR ALTERING A CERTIFICATE AND USING OR POSSESSING A FALSE CERTIFICATE
©CROWN COPYRIGHT
WARNING: A CERTIFICATE IS NOT EVIDENCE OF IDENTITY.

SA Series Dd 0648 2M 9/00 SPSL(207198)

GENERAL REGISTER OFFICE ENGLAND

Figure 10 Death certificate of Capt. the Hon. Fergus Bowes-Lyon, 1915, extracted from Army War Records. One of the four older brothers of HM Queen Elizabeth the Queen Mother, he was 26 when he was killed. He is commemorated by a memorial at Loos, in France.

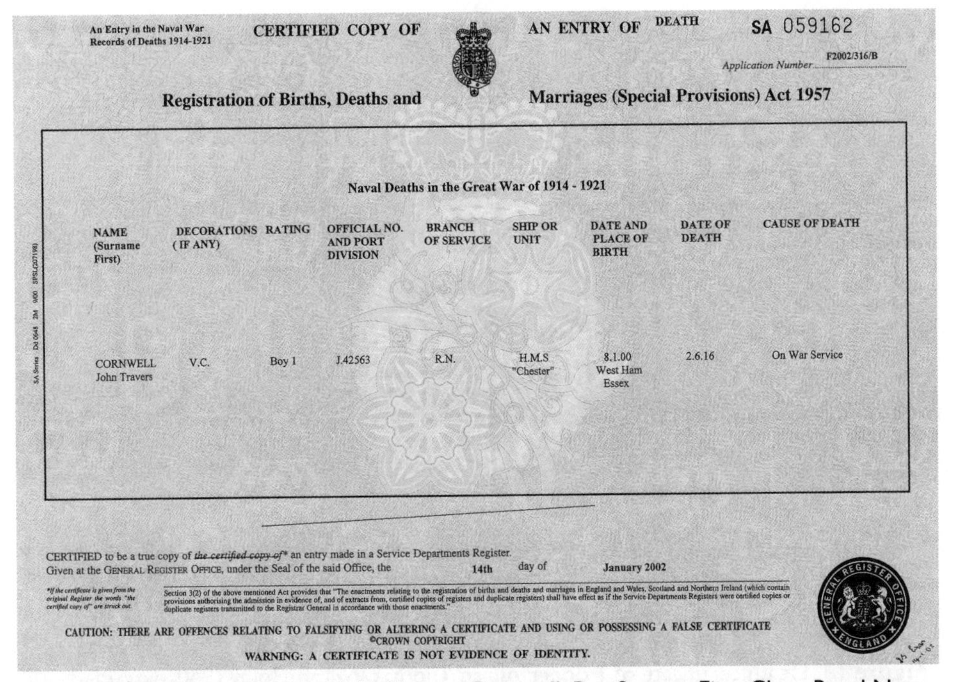

An Entry in the Naval War Records of Deaths 1914-1921

CERTIFIED COPY OF AN ENTRY OF DEATH SA 059162

Application Number F2002/316/B

Registration of Births, Deaths and Marriages (Special Provisions) Act 1957

Naval Deaths in the Great War of 1914 - 1921

NAME (Surname First)	DECORATIONS (IF ANY)	RATING	OFFICIAL NO. AND PORT DIVISION	BRANCH OF SERVICE	SHIP OR UNIT	DATE AND PLACE OF BIRTH	DATE OF DEATH	CAUSE OF DEATH
CORNWELL John Travers	V.C.	Boy 1	J.42563	R.N.	H.M.S "Chester"	8.1.00 West Ham Essex	2.6.16	On War Service

CERTIFIED to be a true copy of ~~the certified copy of~~* an entry made in a Service Departments Register.
Given at the GENERAL REGISTER OFFICE, under the Seal of the said Office, the 14th day of January 2002

*If the certificate is given from the original Register the words "the certified copy of" are struck out.

Section 3(2) of the above mentioned Act provides that "The enactments relating to the registration of births and deaths and marriages in England and Wales, Scotland and Northern Ireland (which contain provisions authorising the admission in evidence of, and of extracts from, certified copies of registers and duplicate registers) shall have effect as if the Service Departments Registers were certified copies or duplicate registers transmitted to the Registrar General in accordance with those enactments."

CAUTION: THERE ARE OFFENCES RELATING TO FALSIFYING OR ALTERING A CERTIFICATE AND USING OR POSSESSING A FALSE CERTIFICATE
©CROWN COPYRIGHT
WARNING: A CERTIFICATE IS NOT EVIDENCE OF IDENTITY.

SA Series Dd 0648 2M 9/00 SPSL(207198)

GENERAL REGISTER OFFICE ENGLAND

Figure 11 Death certificate of John Travers Cornwell, Boy Seaman First Class, Royal Navy, 1916. At the Battle of Jutland, off Denmark, he was mortally wounded but remained standing, awaiting orders, throughout the action. He was buried in Manor Park Cemetery, London, after a funeral with full naval honours. He was posthumously awarded the Victoria Cross.

An Entry in the Army Officers Records of Deaths 1939 - 1948

CERTIFIED COPY OF AN ENTRY OF DEATH

SA 059168

Application Number F2002/316/B

Registration of Births, Deaths and Marriages (Special Provisions) Act 1957

Return of Officers Killed in Action or who have died while on Service Abroad
Between 3rd September 1939 and 30th June 1948 inclusive

Name in full (Surname first)	Rank and Unit	Age	Country of Birth	Date of Death	Place of Death	Cause of Death
SZABO Mrs Violette Reine Elisabeth	Ensign Field Ambulance Nursing Yeomanry	23	France	Between 25th Jan & 5th Feb 1945	Ravensbruck Concentration Camp, Germany	Killed in Action

CERTIFIED to be a true copy of ~~the certified copy of~~* an entry made in a Service Departments Register.
Given at the GENERAL REGISTER OFFICE, under the Seal of the said Office, the 14th day of January 2002

*If the certificate is given from the original Register the words "the certified copy of" are struck out.

Section 3(2) of the above mentioned Act provides that "The enactments relating to the registration of births and deaths and marriages in England and Wales, Scotland and Northern Ireland (which contain provisions authorising the admission in evidence of, and of extracts from, certified copies of registers and duplicate registers) shall have effect as if the Service Departments Registers were certified copies or duplicate registers transmitted to the Registrar General in accordance with those enactments."

CAUTION: THERE ARE OFFENCES RELATING TO FALSIFYING OR ALTERING A CERTIFICATE AND USING OR POSSESSING A FALSE CERTIFICATE
©CROWN COPYRIGHT
WARNING: A CERTIFICATE IS NOT EVIDENCE OF IDENTITY.

GENERAL REGISTER OFFICE ENGLAND

Figure 12 Death certificate of Violette Reine Elisabeth Szabo, 1945, extracted from Army Officers' Records. A member of the Special Operations Executive (SOE), she was captured by the Waffen-SS on 10 June 1944, near Salon-la-Tour, near Limoges, in France. Executed on an unknown date in Ravensbrück concentration camp, she was posthumously awarded the George Cross and the Croix de Guerre.

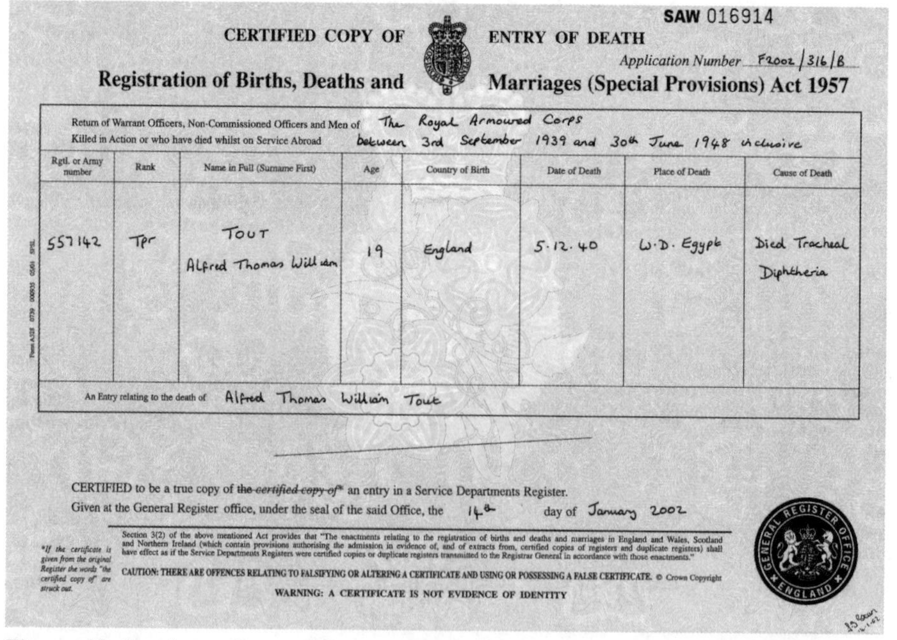

SAW 016914

CERTIFIED COPY OF ENTRY OF DEATH

Application Number F2002/316/B

Registration of Births, Deaths and Marriages (Special Provisions) Act 1957

Return of Warrant Officers, Non-Commissioned Officers and Men of The Royal Armoured Corps
Killed in Action or who have died whilst on Service Abroad between 3rd September 1939 and 30th June 1948 inclusive

Rgtl. or Army number	Rank	Name in Full (Surname First)	Age	Country of Birth	Date of Death	Place of Death	Cause of Death
557142	Tpr	TOUT Alfred Thomas William	19	England	5.12.40	W.D. Egypt	Died Tracheal Diphtheria

An Entry relating to the death of Alfred Thomas William Tout

CERTIFIED to be a true copy of ~~the certified copy of~~* an entry in a Service Departments Register.
Given at the General Register office, under the seal of the said Office, the 14th day of January 2002

*If the certificate is given from the original Register the words "the certified copy of" are struck out.

Section 3(2) of the above mentioned Act provides that "The enactments relating to the registration of births and deaths and marriages in England and Wales, Scotland and Northern Ireland (which contain provisions authorising the admission in evidence of, and of extracts from, certified copies of registers and duplicate registers) shall have effect as if the Service Departments Registers were certified copies or duplicate registers transmitted to the Registrar General in accordance with those enactments."

CAUTION: THERE ARE OFFENCES RELATING TO FALSIFYING OR ALTERING A CERTIFICATE AND USING OR POSSESSING A FALSE CERTIFICATE. © Crown Copyright

WARNING: A CERTIFICATE IS NOT EVIDENCE OF IDENTITY

GENERAL REGISTER OFFICE ENGLAND

Figure 13 Death certificate of Trooper Alfred Thomas William Tout, 1940, extracted from Army Returns. He is commemorated in the El Alamein war cemetery, in Egypt.

Rough Riders, the Imperial Yeomanry and Kitchener's Scouts) and civilians. The indexes give their surnames and initials only, plus the regiment and the page reference of the return.

- **War deaths, Army officers, 1914–21**
  The index to First World War casualties include men commissioned in the Royal Flying Corps and, from 1 April 1918, the Royal Air Force. Each officer's name, rank, unit and year of death, plus volume and page numbers, are included in the index book. For an example of a death certificate, look at that of Captain Fergus Bowes-Lyon, brother of HM Queen Elizabeth the Queen Mother, on p. 59.

- **War deaths, Army other ranks, 1914–21**
  The indexes include RFC and RAF personnel as above. The names of the dead and their rank, number, unit and year of death are given in the indexes, together with the volume and page numbers where the entry can be found.

- **War deaths, Royal Navy officers and ratings, 1914–21**
  The indexes include references to members of the Royal Naval Air Service, Royal Marines and Submariners, but there is no list of men posted missing. You will find details of name, rank or rating, ship or unit and year of death, plus the volume and page numbers of the actual registration. For example:

Name	Rank/rating	Ship/Unit	Year	Volume	Page
Cornwell, John T. (VC)	Boy 1	Chester	1916	RN	875B

  It is also worth scanning the indexes to Marine returns, 1912–18, for people dying on board merchant vessels during the First World War.

- **War deaths, Indian Services, 1914–21**
  The indexes relate to both officers and men, and give the name, rank, regiment, year of death and page number for each registered casualty. The entries also record any gallantry awards, such as the Military Cross (MC). For instance:

Name	Rank	Regt	Year	Page
Acworth, Douglas Harry (MC)	Major	55th Rifles	1919	1

- **War deaths, Army officers, from 3 September 1939 to 20 June 1948**
  This index volume relates to commissioned Army officers killed or dying during the Second World War, or who died as a result of their wounds. An example is:

Name	Rank	Unit	Year	Volume	Page
Szabo, Violette R.E.	Ensign	FANY	1945	44	170

If your relative died as a prisoner of war or engaged in secret operations, then it is worth looking in these indexes. Look also in the microfilmed indexes to miscellaneous foreign returns in PRO series RG 43 (*see* pp. 138–40).

- **War deaths, Army other ranks, from 3 September 1939 to 30 June 1948**
The indexes give the name, rank, number, unit, year, volume and page number for each registered casualty. Women's names may also be found – for instance, those serving in the ATS. You may find an entry complements one for the same person that appears in the indexes to the Army returns, 1936–40, 1941–5 or 1946–50. Thus:

Name	**Rank**	**Number**	**Unit**	**Year**	**Volume**	**Page**
Tout, Alfred T.W.	Tpr	557142	RAC	1940	17	449

also appears in the indexes of Army returns, 1941–5, under:

Name	**Age**	**Station**	**Year**	**Page**
Tout, Alfred T.W.	19	Western Desert	1941	138

So you learn different information from each. Although the year is at odds, a quick look at the Debt of Honour Register on the Commonwealth War Graves Commission website (**www.cwgc.org**) and/or at the *Army Roll of Honour* of officers and men killed during the Second World War (on CD-ROM in the Library and Resource Centre of the PRO, Kew) shows that Trooper Alfred Thomas William Tout, of the 8th King's Royal Irish Hussars, RAC, died on 5 December 1940, aged 20, and lies buried in the El Alamein War Cemetery in Egypt.

- **War deaths of Naval officers, from 3 September 1939 to 30 June 1948**
The time span takes account of commissioned officers who either died on war service or who were reported missing on war service and presumed dead, or who died from other causes. The index includes officers in the WRNS. Casualties are indexed by name and details of decorations, rank, branch of the Service, and ship or unit are included, but no year is given.

- **War deaths of Naval ratings, from 3 September 1939 to 30 June 1948**
Each casualty is named, including members of the WRNS, and in each case the rating, ship or unit, year, and volume and page numbers are given.

- **War deaths, Royal Air Force, all ranks, 1939–48**
The indexes note name, rank, number, unit and year, plus volume and page numbers, for each registered casualty, regardless of rank.

- **War deaths, Indian Services, 1939–48**
  In this volume, the rank, name (in alphabetical order), unit and age of each person are given, but not the year of death.

To obtain a certificate for any of the above, once you have found what you are looking for, copy the relevant information from the index onto an overseas application form and take it with your payment to one of the tills.

War deaths – other sources

There are lots of other avenues to explore if you are trying to trace information about war deaths. You can search *Soldiers Died in the Great War* and *Officers Died in the Great War* or the *Army Roll of Honour* for the Second World War, as appropriate. All three are available on CD-ROM in the Library and Resource Centre of the PRO, Kew. You can also discover more about casualties during the two World Wars by visiting the Debt of Honour Register on the Commonwealth War Graves Commission website at **www.cwgc.org**.

The PRO, Kew, holds a multitude of service and casualty records relating to Army, Royal Navy, Merchant Navy, Royal Marines and Royal Air Force personnel during the First World War. A range of online leaflets giving details about them is available on **www.pro.gov.uk**. To find out what there is for later years, either phone 020 8392 5200 or search the PRO's online catalogue, or send an email to **enquiry@pro.gov.uk**. Further information is provided in *Tracing Your Ancestors in the Public Record Office*.

The Scottish Link

In the past, people with Scottish ancestry had to travel to Edinburgh to do most of their research, but that is no longer the case. Although the original records are still in Scotland (mainly in the General Register Office and the National Archives, or in the regional record offices), more and more of them are being made accessible via the internet or on CD-ROM and, at the Family Records Centre, via the Scottish Link. This computerized link to the GRO in Edinburgh is situated on the ground floor of the FRC (*see* plan on p. 32).

If you are a beginner, you may find it helpful to buy one of the guides to Scottish genealogy from the FRC bookshop, or to look at one or two of them in the library in the General Reference area on the first floor. This will give you a good idea of the available sources and their contents, before you embark on your research.

The important thing to remember about the Scottish Link is that it comprises **indexes only** – so, in order to obtain a certificate, you will have to complete one of the application forms displayed near the computer terminals and send it with your payment to the General Register Office for Scotland, New Register House, Edinburgh EH1 3YT. If you have any enquiries about your application, phone 0131 334 0380 or send an email to **nrh.gros@gt.net.gov.uk**.

To book one of the Scottish Link computer terminals, phone 020 7533 6438 or ask at the Customer Services Desk. The second one is not bookable. You can use them for up to two hours at a time, paying £4 per half hour (there are card dispensers by the terminals).

Scottish indexes

Currently, the Scottish Link has **computerized indexes** for:

- **Births, marriages and deaths registered from 1 January 1855 to date**

- **Adoptions from 1930 onwards**. These are merged with the indexes to births, and are listed under the adopted name. The certificate itself will not reveal the names of natural parents or original birth name (*see* p. 49 for information about Birth Link).

- **Divorces from 1 May 1984 onwards**. You can search under surname, forename and year, and the screen will display the other spouse's name and the date of marriage, together with the divorce year, court, and serial number. Earlier decrees of divorce granted by the Court of Session were noted on the marriage registration itself.

- **Old Parochial Registers of births/baptisms and marriages, 1553–1854.** These relate to the established Church of Scotland only, and no burials are included. Where both birth and baptism were recorded in a register entry, the date included in the index is invariably that of the birth. You can search the *Scottish Old Parochial Registers* index for Scotland as a whole or by county, and by decade. This index is also accessible (*see* pp. 75–6) as part of *FamilySearch*, one of the online Family History Databases which you can use, without charge, on the first floor of the FRC. (For births, baptisms and marriages registered by other congregations, try the National Archives of Scotland, HM General Register House, Edinburgh EH1 3YY, telephone 0131 535 1314, email **research@nas.gov.uk**. The NAS website can be accessed via **www.familyrecords.gov.uk**.)

- **1881, 1891 and 1901 Scottish census returns.** These are personal-name indexes giving name, age and sex and the county and registration district where the person was resident on the night the census was taken (3 April 1881, 5 April 1891 and 31 March 1901). To obtain full information about the entire household, including occupations and places of birth, you will need to go up to the first floor of the FRC and use the online Family History Database for the 1881 census. For the 1891 and

1901 census returns, you can view the digitized images by visiting **www.scotsorigins.com**, which is a charged service run in collaboration with the Scottish GRO. Otherwise, complete the appropriate application form in the Scottish Link area and send a fee to the GRO for a copy of the enumeration entry.

Copies of all the above original records can be ordered for a fee direct from the Scottish GRO, using the application forms provided in the Scottish Link area.

Northern Ireland birth indexes

You can search computerized indexes of birth registrations in Northern Ireland, from 1 January 1922 to date, on a terminal in the Scottish Link area. You don't need to book or pay to search these, but to obtain a certificate you will have to post your application and fee direct to the General Register Office in Belfast. There is a sample application form displayed in the Scottish Link area, with details of fees and of other civil-registration records held by the GRO, Belfast.

Other information in the Scottish Link

Indexes to marriages registered in England and Wales from 1969 to 2000 are kept in this area. There is also a computerized index of registrations in England and Wales of births and deaths from 1984 to 1992 and marriages from 1984 to 1993. Ask at the Customer Services Desk if you wish to use this. It is planned to make the indexes of overseas registrations of Britons (*see* pp. 50–2) similarly available.

Microfiche copies of the indexes of birth, marriage and death registrations in England and Wales from 1 July 1837 to 31 December 1983 and overseas registrations up to 1994 are available for people who have difficulty using the index books, or when volumes have been removed for repair. If you need them, ask at the Customer Services Desk.

Information about civil-registration start dates, access to personal-name indexes, contact details and cost of searches and certificates in the Republic of Ireland, Guernsey, Jersey and Isle of Man are displayed in the Scottish Link area (*see also* Useful addresses and websites, on pp. 165–8).

If you can't visit the FRC

As explained in more detail on pp. 33–5, you can consult the indexes to births, marriages and deaths in England and Wales locally and then send off for certificates or download an application form from **www.statistics.gov.uk** or **www.familyrecords.**

gov.uk. For information about the holdings of local libraries that have copies of these indexes, visit **www.familia.org.uk**. The overseas indexes may be available locally, too. If you choose to order a certificate direct from the relevant local Register Office instead, remember that the GRO references before 1993 will be of no use. Some of the registration districts have altered or been abolished over time, so find out if they are still appropriate (*see* p. 37).

You can search these indexes at many of the LDS Family History Centres (*see* p. 4). Details of those in your area can be found on **www.familysearch.org**.

If you have access to the internet, visit **www.scotsorigins.com**, where you can scan the indexes of Scottish Old Parochial Registers, Scottish births and marriages registered from 1 January 1855 until 1900 and Scottish deaths registered from 1855 until 1925, then order a certificate online using the credit card facility.

If you want to engage a professional to research your family's history, you can choose one from among the many who advertise in family history magazines or contact a member of the Association of Genealogists and Researchers in Archives (AGRA) via **www.agra.org.uk**. But be wary – the cheapest may not necessarily be the best! Besides, it is much more fun to do it yourself, and personal discoveries about your family's past are likely to be the ones you will cherish most.

3 The Public Record Office Census and Wills Reading Room

The PRO search area

No original records are kept in the PRO search area on the first floor of the FRC. You can study everything free of charge, except for the online 1901 census returns and digitized Prerogative Court of Canterbury wills. Except for on-the-day tickets for the 1901 census terminals during busy periods, you do not need to book a seat.

As you walk towards the search area, you will pass the entrance to the Meetings Room and a small exhibition about genealogical sources, which includes displays of family histories of famous people drawn from FRC material. In this area too are **Family Research Interest Registers**, in which you are invited to record your own details. You may also want to browse through them to see if anyone is already digging into your family's ancestry.

Sources you can search

Family history sources on the internet

- You can surf the internet on one of the four computer terminals at the Internet Access Point in the first-floor lobby. Each computer is connected to a machine that accepts coins and Copycards (*see* p. 70). The fee is 50p for 15 minutes, or £2 per hour. The cards can be recharged here or at the Copy Service Desk.

Family History Databases

You can search the following databases online, using one of 16 computer terminals:

- *FamilySearch* – including the *International Genealogical Index*
- The *British Isles Vital Records Index*
- The *National Burial Index*
- 1881 census indexes and transcripts for England, Wales, Channel Islands, Isle of Man and Scotland
- Various trade directories around the census years
- PRO Online Resources – offering access to the PRO website (**www.pro.gov.uk**), the PCC wills database (at **www.pro-online.pro.gov.uk**) and a variety of other resources, including **www.familyrecords.gov.uk**, which provides links to the websites of all of the UK national archives.

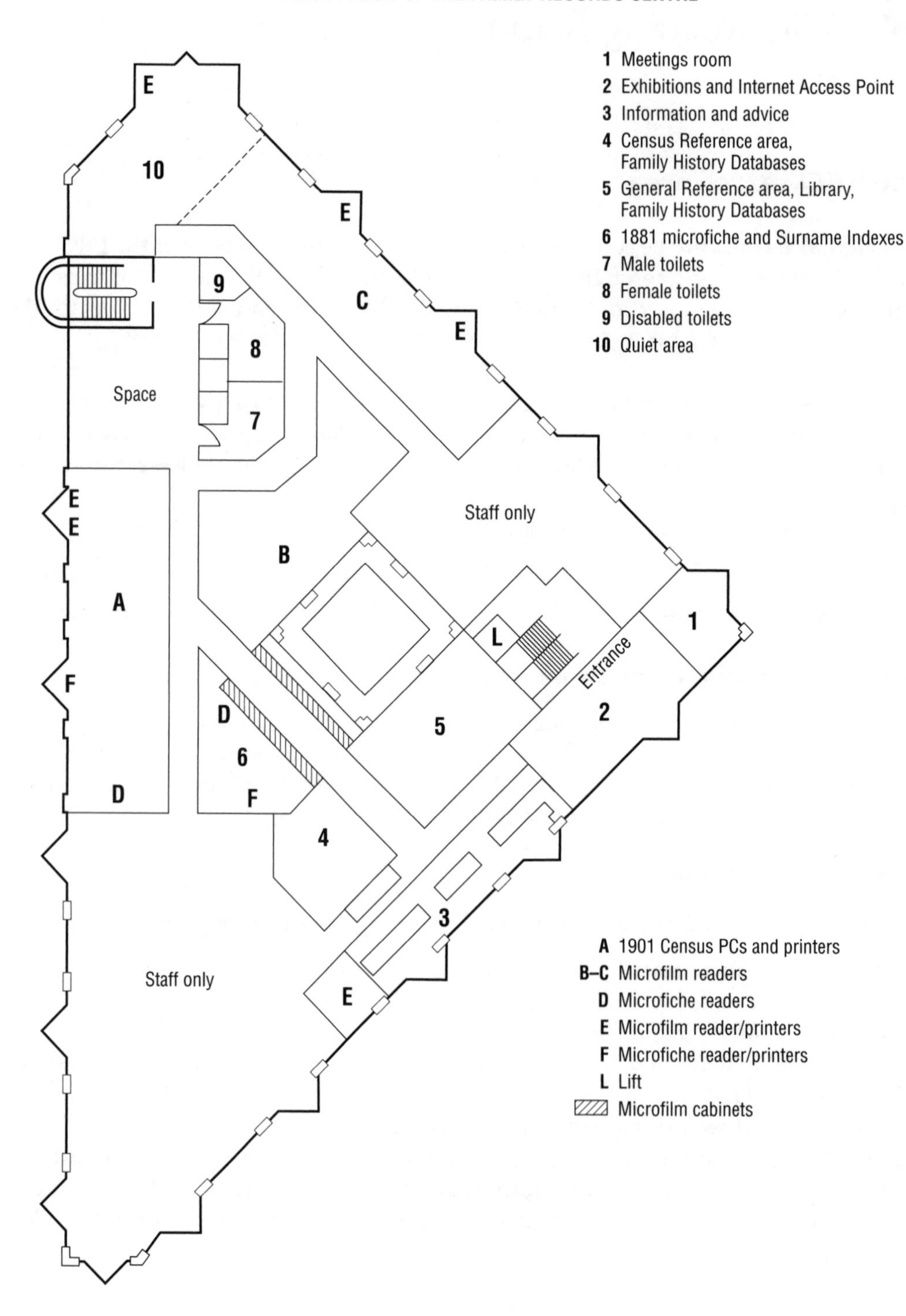
FIRST FLOOR OF THE FAMILY RECORDS CENTRE
1 Meetings room
2 Exhibitions and Internet Access Point
3 Information and advice
4 Census Reference area, Family History Databases
5 General Reference area, Library, Family History Databases
6 1881 microfiche and Surname Indexes
7 Male toilets
8 Female toilets
9 Disabled toilets
10 Quiet area
Space
Staff only
Entrance
Staff only
A 1901 Census PCs and printers
B–C Microfilm readers
D Microfiche readers
E Microfilm reader/printers
F Microfiche reader/printers
L Lift
Microfilm cabinets

There is also a series of CD-ROMs containing:

- Census Surname Indexes
- The consolidated index to the *Genealogical Research Directory*, 1990–9 (*see* pp. 2–3)
- The *Mormon Immigration Index* (USA), 1840–90
- *Who's Who* entries, 1897–1996

These can be used at a special computer terminal in the same area as the Family History Databases. Ask for the CD-ROM pack at the Research Enquiries Desk.

1901 census returns

- Digital images of the 1901 census returns for England, Wales, Channel Islands and Isle of Man (**www.census.pro.gov.uk**) are available online, as a charged service. You will be given a ticket to use one of the 48 numbered computer terminals to access the 1901 census. The tickets are issued on a 'first come, first served' basis, and are valid for an hour.

PRO records on microfilm or microfiche and facsimile maps

You can search microform copies of the following PRO records:

- Census returns for England and Wales, Channel Islands and Isle of Man, 1841, 1851, 1861, 1871, 1881 and 1891
- Wills proved in the Prerogative Court of Canterbury, 1384–1858, and administration grants, 1559–1858
- Death Duty registers, 1796–1857, and indexes, 1796–1903
- Divorces in England and Wales, indexes only, 1858–1958
- Non-parochial registers of births/baptisms and burials, 1567–1970 (including those of foreign Protestant congregations in England and of the Russian Orthodox Church in London)
- Births of dissenters registered at Dr Williams's Library, 1742–1837, and Wesleyan Methodist Metropolitan Registry, 1818–40
- Births, marriages and deaths recorded at monthly meetings and other records of the Religious Society of Friends, 1578–1841
- Clandestine and irregular marriage registers (including 'Fleet marriage' registers), 1667–1754
- Registrar general's miscellaneous non-statutory returns of births, baptisms, marriages and deaths of Britons abroad, 1627–1965, indexed 1627–1960
- Maps of registration districts for England and Wales (these are full-size colour facsimiles)

All the above, with the exception of the census returns, can also be searched at the PRO, Kew.

Non-PRO indexes on microfiche

The following microfiche personal-name indexes are to records **not** held by the PRO:

- The *National Probate Indexes* of wills and administration grants, 1858–1943
- The *International Genealogical Index* for the British Isles only (including Ireland), March 1992 edition, plus the *Vital Records Listing* (at July 1993)
- The *British Isles Genealogical Register*, 1997 and 2000 editions

It may take you a while to find your way round – but remember there is a first time for everything, and with a little patience and perseverance you will soon be experiencing the thrill of original research.

How the system works

As much as possible is self-service. There are 'How to use' leaflets near the General Reference area, explaining how to get the best out of your visit and showing how to use microfilm and microfiche machines. As you enter the PRO search area, you will see a line of staffed desks on your left. The first is for **Information and New Customers**, and the second for **Research Enquiries**. The third offers a **Copy Service**. Beyond the Copy Service Desk are four self-service photocopiers, with another in front of the desk itself. Other self-service copiers are dotted around each search section. If you have any problems, these are the desks to head for.

Buying photocopies

You can select whether to make A3 or (smaller) A4 photocopies. Generally, an A3 copy is more suitable for census returns and wills. Using coins, an A3 or A4 photocopy from a microfilm or microfiche will cost 25p. If you want to make photocopies of pages from a book, there is a self-service photocopier in the General Reference area, for which the charge is 20p for an A3 copy or 10p for an A4 copy.

However, you can buy a **Copycard** at the Copy Service Desk for £5. The initial price includes an 80p charge for the manufacture and programming of the card. When you first insert the card in one of the copiers, the display will show you have £4.20 credit. The cost of every photocopy using a Copycard is 20p. You can recharge this card at any of the self-service copiers near the Copy Service Desk, or a member of staff will do this for you at the desk. Copycards can be purchased with cash or a cheque or credit card; cheques should be made payable to the Public Record Office. The Copycard may also be used for self-service photocopying at the PRO, Kew. Store your Copycard carefully, making sure the magnetic strip does not come into contact with the strip on other cards.

If you would prefer a member of the staff to copy microfilm for you, write down the full reference of the relevant film, plus the folio(s) and page(s) you want copied and take the film to the Copy Service Desk with your request. A3 copies can be made while you wait. If you are paying by credit card, the minimum charge will be £5; otherwise, it will be 35p per page.

Where can I sit?

Look straight ahead and you will see a sign indicating where to collect your **seat box** when you are ready to use a **microfilm machine**. The numbers are inscribed on **colour-coded boxes** and are prefixed by a letter A, B or C, each representing a particular section of the PRO search area. If you want to use a motorized microfilm machine, which is quicker and has a larger display screen, choose one of the boxes with 'motorized' written on it. If you prefer to sit in the special quiet area, then opt for one of the C numbers with 'quiet area' marked on it. Sections A and B are nearest to the microfilm and microfiche cabinets, and Section C is the furthest away. There are

Figure 14 One of the self-service reader/printers, in the PRO search area of the FRC, that enable you to make copies of microfilm pages. Each page has a full PRO archival reference at the bottom. The printers operate on a cash or Copycard basis (part of the cash/card dispenser is visible on the right).

also some motorized readers set aside for people with special needs (ask at the Information Desk about these).

Each time you remove a boxed film from a cabinet, put your box in the microfilm drawer as a marker. We ask that you take only one microfilm box at a time. When you have finished with the film, rewind the reel, put the spool back in its box, and replace the box in the drawer – retrieving your marker box, so you can repeat the process for the next film. When you no longer want to occupy your seat, restore the box to its rightful place on the seat boxes shelves.

To use a **microfiche reader** in Section A, find one with an **orange card** in front of it giving its section letter and seat number. Every time you remove a microfiche, use this card as a marker, so you know where to replace the fiche when you have finished with it. When you leave, put the **marker card** back in front of the reader.

If you want to sit at one of the computer terminals for the 1901 census, you will need to obtain a ticket from the **1901 Census Ticket Desk**. There is a time restriction of an hour, and tickets are issued on a 'first come, first served' basis. The Family History Databases on the terminals in the reference areas operate on a 'first come, first served' basis, too, but you do not need a ticket for them and they have no time restriction.

As you go past the staffed desks, the search area opens up before you. Here you will find some of the terminals for searching the **Family History Databases**. This is also the **Census Reference area**, containing the finding aids for the 10-yearly census returns between 1841 and 1891, plus some London and county directories of names, published close to census years.

To the right is the **General Reference area**, where you will find shelves containing the finding aids to the Death Duty registers, Prerogative Court of Canterbury wills and administration grants, non-parochial registers, indexes to divorces, and the Registrar General's miscellaneous returns of births, marriages and deaths of Britons abroad, plus more terminals for searching the **Family History Databases**, finding aids to registration-district maps, copies of maps, and the **Library**.

The Library

This area contains a number of printed research guides and includes personal-name indexes to wills proved in various church courts in England and Wales before 1858 (*see* p. 27), some personal-name indexes to marriage licence allegations, published indexes to immigrant settlers' denizations and naturalizations as British subjects, 1509–1936, and other sources. You may browse through back numbers of various family history periodicals, such as *Family Tree Magazine, Practical Family History, Family History*

Monthly, *Genealogists' Magazine*, and *Family History News and Digest*. There are copies of the annual *Genealogical Research Directory, International and National* from 1993 onwards, a set of *The Dictionary of National Biography*, and various topographical dictionaries and gazetteers to help ease your way around. Ask at the Research Enquiries Desk if there is a particular book you require, or search the online library catalogue at **www.pro.gov.uk**.

Searching the sources

You cannot go directly to the microfilms or microfiches without a specific reference. Each series of records has its own coded reference system. The next sections will explain what these are and how to find what you want quickly and simply.

If you have access to the internet, you may be able to find the reference you need by searching the PRO's online catalogue on **www.pro.gov.uk** before you visit the FRC; or perhaps you may have found your reference in a published personal-name index or elsewhere. All you then need to do is to collect your **seat box**, or an **orange marker card** (*see* pp. 71–2).

Let's assume that you are starting from scratch. You may prefer to begin with the **Family History Databases**. Find yourself a seat at one of the terminals and click on each option in turn, following the instructions displayed on the screen. The databases are quick and simple to use – and you may be surprised at what you are able to find!

Using a Copycard and the self-service printer near the terminals (which is operated by a touch mechanism), you can print A4 copies of pages from the databases for 10p apiece (though you can't print copies from *FamilySearch*). Copycards may be purchased at the Copy Service Desk for £5 (*see* p. 70); or you may prefer to hire a loan Copycard for £2.50, which allows you to make four copies (you then receive a £2 refund from the Copy Service Desk). When your Copycard needs recharging, you can take it to the Copy Service Desk or go to a microfilm or microfiche printer and recharge it there.

The Family History Databases

FamilySearch – including the International Genealogical Index (IGI)

FamilySearch consists of six independent databases. No living people are included in any of them. The first of these databases, the *Ancestral File*, contains unauthenticated family-group sheets and pedigree charts deposited both by patrons of the Family History Library of the Church of Jesus Christ of Latter-day Saints (LDS), in Salt Lake

City, Utah, and by others, up to 5 January 1998. You cannot contact the contributors for more information, but merely tap into the family trees they are sharing with you. You are strongly advised to double-check each detail against original records to satisfy yourself that the statements are correct and nothing has been missed out.

The second database is the March 1993 edition of and January 2000 *Addendum* to the *International Genealogical Index (IGI)*. This is made up of hundreds of millions of entries of births, baptisms and marriages extracted from parish church registers and other vital records throughout the world, plus researched information submitted by members of the LDS. The time span covers roughly 1538 to 1888, but there are some later entries (though none about living people). You select the region you want, say the British Isles, request a search for a named individual's birth or baptism, a marriage, or all the children of a particular set of parents, then choose a date or date range you want retrieved, and the computer will do the rest. Similar given names and surnames are grouped under standardized spellings and are retrieved for you. After a short interval, the results are displayed on the screen. Click on the relevant entry to obtain more details, including the source of the information and, where appropriate, an LDS Library call number. To access the *Addendum*, which has to be searched separately, press key F9 on the keyboard.

Use the *IGI* as a signpost only. It is not a source in itself. Not every parish or every entry from a parish register has been included in it, and some counties have only been thinly covered. You can identify which parishes and events are in the *IGI* by looking at the *Family History Library Catalog* (*see* p. 76), which also tells you the whereabouts of the filmed parish registers. The *IGI* is an excellent research tool for finding people who have strayed from their home beat, and for tracking surname distributions over time. It also provides a bridge into the tricky period before the start of central civil registration.

In the *IGI*, details are pared down to reveal only the name of the person born or baptized and those of his or her recorded parents, plus the date and place of the event, or the names of the bride and groom (and vice versa) and their date and place of marriage. There is frequently far more information to be found in the original records. Sometimes names or dates have been misread, so there may be mistakes in the database. If you look at the original registers, you may be able to pick up siblings whose names have been omitted from the *IGI*. It is also worth checking the burial entries, which were not extracted for use in the database; this is important, because the person you thought was your ancestor may turn out to have died young or in infancy. But, although the details on the *IGI* should always be checked, it may sometimes save you a lot of time searching the GRO indexes for a particular marriage or birth registration. If you can find the one you want in the database, you then have a date and place to work from. The *IGI* may also clarify parentage before you purchase a GRO birth certificate or spend money on a reference check of several likely index entries. However, you will still need to order a certificate to verify and supply all the information you require, since the *IGI* will not disclose such key details as a bridal couple's ages, occupations, places of residence, or fathers' names. Nor will it reveal the maiden surname and usual abode of a baby's mother or the father's occupation.

You can also search the March 1992 edition of the *IGI* on microfiche in Section A. This covers the British Isles and Ireland only. It is organized by county, and for Wales there is a given name index as well, to take account of the use of changing patronymics (*see* pp. 7–8). Middlesex is included under 'London'. There is a set of microfiches for Ireland ('All counties'), besides the individual county series, and it embraces extracts from civil registrations of births in Ireland from 1864 to 1875 and non-Catholic marriages from 1845 to 1863. The *Parish and Vital Records Listing* (as of July 1993), also on microfiche, is the key to the contents of this edition. You will see that the alphabetical entries are listed chronologically by date, with the earliest date first, regardless of whether they relate to births, baptisms or weddings. There will obviously be far fewer marriage entries, because a single union might produce many offspring. Groups of variant phonetic spellings of surnames are listed together or cross-referenced, but forenames are 'as found' and are listed strictly alphabetically. The microfiche edition will not be such a good option if your surname was a common one, especially if you are trying to find all the children of a particular marriage. If your family spilled over into other counties, the online database will do all the hard work of tracking them down for you.

Another *FamilySearch* database is the *U.S. Social Security Death Index*, which ranges from 1937 to 1999, though most of the 63 million or so entries date from after 1962. This is a handy method of tracing relatives who moved to America, because it reveals their birth and death dates, their last address, the place to which the death payment was sent, the deceased's Social Security number, and the state where he or she lived when it was issued.

The *U.S. Military Index* enshrines the deaths of about 100,000 American servicemen and women in the Korean and Vietnam Wars, 1950–75. Again, birth and death dates are included, with rank and service number, place of residence and place of death; plus for Vietnam casualties, religious affiliation, marital status, race, and Vietnam Memorial plaque number.

Scottish Old Parochial Registers, 1553–1854, is an index of about 10 million births or baptisms and marriages extracted from the registers of the established (Presbyterian) Church of Scotland. This is identical to the computerized index in the Scottish Link on the ground floor of the FRC. As with the *IGI*, you can conduct individual birth or baptism, marriage and parent searches. Once you have found an entry, try the *IGI* to see if more information is forthcoming. If not, you will need to write to the General Register Office in Edinburgh (*see* p. 64) or consult the *Family History Library Catalog* (*see below*) to find out whether there is an LDS microfilm copy of the register that can be hired in for you, for a fee, at an LDS Family History Centre.

The *Family History Library Catalog* (*FHLC*) lists more than 3 million books, microfilms, fiches and maps. The date of the online edition is specified on the screen (currently 31 March 1997). There is also a CD-ROM version, of which a new edition is due out early in 2002. You can choose a surname or locality or a film number, and see what comes up. The LDS Library call number can then be used to order a specific item at your local Family History Centre. The *FHLC* indicates which Family History Centres hold copies of films.

You can access all the *FamilySearch* programs except *Scottish Old Parochial Registers* on **www.familysearch.org** – which also encompasses the *Pedigree Resource File*, a more up-to-date series of submitted family group sheets.

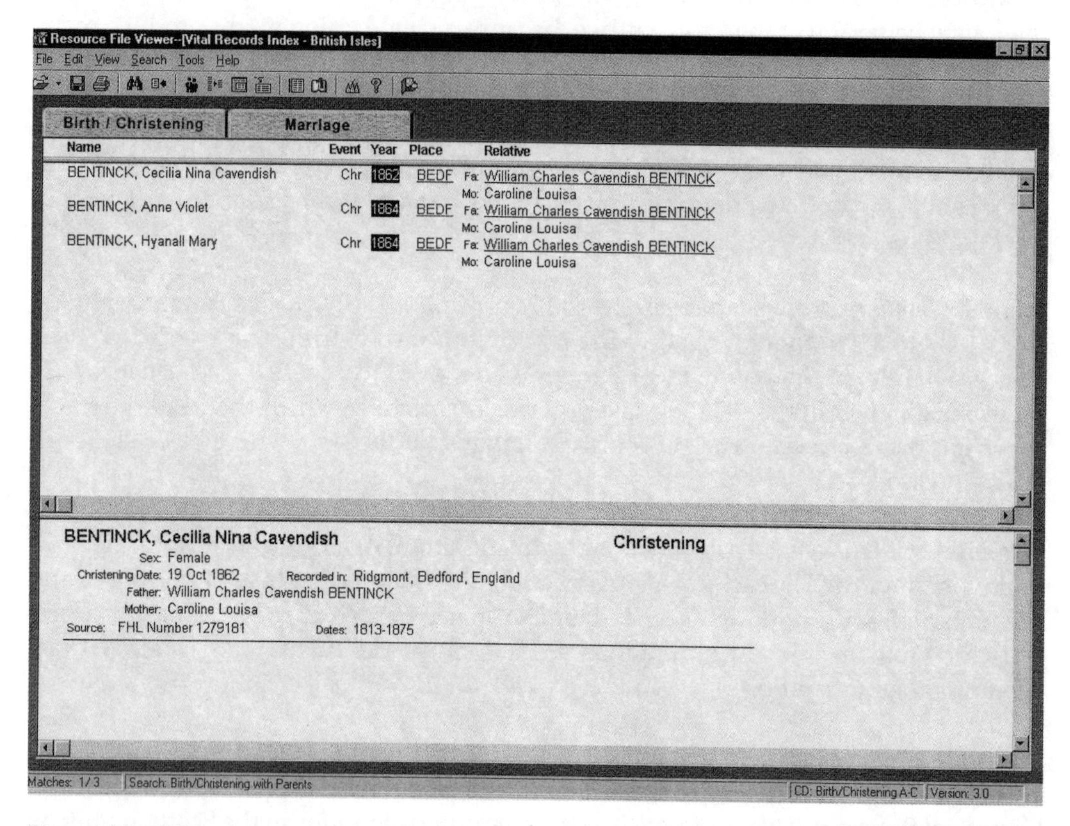

Figure 15 *BIVRI* baptism entries for Cecilia Nina Cavendish Bentinck and her twin sisters. You can use this database to find details of all the children of each set of parents. The source number at the bottom of the full entry about Cecilia Nina relates to material held by the Family History Library of the Church of Jesus Christ of Latter-day Saints, in Salt Lake City, Utah.

British Isles Vital Records Index (BIVRI)

The *British Isles Vital Records Index*, another of the LDS databases, is an updated edition of the *IGI* (currently 1998, but a new edition is due early in 2002), except that it is confined solely to births, baptisms and marriages extracted from parish registers and vital records not previously in the *IGI*. Fill in the boxes with the name, type of event (birth/baptism or marriage), date range, place, country and/or county of choice, and the name of the spouse (optional). Then, when you are ready, click on 'Search'. The screen will display the results, in the same format as for the *IGI*. You can click on the names of the parents for details about other offspring. What makes this database especially valuable is that, from 1 July 1837, marriage details record the father's name for both parties, enabling you to track down the births and baptisms of siblings as well as the groom or bride's own births or baptisms. To find out which places, events and dates are covered, click on the 'Integral Collection' option. The LDS plans to make this database available on **www.familysearch.org**.

National Burial Index (NBI)

The *National Burial Index* is a project of the Federation of Family History Societies (FFHS) and associates. One edition has so far been issued, in April 2001. It contains almost 5½ million names of people buried in 4,440 English and Welsh churchyards and nonconformist burial grounds or cemeteries between 1538 and 2000. No death registrations or gravestone inscriptions are included. Coverage is best for the first half of the nineteenth century, especially 1813–37, but it varies from area to area. Not all counties are included and some have better coverage than others – however, it is planned that eventually every English and Welsh churchyard and cemetery will be represented. The present edition covers burials in Bedfordshire, Berkshire, Buckinghamshire, Cambridgeshire, Cardiganshire, Cheshire, Derbyshire, Dorset, Durham, Essex, Glamorganshire, Gloucestershire, Herefordshire, Hertfordshire, Huntingdonshire, Kent, Lancashire, Leicestershire, Lincolnshire, Middlesex, Montgomeryshire, Norfolk, Northamptonshire, Northumberland, Oxfordshire, Radnorshire, Shropshire, Staffordshire, Suffolk, Surrey, Warwickshire, Wiltshire, Worcestershire and Yorkshire. If you want to discover what places, period and denominations are integrated into the database, click on the 'Reference' menu tab at the top of the screen and follow the instructions. Click on the binoculars symbol (also at the top of the screen) and in the relevant boxes you can insert the person's name, the place or county where you would expect him or her to be buried, and a likely date. The screen will display the person's name, age and date of burial, together with the parish or cemetery and county where interred, and will identify the society or group that transcribed the information. Wherever possible, check the original records for the accuracy and completeness of the indexed entries.

You can buy the two CDs for £30 from FFHS (Publications) Ltd., Units 15–16, Chesham Industrial Centre, Oram Street, Bury, Lancashire BL9 6EN (telephone 0161 797 3843, website **www.familyhistorybooks.co.uk**).

A similar index is in preparation for Scotland, under the auspices of the Scottish Association of Family History Societies.

The 1881 census database

The 1881 census database contains a complete personal-name index of almost 30 million people in England, Wales, Channel Islands, Isle of Man and Scotland who were 'enumerated' where they slept on the night of 3 April 1881. You can choose the **British Census Index** (which is divided into counties) or the **British Census – National Index** (which is the complete index). If you select the first option, fill in the boxes on the screen with the details you want searched, including the person's expected birth year, birthplace (city, town or county), census region, county, country, city or town, if you know them. Click on the 'Search' button and the results will be displayed on the screen. This will reveal the name, relationship to the head of household, year of birth, birthplace and county, and census place and county of each individual. There may be several similar entries, so highlight the most likely one, and full information about that person and household will be set out lower down on the screen. This is a transcript of the census return for that household, and will record the given address or house name, relationship of each named person to the head of the household, marital status, age, occupation and birthplace, plus the PRO microfilm, folio and page references. The PRO code for the 1881 census returns is RG 11, followed by the film number, folio and page, so you can check the original return for yourself. The other given number is the LDS *Family History Library Catalog* reference.

You can then click on, to inspect the neighbours! If you want to find others of the same occupation, you can click on the 'Advance Query' option. This data will be retrieved only from the same area or region of the household you had on the screen when you made the request.

The 1881 personal-name index and transcripts can also be consulted on CD-ROM in the Library and Resource Centre at the PRO, Kew, in many local libraries and record offices, and at LDS Family History Centres. You may want to buy the database to use at home. It is available on 25 CD-ROMs from the LDS Distribution Centre, 399 Garretts Green Lane, Sheldon, Birmingham B33 0UH (telephone 0121 785 2200). Cheques should be made payable to the LDS Distribution Centre, and credit card orders can be placed by phoning 08700 102051. The complete set costs £29.95, or you can buy a region for £15.

The undermentioned Houses are situate within the Boundaries of the [Page 3

Civil Parish [or Township] of: St Georges Han Sq | City or Municipal Borough of: Westminster | Municipal Ward of: Knightsbridge | Parliamentary Borough of: Westminster | Town or Village or Hamlet of: | Urban Sanitary District of: St Georges Han Sq | Rural Sanitary District of: 114 | Ecclesiastical Parish or District of: St Peters

No. of Schedule	ROAD, STREET, &c., and No. or NAME of HOUSE	HOUSES In-habited	HOUSES Unin-habited (U.), or Building (B.)	NAME and Surname of each Person	RELATION to Head of Family	CONDITION as to Marriage	AGE last Birthday of Males	AGE last Birthday of Females	Rank, Profession, or OCCUPATION	WHERE BORN	(1) Deaf-and-Dumb (2) Blind (3) Imbecile or Idiot (4) Lunatic
7	42 Grosvenor Place	1		Mary Anne Curwen	Head	Widow		62		India	
				Margaret Goodlake	Daug	Mar		42		Portland Glen Kent	
				Gerald Goodlake	Son in Law	Mar	48		Major General Coldstream Gds	Berks Faringdon	
				Mary Anne Janson	Visitor	Unm		61		City of London	
				Sarah Howe	Servant Domestic	Do		75	Housekeeper	Essex Boxted	
				Mary Smith	Do	Do		40	Ladys Maid	Surrey Horsham	
				Julie D'Or	Do	Do		29	Do Do	France Lyons	
				Sarah Davis	Do	Do		26	House Maid	Staffordshire Pattingham	
				Elizabeth Brydon	Do	Do		26	Cook	Surrey Red Hill	
				Kate Pound	Do	Do		25	House Maid	Surrey Guildford	
				Elizabeth Larkin	Do	Do		20	Kitchen Maid	Cambridge Chesterton	
				Amy Cox	Do	Do		17	Scullery Maid	Middlesex London	
				Henry Martin	Do	Do	28		Butler	Titchfield Hants	
				William Hare	Do	Do	24		Footman	Somersetshire Radstock	
				Edward Payne	Do	Do	19		Footman	Chelsea London	
8	43 Grosvenor Place	1		Anne Driver	Servant Domestic	Widow		53	Housekeeper	Holme Huntingdon	
				Elizabeth Burroughs	Do	Unm		19	Housemaid	London St Georges	
9	44 Do	1		Susannah Fleming	Do	Do		22	Cook	Far End Coniston Lancashire	
				Annie Tilling	Do	Do		31	Housemaid	Avening Gloucestershire	
				Mary Anne Freeman	Do	Do		14	Kitchen Maid	Kings Rd Chelsea	
				Elizabeth Coder	Do	Do		19	Housemaid	Smith Sq Westminster	107
				Joseph Mitcham	Do	Mar	29	~~29~~	Butler	North Petherton Somerset	
10	45 "	1		Harry Warren Scott	Head	Mar	47		Gentleman J.P.	Scotland	
				Caroline Louisa Scott	Wife	Mar		45		Leicestershire	
				Cecilia Nina Cavendish Bentinck	Daur	Unm		18		London	
	Total of Houses...	4				Total of Males and Females...	~~5~~ 6	~~20~~ 19			

NOTE.—*Draw the pen through such of the words of the headings as are inappropriate.* Eng– Sheet F.

Page 4] The undermentioned Houses are situate within the Boundaries of the

Civil Parish [or Township] of: St Georges Han Sq | City or Municipal Borough of: Westminster | Municipal Ward of: Knightsbridge | Parliamentary Borough of: Westminster | Town or Village or Hamlet of: | Urban Sanitary District of: St Georges Han Sq | Rural Sanitary District of: | Ecclesiastical Parish or District of: St Peters

No. of Schedule	ROAD, STREET, &c., and No. or NAME of HOUSE	HOUSES In-habited	HOUSES Unin-habited (U.), or Building (B.)	NAME and Surname of each Person	RELATION to Head of Family	CONDITION as to Marriage	AGE last Birthday of Males	AGE last Birthday of Females	Rank, Profession, or OCCUPATION	WHERE BORN	(1) Deaf-and-Dumb (2) Blind (3) Imbecile or Idiot (4) Lunatic
10	45 Grosvenor Place (Con)			Anne Violet Cavendish Bentinck	Daur	Unm		17		Bedfordshire	
				Hyacinth Cavendish Bentinck	Daur	Unm		17		Bedfordshire	
				Helen Heinman	Servant	Do		49	Domestic Servant	Scotland	
				Lydia Sadler	Do	Do		28	Do Do	Cambridge	
				Ada Howes	Do	Do		22	Do Do	Felsham Suffolk	
				Lizzie Sadler	Do	Do		24	Do Do	Cambridge	
				John Purves	Do	Do	28	~~28~~	Do Do	Coldingham Berwick	
				Elizabeth Hemming	Do	Do		44	Do Do	Stow on the Wold Gloucestershire	
				Robina Lindsay	Do	Do		18	Do Do	Aberdeen Scotland	
				Martha Parker	Do	Do		23	Do Do	Staffordshire	
				Phillip Postell	Do	Do	21		Do Do	Shipton	
				Annie West	Do	Do		27	Do Do	Ham Surrey	
				Edward Botting	Do	Do	32	~~32~~	Do Do	Sussex Hitching	
11	46 Grosvenor Place	1		Cornwallis Ricketts	Head	Mar	78		Baronet Magistrate for Leicester, Admiral Ret List	Plympton Devon	
				Caroline Ricketts	Wife	Mar		62	Right Honorable Lady [illegible]	[illegible]	
				Evelyn [illegible] Ricketts	Daur	Unm		27		Upper Belgrave St London	
				Constance CA Ricketts	Daur	Unm		25		Upper Belgrave St London	
				Gertrude CE Ricketts	Daur	Unm		21		46 Grosvenor Place London	
				Mildred M Ricketts	Daur	Unm		18		46 Grosvenor Place London	
				Emma Green	Dom Servant	Unm		40	Ladys Maid	Lenstead Kent	
				Elizabeth Wigg	do do	Unm		32	Ladys Maid	Cookham Berks	
				Eliza Blair	do do	Unm		28	Ladys Maid	Fulham Middlesex	
				Sarah A Rayner	do do	Widow		37	Cook	Fakenham Norfolk	
				Alice Hill	do do	Unm		18	Kitchen Maid	Nettleton Suffolk	
				Emma Bond	Do Do			30	Housemaid	Tetbury Gloucester	
	Total of Houses...	1				Total of Males and Females...	4	21			

NOTE.—*Draw the pen through such of the words of the headings as are inappropriate.*

Figure 16 The 1881 census return for 45 Grosvenor Place, in the civil parish of St George's Hanover Square, Westminster. The Queen's grandmother, Cecilia Nina Cavendish Bentinck, is listed with her stepfather and mother, her two younger sisters, and their 11 servants. (RG 11/98, f. 114, pp. 3 and 4)

If you can't find your ancestor in the database, this may be because the computer has not been able to match your information with the stored data, so try the microfiche version (on your left as you enter the census search area). With microfiche, what you see is what you get. There are complete national and county by county personal-name indexes. London is included as part of Middlesex. There is no microfiche index for Scotland. When you have found the person you want, you can look at the original census returns for the relevant address on microfilm in series RG 11, using the PRO reference numbers given at the far right of the index entry as the key. Ignore the final number, as this is the LDS call number for people wishing to use a microfilm copy at a Family History Centre. If you cannot find someone in the personal-name index but have an address, try the finding aids (*see* pp. 88–94) in the **Census Reference area**.

Trade directories

Click on this option, and select the county, and then the particular directory you want. Most of the directories date from the 1850s onwards.

PRO Online Resources

The PRO's public screens, which are accessible both at the FRC and at Kew, offer a choice of four options: Advanced Document Ordering, the PRO website, Electronic Records, and Other Useful Websites. At the FRC, click on PRO Online Resources, on one of the Family History Database terminals. Included is the PRO's online catalogue (PROCAT), which contains more than 9½ million document references. The online catalogue is a highly sophisticated search tool, making it easy to identify the PRO references to records from your chosen keywords and dates taken from the catalogue descriptions. It is not a personal-name index, but by skilful searches of the places where people lived you can often circumvent this. You may order up to three documents to search at Kew, so long as you do this at least a day ahead of your visit; these will then be waiting for you on arrival.

The public screens single out a variety of useful websites, which you can click on for direct access. They are arranged under headings: Archives, Family History, Libraries, Museums, Online Publications, and Reference. Among them you will find the Commonwealth War Graves Commission's Debt of Honour Register commemorating casualties in the First and Second World Wars, at **www.cwgc.org**; the UK public libraries network's listing of their most popular family history resources, at **www.familia.org.uk**; the Society of Genealogists' website, at **www.sog.org.uk**; that of the Federation of Family History Societies, at **www.ffhs.org.uk**; the server for a number of Scottish General Register Office indexes, at **www.scotsorigins.com**; a compilation of English and Welsh birth, marriage and death indexes at

http://freebmd.rootsweb.com; a detailed map of the UK at **http://uk.multimap.com**; a database of names, descriptions and characteristics of over 165,000 places throughout the world at **www.columbiagazetteer.org**; and the UK telephone directory at **www.bt.com/index.jsp**. If you want to discover more about archive repositories in the UK and overseas, click on **www.archivesinfo.net**.

It is worth visiting the PRO's own website (**www.pro.gov.uk**). Of special interest are the sections specifically designed for family historians, the 1901 online exhibition of life at the turn of the century, and the extensive range of leaflets accessed by clicking on the 'Leaflets Index'. You can also use it to access PRO On-line (**www.pro-online.pro.gov.uk**), which contains the PCC wills database and digital images of other PRO records. The PRO Resource Centre and library catalogue are being loaded onto the website, making it possible to find out which books, periodicals and CD-ROMs are available; and you can place online orders for PRO publications, many of which are designed with the genealogist in mind, at **www.pro.gov.uk/bookshop**. The PRO website also provides a link to **www.familyrecords.gov.uk**, the portal site for all the UK national archives. If you don't have time to continue your research yourself or would prefer to hire a professional, there are themed lists of independent researchers on the PRO website, too.

Nineteenth-century Prerogative Court of Canterbury (PCC) wills

By clicking on **www.pro-online.pro.gov.uk**, then on 'Search', and choosing 'Probate Wills' in the 'Collections' box, you can search the personal-name index and digitized images of wills proved in the chief church court of England and Wales, the Prerogative Court of Canterbury, between 1850 and 11 January 1858. It is planned to incorporate all the earlier wills into the database, beginning with 1830–49 (due on the internet in April 2002) and working backwards. No administration grants are included.

The personal-name index is free, but there is a flat fee of £3 for viewing the will itself (either at the FRC or if you download the images at home), regardless of how many pages your chosen will runs to. At the FRC, you may prefer to search the index, find the PRO microfilm and quire-range reference (each quire comprises 16 pages, and each film contains a number of these), then check this against the Register Book or index entry to identify the precise quire number before helping yourself to the film (*see* pp. 105–7). You can obtain photocopies of the will, just as you would with any other item in the FRC.

The PCC, which functioned under the auspices of the Archbishop of Canterbury, dealt with the estates of people whose possessions lay in more than one diocese and exceeded a certain value. This meant that originally it dealt mainly with the estates of the rich, but by the 1830s it was handling about a third of the country's probate business (*see* p. 103). It was abolished early in 1858, together with other church courts, so this database covers its terminal years.

Fill in the boxes, with the person's surname and forename, plus any known details, such as occupation, parish or place and county or country, then click on 'Search'. The screen will display the result and, if you are happy that this is the will you want, you can then find the microfilm itself or, if you're at home, request the digital images by supplying your credit card details.

Miscellaneous databases on CD-ROM

You can search a growing number of county personal-name indexes on CD-ROM for various census years, which will save you time trying to locate people in the filmed indexes. There is also a consolidated index of the entries and contributors to the *Genealogical Research Directory*, 1990–9, which may reveal who else is tracing your family's ancestry (*see* pp. 2–3). The *Mormon Immigration Index*, 1840–90, lists immigrants to America and enables you to discover who was on the same ship. *Who's Who*, 1877–1996, offers biographies of notable public figures, including dates of death.

The 1901 census of England and Wales

The 1901 census for England, Wales, the Channel Islands and the Isle of Man (held on 31 March 1901) is available on the internet on the PRO's census website, **www.census.pro.gov.uk**. It is planned to make earlier census returns accessible in the same way, commencing with 1891; this will be county by county, commencing with London, and is due for completion early in 2003. The 1881 census returns will then, in turn, be made available digitally, probably by the end of 2002.

You can access the 1901 census online at the Family Records Centre – where there are 48 computer terminals in Section A of the PRO search area (*see* p. 68) – and anywhere else that offers internet access. If you have the internet at home, you can access it 24 hours a day at your convenience. There is a charge for parts of the service, but the index (which gives you access to a database containing details of over 32 million people) is free and can be searched in a variety of ways. To view an image of a census page costs 75p; to view a transcription of the details of an individual costs 50p; and if you wish to see a transcription for an entire household, the cost is a further 50p.

You can pay for the charged part of the service in two ways – by voucher or credit or debit card. You can buy a voucher at the Copy Service Desk or the bookshop, which will be valid for six months from the moment you begin to use it. The vouchers run in £5, £10 or £50 units. The PRO website lists other bodies selling these vouchers.

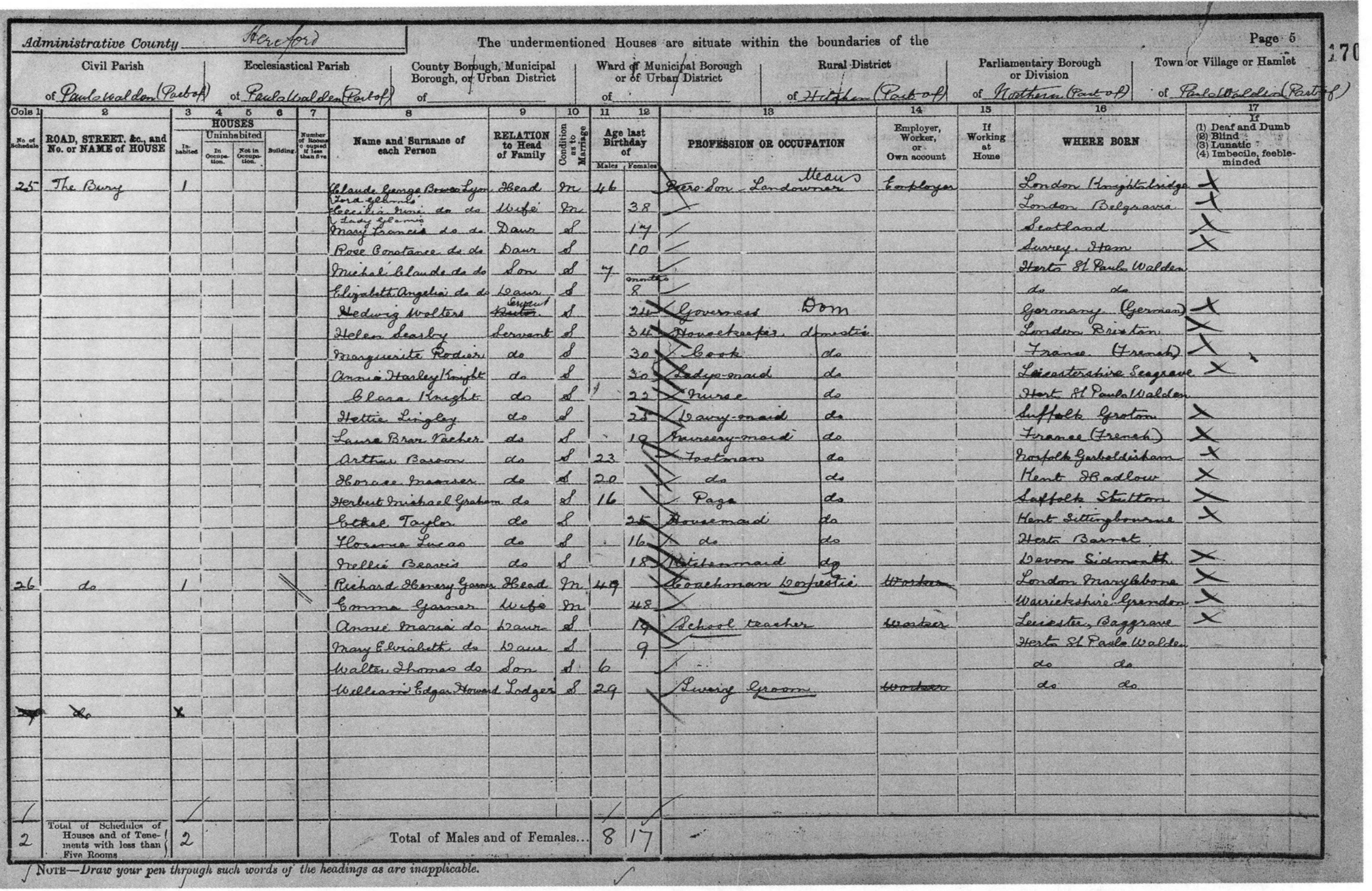

Administrative County Hereford — The undermentioned Houses are situate within the boundaries of the — Page 5 — 170

Civil Parish of Paulswalden (Part of) | Ecclesiastical Parish of Paulswalden (Part of) | County Borough, Municipal Borough, or Urban District of | Ward of Municipal Borough or of Urban District of | Rural District of Hitchin (Part of) | Parliamentary Borough or Division of Northern (Part of) | Town or Village or Hamlet of Paulswalden (Part of)

1 No. of Schedule	2 ROAD, STREET, &c., and No. or NAME of HOUSE	3 HOUSES Inhabited	4 Uninhabited In Occupation	5 Uninhabited Not in Occupation	6 Building	7 Number of Rooms occupied if less than five	8 Name and Surname of each Person	9 RELATION to Head of Family	10 Condition as to Marriage	11 Age last Birthday of Males	12 Age last Birthday of Females	13 PROFESSION OR OCCUPATION	14 Employer, Worker, or Own account	15 If Working at Home	16 WHERE BORN	17 If (1) Deaf and Dumb (2) Blind (3) Lunatic (4) Imbecile, feeble-minded
25	The Bury	1					Claude George Bowes-Lyon (Lord Glamis)	Head	M	46		Peer's Son Landowner Means	Employer		London Knightsbridge	X
							Cecilia Nina do do (Lady Glamis)	Wife	M		38				London Belgravia	X
							Mary Frances do do	Daur	S		17				Scotland	X
							Rose Constance do do	Daur	S		10				Surrey Ham	X
							Michael Claude do do	Son	S	7					Herts St Pauls Walden	
							Elizabeth Angelia do do	Daur	S		8 months				do do	
							Hedwig Walters	Expert Gov	S		24	Governess Dom			Germany (German)	X
							Helen Searly	Servant	S		34	Housekeeper domestic			London Brixton	X
							Marguerite Rodier	do	S		30	Cook do			France (French)	X
							Annie Harley Knight	do	S		30	Ladys-maid do			Leicestershire Seagrave	X
							Clara Knight	do	S		22	Nurse do			Herts St Pauls Walden	
							Hettie Lingley	do	S		23	Dairy-maid do			Suffolk Groton	X
							Laura Bran Vacher	do	S		19	Nursery-maid do			France (French)	X
							Arthur Bason	do	S	23		Footman do			Norfolk Garboldisham	X
							Horace Measer	do	S	20		do do			Kent Hadlow	X
							Herbert Michael Graham	do	S	16		Page do			Suffolk Stutton	X
							Ethel Taylor	do	S		25	Housemaid do			Kent Sittingbourne	X
							Florence Lucas	do	S		16	do do			Herts Barnet	
							Nellie Beavis	do	S		18	Kitchenmaid do			Devon Sidmouth	X
26	do	1					Richard Henery Garner	Head	M	49		Coachman Domestic	Worker		London Marylebone	X
							Emma Garner	Wife	M		48				Warwickshire Grendon	X
							Annie Maria do	Daur	S		19	School teacher	Worker		Leicester, Baggrave	X
							Mary Elizabeth do	Daur	S		9				Herts St Pauls Walden	
							Walter Thomas do	Son	S	6					do do	
							William Edgar Howard	Lodger	S	29		Livery Groom	Worker		do do	
	do	X														
2	Total of Schedules of Houses and of Tenements with less than Five Rooms	2					Total of Males and of Females			8	17					

NOTE—Draw your pen through such words of the headings as are inapplicable.

Figure 17 Lord and Lady Glamis, with four of their eight surviving children and their retinue of servants, enumerated at their Georgian country house (The Bury) in Hertfordshire in the 1901 census returns. Baby Elizabeth (the future Queen Mother) is listed as eight months old. Her nurse, Clara Knight, known as 'Allah', later served as nanny to her own daughters. (RG 13/1300, f. 170, p. 5)

Discounts are offered on bulk purchases of vouchers worth £100 or more, but you have to order these online. There is an application form available on **www.census.pro.gov.uk**. For overseas users wishing to buy vouchers, there is online advice on how to proceed. If you elect to use your credit card, the minimum fee is £5 per session and this must be spent within 48 hours of logging on. After this you will be charged at cost, based on 50p per transcript viewed and 75p per digital image. If the household you want to view spreads over more than one page, the cost will be £1.50. You will be charged only once for each image or transcript viewed during the session, no matter how many times you return to it. You can print out the images on one of the A3 laser printers for 20p a page, using a Copycard (*see* pp. 70–1).

To log on and open your account, click on 'Open/Resume' – or wait until your first request to use the charged service. Enter your credit card or debit card or voucher details. You will then be allocated a session ID number, which is valid until the end of the session or you log out. If you are using a credit card or debit card, you have to set an upper limit on what you want to spend. If you want to exceed this, you will have to log out and start again. Each new session with a credit or debit card automatically incurs a £5 minimum charge, whether you use it all up or not. For voucher users, the limit has already been set at the time of purchase, and any balance will be shown each time you log on during the six-month period of its validity. You can also share your vouchers with friends. To keep track of your outlay, click on 'My Account'. At the end of the session, the charges are debited from your account or deducted from the voucher value.

If you are using a credit card and want to take a break or look at an image or transcript again, click on 'Suspend' and the time will stop. When you click on 'Resume' the clock will start ticking again, and in any event your session must still be within 48 hours of having logged on. Click on 'Log Out' to end the session. You will then be shown a summary of the charges. It is a good idea to print this out or save it, in case you need to query anything. If using a credit or debit card at a public computer terminal, always remember to log out to stop anyone making use of your remaining credit balance. Should you leave your session for more than 30 minutes, there will be a 'Time Out' warning. Conversely, if you spend a long time looking at an image you may be timed out. Click on 'Resume' to start again.

1901 census searches

You can choose from several options: Person Search, Address Search, Place Search, Institution Search, Vessel Search, or Direct Search. As a family historian, it is likely you will want to try Person Search first. You can do separate searches by surname (Last Name search) or by forename (First Name search). For the Last Name search the only mandatory box is the one for surname; for a First Name search the mandatory boxes are first name, age and place of birth. For a double-barrelled name, you may have to make separate searches under each part of the surname. Surnames and forenames may occasionally have been recorded in reverse, or a person's title inserted in the 'Given Name' box. A search for synonyms and abbreviations can be obtained through the 'Advanced Person Search' facility. If you are unsure about spellings, try a wild-card search using * to represent more than one uncertain letter and _ under a single letter that is in doubt.

The results will be displayed on the screen, perhaps giving you a multiple choice of entry to pursue further into the charged areas of the database. If you want to view the transcription, click on the relevant option. You will then see full details (name, age, where born, county, civil parish, and occupation at the time of the census) for that individual only. By paying another 50p, you can see a transcription for the entire household. The same applies for viewing the neighbours' details. You may prefer to go straight to the digitized image, so click on 'Images' to see the entire page on which a person's name was enumerated. You can also search the index for specific addresses, for the whereabouts of particular places in the census enumerators' books, and for institutions (such as schools, barracks, prisons and hospitals) and vessels. If you already have a PRO reference for the enumerator's book, including the folio and page, you can go direct to the image for 75p, using the 'Direct Search' option. There is a facility for magnifying the images on the screen.

If you have internet access at home, then the process is just as simple, and you can start the clock at your own convenience, not limited by FRC opening hours. If you have a printer, you can print off a page; or you may want to download the image, or save it as part of your personal electronic archive. If you do not have a printer, you can place an online order for a copy by clicking on 'Print Request' and build up a shopping basket of items for photocopying. Each page costs 50p a copy, plus postage and packing; when you are ready, click on 'Submit' and the amount will be added to your total expenditure during your session. If you log off or fail to click on 'Submit', you will not be charged and no copying order will have been placed.

If you have any difficulties, there is a comprehensive online help facility giving lots of tips and advice on how to conduct your searches and get the best out of the online service. If you need further help, or advice about vouchers, contact the Census Help Desk. You can do this by emailing **support@censushelpdesk.co.uk**; alternatively, phone 01684 585298/585299, or fax 01684 585372; or write to Census Help Desk, PO Box 1901, Malvern, Worcestershire WR14 3YB. The Help Desk is open Monday to Friday from 9 a.m. to 7 p.m., and on Saturdays (except UK public holidays) from 9 a.m. to 5 p.m. Any technical problems should be referred to your Internet Service Provider or PC software supplier.

The online service is available in many local libraries and record offices. There is a list of these on **www.census.pro.gov.uk**. Some record offices, libraries and family history societies – which are listed on **www.census.pro.gov.uk** – have microfilm or microfiche copies of local 1901 census returns, instead. There is also a list of London reference libraries, record offices and organizations with an online service and/or copies of local returns available at the Research Enquiries, New Customers and Copy Service desks. Local finding aids and street indexes will help you find the relevant microform. You won't be able to use the online personal-name index to obtain the film/fiche, folio and page reference of the entry you want, but you will be able to confirm that the person's name is recorded, plus the age, birthplace, county, civil parish and occupation given in 1901.

You can search the 1901 census returns on microfiche at the PRO, Kew, using finding aids and street indexes similar to those for the 1851–91 returns. The PRO code for the 1901 census is RG 13, and you will need a third, unique, reference number for the precise address or part of a city, town, village or hamlet you'd like to search. The street indexes relate to towns with populations over 40,000 and indicate the folios on which a particular address is located. There is a set of 1901 Reference Book Districts, with PRO archival references, available at the Research Enquiries Desk, so you can identify the relevant microfilm or microfiche for a particular place or institution.

Census returns for England and Wales, Channel Islands and Isle of Man, 1841–91

The Victorian census returns provide the vital link between centralized and local records about people, because they tell you approximately when and where they were born before civil registration began in 1837. The returns also yield pointers to likely birth, marriage and death years after 1837 that are helpful for GRO index searches. Unfortunately, the registration districts given in the GRO indexes cover a far wider area than their names suggest, so cannot be used to home in on census places. There are, however, a number of personal-name indexes to help you locate people's whereabouts, many of which can be consulted at the FRC (*see* pp. 88–9). Look in the county by county listing in J. Gibson and E. Hampson, *Marriage and Census Indexes for Family Historians* (FFHS, 8th edn 2000) to see what exists.

The census is a dwelling by dwelling survey counting every person 'at home' there on the appointed day, including those involved in night work. The first census in the United Kingdom was undertaken in 1801, but the first one to systematically record people's names and personal details was that of 1841. Since then, a complete national census has been taken every 10 years, except in 1941.

To protect the private nature of their contents, you are not allowed to inspect census returns until they are 100 years old. Available returns list almost everyone in England, Wales, the Channel Islands and the Isle of Man, in the households where they slept on the nights of:

Sunday	**6 June**	1841
Sunday	**30 March**	1851
Sunday	**7 April**	1861
Sunday	**2 April**	1871
Sunday	**3 April**	1881
Sunday	**5 April**	1891
Sunday	**31 March**	1901

Whereas birth, marriage and death certificates record only two generations in a family, or three at most, the census returns offer a series of 10-yearly snapshots recording the evolution of a family over time. A sequence of all seven returns spanning six decades enables you to trace a child from infancy, through young adulthood, to marriage, parenthood and old age, until he or she disappears and death is presumed. The census supplies clues on when and where to start looking for births, baptisms, marriages, deaths and burials. Searches of given birthplaces may be keys to the current whereabouts of other family members, or to the same people or other relatives 10, 20 or 30 years before.

You can search microfilm copies of the returns for 1841–91 in the PRO search area, on the first floor of the FRC. There is a database for the 1881 census returns (*see* pp. 78–80 above), which includes Scotland. It is planned to make indexes and digital images of the English and Welsh census returns available on the internet, beginning with those for 1891 and 1881. During 2002, the counties of London, Lancashire, Yorkshire and Norfolk are likely to be the first of the 1891 returns to become accessible online. Currently, you can search the FreeCEN website (**http://freecen.rootsweb.com**), compiled with the collaboration of the LDS, which plans to provide online personal-name indexes and transcripts of English and Welsh census returns between 1841 and 1891, starting with the Cornish returns from 1841 and then both Devon and Cornwall from 1891.

Indexes to the Scottish census returns of 1881, 1891 and 1901 can be accessed via the Scottish Link, in the GRO search area on the ground floor of the FRC. Digital images of the 1891 and 1901 Scottish census returns are available using the charged service on **www.scotsorigins.com**. For details and call numbers of microfilm copies of surviving Irish census returns for 1901 and 1911, consult the LDS *Family History Library Catalog* (*see* p. 76). The original Irish enumerators' books are kept in the National Archives in Dublin; and there are copies for Northern Irish counties in the Public Record Office of Northern Ireland (PRONI), in Belfast. For more information about access to Scottish and Irish census returns in the respective National Archives, visit **www.familyrecords.gov.uk**.

Microfilm or microfiche copies of local census returns for the above years are held by many record offices and libraries, and they may also hold compiled personal-name indexes to them. To check library holdings, visit **www.familia.org.uk** or consult J. Gibson and E. Hampson, *Census Returns, 1841–1891 on Microform: a directory to local holdings in Great Britain, Channel Islands, Isle of Man* (FFHS, 6th edn 1994, reprinted 1997), which is a county by county listing of local copies. There are copies in the library in the General Reference area, on the first floor of the FRC. A small fee is payable to hire in a microfilm copy of any of the above census returns at an LDS Family History Centre.

If you are interested in census returns that have survived from before 1841, consult J. Gibson and M. Medlycott, *Local Census Listings, 1522–1930, Holdings in the British Isles* (FFHS, 3rd edn 1997).

Finding a census entry

Unlike the GRO birth, marriage and death indexes, which are listed alphabetically by personal name, the censuses are arranged by place. You will therefore need to have an address if your family lived in a city or large town; or (outside the major conurbations) the name of the town, village or hamlet, plus the county (except for the 1881 census). Don't rely on a registration district given in these indexes as your census address, because each district will contain about seven parishes or places, and the urban districts frequently embrace a huge population. For details about how to discover which civil parishes, townships and places were included in each registrar's sub-district and superintendent registrar's district, look in the relevant Reference Books (*see* pp. 90–4).

The finding aids are designed to help you identify the microfilm you need. Each census year has its own set of finding aids, all of which are similar except for those relating to the 1841 census (*see* pp. 90–1). The finding-aid books are colour-coded for each census year (**green** for 1841, **red** for 1851, **blue** for 1861, **brown** for 1871, **yellow** for 1881, and **black** for 1891).

Surname Indexes

The 1901 and 1881 census returns have been completely indexed. After these, the next best coverage is of 1851. In some cases, such as Devon, Glamorgan, Norfolk, Suffolk and Warwickshire, the entire county has been indexed. The first census year in which exact ages and places of birth were recorded was 1851 – including details about many people born long before the onset of civil registration in 1837. If you can locate their names in one of these indexes, you can quickly and easily learn who shared the household with them on census night, and then go straight to the Family History Databases and see if you can find their births, baptisms or marriages in the *IGI* (*see* pp. 73–5) or *BIVRI* (*see* p. 77).

Start by going to the shelves containing the census finding aids for your chosen year. The finding aids are in colour-coded binders (**green** for 1841, **red** for 1851, **blue** for 1861, **brown** for 1881, and **black** for 1891). Find the book with the blue label marked 'Index to Surname Indexes (by Place)' on its spine. Look for the city, town or village you are after, and if there is a personal-name index in the search area it will be allotted a number – with the prefix F if the index is on microfiche. Note down this number and then go into the census search area and find the numbered wallet in the relevant census year drawers in the index cabinets (which are immediately behind the microfilm cabinets, on your left). There are duplicate copies of the Index to Surname Indexes in the adjacent bookcase, along with some labelled Surname Index volumes. If the entry in the Index to Surname Indexes has an 'F' before the numbered Surname Index, go to the two 1841–91 microfiche carousels (to your left as you enter the census area). The carousel on the left is for 1851 census indexes only, the one on the right for other years. There are county tabs to help you find the correct numbered microfiche (don't forget to tuck one of those orange marker cards in its place!). In this area, too, you will find the two carousels for the microfiche containing the national index and county by county index to the 1881 census.

Read the indexer's introductory notes at the beginning of each index, explaining how it works. Each indexing system is different, so you need to understand what your particular reference means. Then you can swiftly find the correct film and folios you want. Some census indexes are on CD-ROM (*see* p. 82). You may know of a census personal-name index, but cannot find it listed; in which case, ask at the Research Enquiries Desk or refer to J. Gibson and E. Hampson, *Marriage and Census Indexes for Family Historians* for details of its whereabouts. Some of these indexes are in private hands, and searches of them can be done for you for a moderate fee – which may save you time and travel costs if you have a large area to search and not much idea where someone lived.

If you can find nothing in the personal-name index or Index to Surname Indexes for the year in question but from a birth, marriage or death certificate, or some other source, know in which street, house, public house or institution someone resided in or around a census year, it is worth looking at the Street Indexes.

Street Indexes

Trawl down the list of towns and cities to find the number of the Street Index for the census year. A list is posted next to the relevant finding-aid shelves. Now look for the books with 'Street Index Districts' written on white labels on their spines. Retrieve the right book, and find the appropriate numbered section in the index. Search for the street name, house or institution, against which will be the appropriate film and folio numbers. Note down these references, collect your seat box to act as a marker, then remove the film you wish to use from the labelled drawers in the nearby microfilm cabinets.

If you don't know exactly where someone was living but they had a profession or trade, it is worth having a look at a London or county directory (*see* pp. 99–100). London directories, in particular, are arranged in street order and include trade and court sections as well as a commercial section listing the names of heads of household. The street-index segment indicates intersections with other streets, some of which may be too small to be mentioned in the PRO census Street Indexes. A series of *Post Office London Directories*, published in each census year or the year following, is kept on the appropriate finding-aid shelves. All these directories are labelled in red.

Some London streets and alleys have been omitted from the census Street Indexes. To determine which locality and parish they were in, look at the green-labelled *Names of London Streets and Places and their Localities* (London, 1887) on the finding-aid shelves for each census year. This is an alphabetical list. Note down the locality and seek out this street or road in the same numbered Street Index you had before, or in the one covering the relevant parish, and this time you should be successful. For 1861, however, the returns for certain parts of London no longer survive. Ask at the Research Enquiries Desk if you are in any doubt.

The *List of the Streets and Places within the Administrative County of London* (London, 1912), *Abolished London Street Names and alterations in street nomenclature and numbering since 1856* (London, 1912) and the *List of London Divided Streets*, on the open shelves between the 1881 and 1891 finding aids, may supply answers, too. Copies are also kept at the Research Enquiries Desks, together with *London Terraced Streets*. You may need to look at the census Place Name Indexes and then the Reference Books in order to determine whether there is a Street Index or an institutional return.

Place Name Indexes and Reference Books

The Place Name Indexes are labelled in pink on their spine. This is a complete alphabetical list of cities, city wards, towns, villages and hamlets, and their counties, with their census-district reference numbers highlighted in yellow. Note these numbers down.

For the 1841 census only, the highlighted number refers to the page in the accompanying yellow-labelled Reference Book where the city, city ward, town, village or hamlet will be found again. The highlighted numbers are at the bottom of each page. For the 1851 census and later returns, the yellow-highlighted numbers in the Place Name Indexes refer to the registration districts – which are, in turn, highlighted in yellow in the Reference Books. Otherwise, the process is the same as for 1841.

Pore over the page for the place you want, and in the left-hand margin you will see the relevant PRO microfilm reference. At the top left-hand corner of each Reference Book page you will spot the PRO code for the census year, which is the key to the drawers of films. If you cannot remember the census year relevant to your notes or photocopy, this code will identify it for you. So, HO 107 is the code for 1841 and 1851 census returns (as you will see from the examples on p. 96, the format of these returns differs in several important respects, so there will be no problem in sorting out which year is which). RG 9 is the code for 1861, RG 10 for 1871, RG 11 for 1881, and RG 12 for 1891. At Kew, the 1901 census returns are on microfiche in series RG 13.

Look at the sample Reference Book page reproduced on p. 92. At the top you will see the letter code and series number; and in the left-hand column, underneath, is the film number indicating where the places listed in the other columns will be found. The code is HO 107, because the census year is 1851.

Each film will encompass a number of enumeration districts (*see* p. 94) – so if you see where in the Reference Book list your district appears, you will have a good idea of how much film you need to wind on to locate it. For 1841, the number of the enumerator's book containing your chosen place will be indicated, too; and when you come to use the film, you will notice that every frame is stamped with the full film and book reference, to tell you where you are.

The registration-district name appears in the next column in from the film number. The Reference Books reveal what parishes and townships each registration district contained in a particular census year. When you are faced with several alternative indexed birth registrations, this can help in sorting out which are most likely to be relevant. If there is a Street Index, this will be indicated in brackets below the name of the registration district. Displayed near to the Reference Books is an alphabetical list of towns and wards showing their Street Index numbers (though this list does not include suburbs, whereas the Reference Books do). To identify the film and folio references for your street or house, help yourself to the numbered Street Index on the same set of shelves.

Sometimes your Place Name Index search will be unsuccessful. The Victorian period was marked by an escalation in population size, and by growing urbanization as people drifted away from the countryside to seek employment in towns and cities. If you are looking for Blackpool, or Torquay, Southend or Bournemouth, Barrow-in-Furness or Southport, you will be disappointed, as they are listed under the parishes

Reference				HO 107
HO 107	Registration District	Registration Sub-District	Parish	Hamlet
		LEICESTERSHIRE – contd.		
2080	410. BILLESDON	1 Billesdon	Noseley	
			Billesdon	Billesdon(3)
				Rolleston
				Goadby
			Skeffington	
			Tugby	Tugby
				Keythorpe
			East Norton	
			Alexton	
			Loddington	
			Launde	
			Withcote	
			Ouston	Newbold-Saucey
			Tilton	Tilton
				Whatborough
				Halstead
				Marefield
			Lowesby	Lowesby
				Cold Newton
			Hungerton	Hungerton
				Baggrave
				Ingarsby
				Quenby
			Rothley (part)*	Keyham
			Scraptoft	
			Humberstone	
			Evington	
			Thurnby	Thurnby
				Stoughton
				Bushby
			Houghton-on-the-Hill	
			Galby	Galby
				Frisby
			Kings Norton	Little Stretton
				Kings-Norton
			Carlton-Curliew	Carlton-Curliew
				Ilston-on-the-Hill
			Burton Overy	
			Glenn Magna	Glenn Magna
				Great Stretton
			Wistow	Wistow
				Newton Harcourt

*Rest is in HO 107/2087 & in Melton Mowbray & Clawson Sub-districts & HO 107/2091/

Figure 18 Page from a Reference Book for the microfilmed 1851 census returns for England and Wales, which shows that the hamlet of Baggrave was in the parish of Hungerton, in registration district 410 (Billesdon, in Leicestershire). The microfilm reference is HO 107/2080. The number in brackets (3) indicates the return for the Poor Law union workhouse situated in Billesdon itself. Personal-name indexes published by the Leicestershire and Rutland Family History Society for this and other registration districts in the area are available at the FRC.

to which they belonged. Blackpool residents are listed under Poulton le Fylde, Torquay inhabitants under Tormoham, Southend people under Prittlewell, and Bournemouth folk under Christchurch; Barrow-in-Furness appears as part of Dalton-in-Furness, and Southport as North Meols. Ask at the Research Enquiries Desk if the place you are searching for appears to be absent from the Place Name Index.

Welsh place names are notoriously difficult to pin down, because of varying spelling, but there are place-name indexes, topographical dictionaries (for instance, S. Lewis, *Topographical Dictionary of Wales* (London, 3rd edn 1843)), atlases and maps (for example, the *Landranger Series*, published between 1974 and 1993) and the online *National Gazetteer of Wales* (**www.gazetteer-wales.co.uk**) to help. Ask the staff of the FRC about these.

If all you know is the parish where someone lived or worshipped, then *Lists of Churches and Chapels where marriages are solemnized according to the Rites of the Established Church, and of places of public worship* (London, corrected to 1 January 1871) will reveal their whereabouts and religious denomination, plus their superintendent registration district and district numbers. *London Ecclesiastical Parishes,* which covers all the London registration districts except Camberwell, Greenwich, Lewisham and Woolwich, is an index of churches in 1891, with film and folio references to the 1891 census. This is kept at the Research Enquiries Desk.

The Survey Gazetteer of the British Isles, edited by J. G. Bartholomew (London, 3 vols, 1904), the *Bartholomew Gazetteer of Places in Britain*, compiled by O. Mason (Edinburgh, 2nd edn 1986) and the PRO's *Hamlet Index* can help identify small communities and the places they were combined with for census purposes. The Ordnance Survey maps (*see* pp. 98–9) can also be used to identify the enumeration districts to which particular hamlets belonged.

The entries in the Reference Books sometimes include a number in brackets against a particular place name. These numbers refer to different types of institution listed separately at the end of the returns for that place. As a rule of thumb, an institution would have had to have a hundred residents or more to be listed in this way. As a sign at the Research Enquiries Desk explains, the numbers indicate the following categories:

1 = Barracks and military quarters
2 = HM ships at home
3 = Workhouses (including pauper schools)
4 = Hospitals (sick, convalescence, incurable)
5 = Lunatic asylums (public and private)
6 = Prisons
7 = Certified reformatories and industrial schools
8 = Merchant vessels
9 = Schools

Returns relating to Royal Naval and merchant shipping rarely survive before 1861. These were filed with the customs officers of the ports where the ships were docked or put into harbour during a longer enumeration period. There is a microfiche index, available from the Research Enquiries Desk, to passengers and crew on ships enumerated in 1861. Names of people on board ship appear in the 1881 database, too.

What the census returns contain

The census returns demarcate every enumerated inhabited building and the households within. In towns and cities you are likely to find buildings occupied by many independent households. The entire country was divided up into administrative units – based on the civil Poor Law unions set up in 1834 – out of which evolved the superintendent registration districts established when civil registration of births, marriages and deaths commenced on 1 July 1837. Each of these was in turn divided into a series of registration districts, further broken down into smaller enumeration districts consisting of about 200 households. The district registrars were responsible for appointing the census enumerators, and the enumeration-district boundaries were set out on a map.

The enumerators delivered a numbered census schedule to every head of household, who was expected to fill in the various printed columns about the people residing in that household over census night. If the head of a household was illiterate or didn't understand the instructions, then the details might have to be written onto the schedule by the enumerator. The completed schedules were collected by the enumerators, who were tasked with transferring the required information into the census enumerators' books (CEBs), making sure that each household's number corresponded with that on the original schedule.

The 1841 census is less instructive. No schedule numbers are given, and precise addresses are unusual. Each inhabited dwelling is separated by //, drawn through the vertical column immediately to the left of the people's names; and each household within it is separated by / drawn through the same column. The relationship of the various members of the household to its head was not recorded, nor current marital status, or birthplace beyond whether it was (Y) or was not (N) in the same county where the person spent census night, or in Scotland (S), Ireland (I), or Foreign Parts (F, and a non-British subject). So you will merely find the name of each person, age (rounded down to the nearest five years if 15 or older), occupation, and whether or not the person was born in the county. The enumerators were instructed to write in only the surname and first name of each individual, with initials for other forenames. Inmates of prisons and asylums are invariably identified only by their initials.

FILLING UP THE CENSUS PAPER.

Wife of his Bosom. "UPON MY WORD, MR. PEEWITT! IS THIS THE WAY YOU FILL UP YOUR CENSUS? SO YOU CALL YOURSELF THE 'HEAD OF THE FAMILY'—DO YOU—AND ME A 'FEMALE?'"

Figure 19 Cartoon from *Punch*, inspired by the 1851 census.

In 1841, the given ages are interesting. Sometimes exact ages are given, but generally they will only be noted for children aged 15 or under, down to months, weeks or days for infants under a year old. Thus, someone aged 78 would be recorded as 75 and likewise someone of 76. The ages are placed in either the 'male' or 'female' column, which can be useful if forenames are spelt in a curious way or you are unsure of a person's sex. Occupations might be abbreviated where they were especially prevalent: for instance, 'Ag lab' for agricultural labourer, 'FS' for female servant, 'App' for apprentice, 'J' for journeyman worker, 'M' for manufacturer, and 'FWK' for framework knitter. If you are not sure what an abbreviation means, look at the page of instructions for enumerators at the front of each census book.

In 1851, the quality of information improves dramatically. House names and numbers and road and street names are denoted; and then the names, plus relationship to the head of household, of each person staying overnight, followed by their current marital status, age by sex, occupation, birthplace and county. If an individual was blind, deaf or dumb, there was a column for this too. From 1871, imbeciles, idiots and lunatics are identified as well.

The enumerators' books from 1851 onwards identify every household by its original schedule number; and when each ends, a horizontal line is drawn across the page. You can tell if a particular household was an apartment, rather than an entire house, by looking in the inhabited buildings column, where each dwelling is indicated by /.

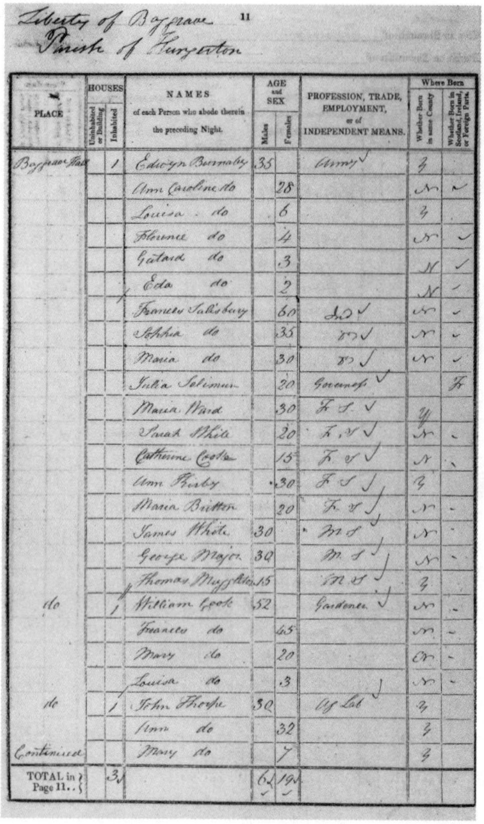

Liberty of Baggrave 11
Parish of Hungerton

PLACE	HOUSES Uninhabited or Building	HOUSES Inhabited	NAMES of each Person who abode therein the preceding Night	AGE and SEX Males	AGE and SEX Females	PROFESSION, TRADE, EMPLOYMENT, or of INDEPENDENT MEANS	Where Born: Whether Born in same County	Whether Born in Scotland, Ireland, or Foreign Parts
Baggrave Hall		1	Edwyn Burnaby	35		Army	y	
			Ann Caroline do		28		n	
			Louisa do		6		y	
			Florence do		4		n	
			Galard do		3			N
			Eda do		2			N
			Frances Salisbury		60	Ind	n	
			Sophia do		35	Ind	n	
			Maria do		30	Ind	n	
			Julia Soliman		20	Governess		F
			Maria Ward		30	F S	y	
			Sarah White		20	F S	n	
			Catherine Cooke		15	F S	n	
			Ann Busby		30	F S	y	
			Maria Britten		20	F S	n	
			James White	30		M S	n	
			George Major	30		M S	n	
			Thomas Muggleton	15		M S	y	
do		1	William Cook	52		Gardener	n	
			Frances do		45		n	
			Mary do		20		n	
			Louisa do		3		n	
do		1	John Thorpe	30		Ag Lab	y	
			Ann do		32		y	
Continued			Mary do		7		y	
TOTAL in Page 11		3		6	19			

Figure 20 The 1841 census return for Baggrave Hall, Baggrave, in the parish of Hungerton, Leicestershire, shows it was occupied by two households. One was headed by the Queen's great-great-grandfather, Edwyn Burnaby, and the second by his mother-in-law, Frances Salisbury. Family relationships, marital condition and exact birthplaces were not recorded in 1841. (HO 107/590/12, f. 2, p. 11)

Figure 21 The Burnaby household at Baggrave Hall, 10 years on, in 1851. Two of the 10 domestic staff are still there, and this time the son and heir is at home, on leave from the Army. His young sister Louisa married Charles William Frederick Cavendish Bentinck in 1859. They were the parents of the Queen's grandmother, Cecilia Nina, born in 1862. (HO 107/2080, f. 119, p. 13)

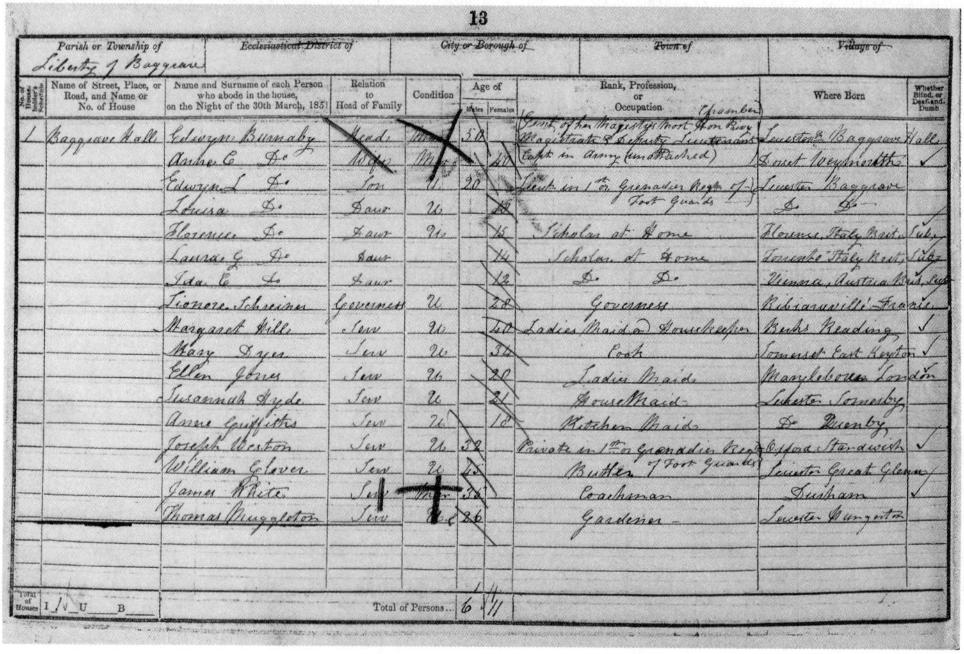

13

Parish or Township of Liberty of Baggrave | Ecclesiastical District of | City or Borough of | Town of | Village of

No. of Householder's Schedule	Name of Street, Place, or Road, and Name or No. of House	Name and Surname of each Person who abode in the house, on the Night of the 30th March, 1851	Relation to Head of Family	Condition	Age of Males	Age of Females	Rank, Profession, or Occupation	Where Born	Whether Blind, or Deaf-and-Dumb
1	Baggrave Hall	Edwyn Burnaby	Head	Mar	50		Gent. of her Majesty's Most Hon. Privy Chamber Magistrate & Deputy Lieutenant	Leicester Baggrave Hall	
		Anne C. Do	Wife	Mar		40	Capt in Army (unattached)	Dorset Weymouth	
		Edwyn L Do	Son	U	20		Lieut in 1st Grenadier Regt of Foot Guards	Leicester Baggrave	
		Louisa Do	Daur	U		16		Do Do	
		Florence Do	Daur	U		15	Scholar at Home	Florence Italy Brit. Sub.	
		Laura G. Do	Daur			14	Scholar at Home	Florence Italy Brit. Sub.	
		Ida C. Do	Daur			12	Do Do	Vienna Austria Brit. Subj	
		Lionore Schreiner	Governess	U		28	Governess	Ribeauvillé France	
		Margaret Hill	Serv	U		40	Ladies Maid & Housekeeper	Berks Reading	
		Mary Dyer	Serv	U		36	Cook	Somerset East Keyton	
		Ellen Jones	Serv	U		20	Ladies Maid	Marylebone London	
		Susannah Hyde	Serv	U		21	House Maid	Leicester Somerby	
		Anne Griffiths	Serv	U		18	Kitchen Maid	Do Quenby	
		Joseph Weston	Serv	U	32		Private in 1st or Grenadier Regt of Foot Guards	Oxford Standwick	
		William Glover	Serv	U	40		Butler	Leicester Great Glenn	
		James White	Serv	Mar	35		Coachman	Durham	
		Thomas Muggleton	Serv	U	26		Gardener	Leicester Hungerton	

Total of Houses I 1 U B | Total of Persons 6 11

Starting in 1891, you can discover how many rooms a specific household occupied, if less than five, and an individual's status as employer or employee or neither. From that year, too, the Welsh returns show whether each person spoke Welsh, or Welsh and English, or English only.

Given names may throw you off the scent, because the instructions were to write only the first forename in full, followed by the initials of other names. If your ancestor wasn't normally known by this first name, his or her identity may thus be obscured. Ages in census returns from 1851 and later may be dubious, as they were provided by the head of household, who might have had only a hazy idea of what they were – so they may not increase or decrease by 10 years between census returns, as you would expect. Birthplaces may also be unreliable, and subject to change with the decades. Given family relationships are those to the head of the household. Although not directly mentioned as relatives, it is often worth pursuing the origins of lodgers, visitors, apprentices and servants, who might be kinsfolk. Farm acreages and numbers of men and boys employed on them will be recorded, as well as adults and apprentices employed in any listed business enterprise. Some occupations may be unfamiliar. If you don't know what they are, ask at the Research Enquiries Desk if you can consult *Instructions to the Clerks Employed in Classifying the Occupations and Ages of the People* (London, 1881). This divides professions and occupations into six classes, ranging from professional people to the unoccupied, and then into sub-groups. There is an index of occupations at the back.

What if I can't read a microfilm?

If a census microfilm is too faint to decipher or the handwriting is illegible, advise a member of staff at the Research Enquiries Desk, who will inspect the relevant part of the film. Sometimes, the answer may be to adjust the magnification, or sit at a microfilm machine in a darker or lighter area, or use a motorized reader. If not, you have a choice: you may be authorized to search the original enumerator's book at the PRO, Kew, or may request a search to be made on your behalf and details sent to you listing all the people at a specific address on that census night. If you wish to inspect the returns yourself, you will be asked to fill in one of the special original document request forms. You will be given a slip with your name, document reference and date of request, and the phone number of the Repository Production Manager (020 8392 5259) to ring at least a week before you plan to visit the PRO. This must be within six months of your application. You will need to take some form of identification, such as a driving licence or bank or credit card (or your passport or national identity card if you are not a British citizen), in order to obtain a reader's ticket on arrival at the PRO. In the search areas, you may use pencils only (not pens). If you want the PRO staff to do the search for you, you will need to complete a different form, giving your name and contact details, the film, folio and page references, and the name and address you wish to have transcribed. The result will usually be posted to you within 10 working days of your application.

Maps

If you have problems following a census enumerator's route or seeing exactly where a street was, or simply want to find out about the lie of the land at the time the census was taken, then a map may provide the answers. If you are researching the London area, browse *The A to Z of Georgian London* (1747; republished by Harry Margary, Lympne Castle, 1981), *The A to Z of Regency London* (3rd edn 1813; Harry Margary in association with the Guildhall Library, 1985), *The A to Z of Victorian London* (1888; Harry Margary and the London Topographical Society, 1987) or the *A–Z Geographers' London Atlas* (Sevenoaks, 1995), as appropriate. All of these are available at the Research Enquiries Desk. It may also be worth going over to the London Metropolitan Archives (*see* p. 17 and map on p. xv), nearby, to pore over its excellent collection of maps and investigate whether there are any surviving deposited photographs of your house or street.

There is a small collection of maps in the library in the General Reference area on the first floor of the FRC. The two main series are the Ordnance Survey (OS) maps and the census registration-district maps (*see below*); there is an index to all the available maps. The maps themselves are stored in the map chests or on the open shelves in the library or can be inspected on request at the Research Enquiries Desk.

A reproduction of all 110 sheets from the 'Old Series' of OS maps, compiled between 1805 and 1874, has been published in 10 volumes by Harry Margary, the first five volumes of which are on the map shelves. Each volume contains a numbered sheet-breakdown map, from which you can identify the sheet you want. A complete set of the 'New Series' OS maps, issued since 1872, is also to be found in the map chests; and there is an index map to these seven volumes. In the map chests there are also two volumes containing London and Middlesex OS street maps, to which there is an index in the first volume. As well as an incomplete set of *Landranger* imprints of OS maps, printed between 1974 and 1993, there is an incomplete set of reproductions of OS street maps dating from 1848 to 1915. Both of these are kept at the Research Enquiries Desk. They are arranged in numerical order, to which there is a key on the back of each map.

The second series of maps comprises the registration-district maps in PRO series RG 18, which are kept in the map chests. They are facsimiles of printed OS and commercially published maps, with manuscript additions and boundaries drawn in coloured ink, indicating registrars' districts and sub-districts. The commercial maps are *Stanford's Library Map of London and its Suburbs*, onto which the boundaries were marked for the 1891 census.

Here is the key to the colours and what they represent:

- **Green circle** = name of the registration district
- **Red spot** = name of the sub-district
- **Red spot surrounded by a green circle** = name of both the registration district and the sub-district
- **Green line** = registration-district boundary
- **Thick red line** = sub-district boundary
- **Thin red line** = civil-parish boundary
- **Red cross** = meaning not yet identified

These annotated maps were utilized for the 1861, 1871 and 1891 censuses. The 1861 series extends to London only; and conversely, the 1871 maps exclude it. There is an incomplete set of OS maps of London and of England and Wales that were used for the 1921 census available at the PRO, Kew.

To get to the map you want, you will need to already know the name of the registration or registration sub-district – which you can find from the Reference Books, using the Place Name Index first to find the correct reference number for the place you are after (*see* pp. 90–4).

Once you have decoded the colours, write down details of the registration district and sub-district for the place you want and then go back to the Place Name Indexes and Reference Books to obtain the correct census-film reference.

Directories

If you don't know which census place to search next, or haven't got an address for someone, or can't find that person at a given address but are aware of his or her trade or profession, or simply want to discover more about the area where your family lived, then it's worth seeing what you can find in London or provincial directories. These listings of residents, produced by a variety of entrepreneurs, can prove invaluable in pinpointing a person in time and place or in tracing a family surname within a particular neighbourhood. They were published virtually every year, and are especially good from the mid nineteenth century. If your ancestor was affluent, or was a farmer, tradesman or professional person, or ran a public house, it is highly likely that one of the directories will list his or her name and home or business address. Bear in mind, though, that the information may have been assembled long before publication and in the meantime he or she might have moved or died. Moreover, some unscrupulous agents and publishers repeated information from earlier editions, or stole entries from other publishers' directories, without checking whether it was up to date.

The PRO has a small collection of nineteenth-century county and urban directories, and an edition of the *Post Office London Directory* for each census year, or the year after, from 1841 to 1891. These and various other directories are now being made available online as another database (*see* p. 80). Consult the binder containing a county by county inventory of the collection in the Census Reference area. The directories are similarly arranged in county order, with the county code stamped on the spine to make your hunt easier. Some directories are only available on microfiche. To see these, you will need to take a microfiche marker card (*see* p. 72) to the Research Enquiries Desk and exchange it for the fiche.

The London directories are housed on the census finding aids shelves, with red labels on their spine. Have a look at the contents page, at the front, and you will be amazed at the wealth of information on offer. Some people are mentioned more than once, in different sections of the directory: as private residents in the commercial section, then under their trade, and then in their street or road. And many are not mentioned at all! If the householder was out, or didn't want his or her name included, then the publisher's agent probably wouldn't have persevered.

If the directory you want isn't listed, then try the London Metropolitan Archives (*see* p. 17) for London directories. If you are after London, provincial or professional directories (for instance, an annual list of lawyers, medical men, clergy, or commissioned officers in the Army, Navy or Royal Air Force), you would be better off visiting the Guildhall Library (*see* p. 158), which has an unrivalled collection. Look at G. Shaw and A. Tipper, *British Directories, A Bibliography and Guide to Directories Published in England and Wales, 1850–1950, Scotland, 1773–1950* (2nd edn, London, 1997) for information about known surviving directories and their whereabouts. A copy is held at the Research Enquiries Desk.

Problems and solutions

1. *You cannot find your village in the Place Name Index.*

   Your place may be a hamlet, perhaps joined with another, under a different name. Try the solutions suggested above (*see* p. 93). The *List of Parishes in England and Wales* (1897) may help, too, as it contains PRO references to 1841–61 census returns. This is on the open shelves between the 1881 and 1891 finding aids, and a copy is kept at the Research Enquiries Desk.

2. *You cannot cope with linking the Place Name Index reference number with the Reference Book entry in order to find the film you want.*

   See the step by step process to success detailed on pp. 90–1. Basically, in the former find the place name and a number, and then do the reverse in the latter. In the left-hand margin, you will find the correct film number.

3. *You aren't sure how to wind microfilm onto the reel, or how to use a microfiche reader.*

   There are instructions by some of the machines. If you get stuck, watch what your neighbour is doing or ask the staff at the Research Enquiries Desk. Sometimes the film has been wrongly rewound. If you think this has happened, take it to the Copy Service Desk and it will be checked and correctly wound onto the reel while you wait. With microfiche, you insert the fiche under the mobile glass slide beneath the screen, with the title facing away from you towards it.

4. *There is no trace of your family at the expected address on census night.*

   They may not be far afield. Try the rest of the street or road, and then the entire enumeration district and the districts on either side of it.

   You may find some members of the family at home, whereas others were temporarily absent, perhaps staying with friends or working away from home, and so were enumerated elsewhere.

   Perhaps the address was short-term – for instance, as a prelude to marriage.

   The street may have been renamed or renumbered or not yet constructed – and the date of the information you have is earlier or later than the census year you've been searching. Follow the advice given on p. 98.

5. *You cannot find a London street in the Street Indexes.*

   The answer may be similar to the one above: it had not yet been built, or was known by some other name. It may have been a cul-de-sac and missed out of the index, so look in *Names of London Streets and Places and their Localities* on the census finding aids shelves or *London Terraced Streets*, available at the Research Enquiries Desk, or *London Street Number Changes*, covering 1841–91, in the library in the General Reference area.

6. *You cannot decipher a name, occupation or address on a film, fiche or certificate.*

   Ask one of the staff at the Research Enquiries Desk for help. You can borrow a magnifying glass; make a photocopy to see if the page of a film or fiche is easier to read; or seek help with the odd word (but not in decoding an entire document).

Giving up altogether

Don't be alarmed if your first foray into the census returns produces nothing. Historical research is never straightforward. Why not tackle some other records, such as the GRO birth, marriage and death indexes for another branch of your family? You could root through the Prerogative Court of Canterbury will indexes and National

Probate Indexes. Or you might just need a break, a cup of tea and a breather, before coming back refreshed for another round. Research can be more tiring than you realize. Try to avoid thrashing around wildly in pursuit of anyone of the same name in the hope that eventually you will hit on the right one. Steer a steady course, focused on the names, dates and places you know about, and then you won't end up climbing someone else's family tree instead of your own!

If you are still keen to learn about your family's history but don't have time to undertake further work yourself, you can hire a researcher to do the work for you. There is a professional organization, the Association of Genealogists and Researchers in Archives. To find out more, visit their website, **www.agra.org.uk**; or email **agra@agra.org.uk**, or write to The Joint Secretaries, AGRA, 29 Badgers Close, Horsham, West Sussex RH12 5RU. Not all professionals belong to AGRA. Ask at the Research Enquiries Desk for further advice.

Wills and administration grants

A will does not take effect until after the death of the person making it. Not everyone makes a will; and even if they do, it may not be 'proved' (i.e. legally approved, or sanctioned by probate). In the past, probably less than 10 per cent of the population left wills that went to probate; also, far fewer women than men left wills. The property of married women was usually disposed of by their husbands, since those married before January 1883 were regarded, together with their goods, as their husband's chattels, unless special provision had been made when they married. However, single women's wills can be really instructive, as they frequently mention many of their kin as beneficiaries.

If someone dies intestate (i.e. no will was made or can be found), the next of kin or creditors may seek a grant of letters of administration, so that the personalty (personal estate) of the deceased person can be distributed according to law once all debts and funeral expenses have been paid. Next of kin and creditors are not legally obliged to obtain an administration grant. Usually grants were only made if the widow or next of kin thought someone else might make a claim on the estate, or there was some need for legal title to be established – for example, by a major creditor.

In England and Wales, until 1858 control over probate of wills and administration grants was vested in a hierarchy of hundreds of local courts; the documentation is therefore scattered widely. Copies of all later probate material, dating from after the abolition of these courts in 1858, can be searched in the Probate Searchroom of the Principal Registry of the Family Division (PRFD), First Avenue House, 42–49 High Holborn, London WC1V 6NP (telephone 020 7947 7022).

Where were wills proved before 1858?

Until 9 January 1858, wills were taken by the executors appointed in them to the ecclesiastical or other court with jurisdiction over where the personal estate lay. At the bottom of the pyramid was the archdeacon's court. If a person's goods and chattels all lay within an archdeaconry, it was to this court that the executors travelled. However, if the property was in more than one archdeaconry, the executors went to the consistory (diocesan) court of the bishop. The wills of people with personal property worth £5 (£10 in London) or over in more than one diocese but in the same Archbishop's See (York or Canterbury) were proved in the relevant Prerogative Court. If there was personal estate in both archbishoprics, then the Prerogative Court of Canterbury was used.

Outside this ecclesiastical hierarchy were various 'Peculiars', ranging from manorial, borough and Royal courts to those run by bishops outside their own dioceses.

The Prerogative Court of York (PCY) claimed jurisdiction over the dioceses of Carlisle, Chester, Durham, Sodor and Man, and York. Records of the PCY between 1388 and 1858 are held by the Borthwick Institute of Historical Research, St Anthony's Hall, Peasholme Green, York YO1 2PW (telephone 01904 642315, website **www.york.ac.uk/inst/bihr**). The rest of the English and Welsh dioceses were controlled by the Prerogative Court of Canterbury (PCC), sitting in Doctors' Commons, in London. This was the most important probate court and had overriding jurisdiction over all the other courts, including the PCY. Between 1653 and 1660 (during the Interregnum) a Court for the Proving of Wills and the Granting of Administrations, in London, dealt with probate for the whole of England and Wales. After the Restoration its records were merged with those of the Prerogative Court of Canterbury, so from 1653 to 1660 the published PCC indexes serve as a countrywide directory. However, many people did not bother with grants of probate or administration during these years, when all the church courts were suspended.

Especially after 1819, wills were sometimes proved in both prerogative courts, the PCY having authority over property within the Province of York and the PCC having authority over property in the Province of Canterbury. Wills of people with property in Scotland or Ireland as well as England were also brought to the PCC. English or Welsh people dying overseas and leaving personal estate in this country generally had their wills proved in the Prerogative Court of Canterbury, or in the diocesan court serving the area where it was held. For alphabetical abstracts, look at P. W. Coldham, *American Wills and Administrations in the Prerogative Court of Canterbury, 1610–1857* (Baltimore, 1989) and *American Wills proved in London, 1611–1775* by the same author (Baltimore, 1992). Wills and administration grants of many ordinary soldiers and sailors are also recorded in the PCC.

From 1812, anyone owning consolidated funds (consols) in the Bank of England was required to have his or her will proved in PCC in order for the funds to be transferred to their nominated beneficiaries. The volume of business thus increased, and after the 1830s it is likely that the court conducted a third of all probate business in England and Wales. The registers of over 61,000 Bank of England will and administration extracts between 1717 and 1845 are in the library of the Society of Genealogists, and indexes to them can be consulted via the charged service offered by **www.english origins.com**. There is a published *Index to the Bank of England Will Extracts 1807–1845* (Society of Genealogists, 1991) available on the probate finding aids shelves in the General Reference area. If you are unsure when someone's will was proved and they may have had Bank of England funds, this is a good source to try first. It includes entries relating to overseas investors, spinsters, widows and servants, and offers a real lucky dip because many saw investment in government stock as a way of providing for their old age. The ledgers themselves, recording the actual stock transfers and any name changes on marriage, are held by the Archive Section, Bank of England, Threadneedle Street, London EC2R 8AH (telephone 020 7601 4889).

Unfortunately, diocesan boundaries do not coincide with those of counties. Look at the county maps in C. R. Humphery-Smith, *Atlas and Index of Parish Registers* to see which pre-1858 probate courts operated for your area. Then scan J. Gibson, *Probate Jurisdictions: Where to Look for Wills* (FFHS, 4th edn 1994, reprinted 1997) to discover the whereabouts of these records and the period they cover, and whether there are any published indexes. Copies of both books are in the library in the General Reference area. There are some printed local will indexes shelved here as well, arranged in alphabetical order of the county where the court sat. You can also consult a typescript index of all the wills proved in Welsh probate courts between 1700 and 1858, which provides references to the records kept in the Department of Manuscripts and Records, National Library of Wales, Aberystwyth SY23 3BU (telephone 01970 632800, email **ymh.lc@llgc.org.uk**). Its website (**www.llgc.org.uk**) can be accessed direct or via **www.familyrecords.gov.uk**. The Society of Genealogists has an excellent collection of copies of probate indexes. For more information about them, consult N. J. N. Newington-Irving, *Will Indexes and Other Probate Material in the Library of the Society of Genealogists* (London, 1996), which is available in the General Reference area. Many wills, indexes and lists have been put on microfilm by the LDS. You can order these to read in your local LDS Family History Centre. For details, search the *Family History Library Catalog* (*see* p. 76).

Prerogative Court of Canterbury (PCC) records

The PCC was the busiest and most important probate court. The PRO holds a number of surviving original wills proved there. These are in series PROB 10 and can be seen only at Kew, though there is a copy of the list in the General Reference area. Some of them are in the handwriting of the testator (holograph wills), and they all bear the signatures or marks of the testator and witnesses. Registered office copies of all PCC wills from 1384 to 9 January 1858 (in PROB 11), all PCC grants of letters of administration from 1559 to 1858 (in PROB 6) and separate Limited Administration Act Books from 1810 to 1858 (in PROB 7) can be searched on microfilm both at the FRC and at Kew.

Probate Act Books from 1526 to 1858 (in PROB 8) and Limited Probate Act Books from 1781 to 1858 (in PROB 9), which identify the parish where the testator died, are at present available only at Kew, along with Probate Inventories of personal possessions and debts owed to the deceased, executors' and administrators' bonds and warrants, and litigation papers relating to disputed wills and administration grants. For information about these other sources, read M. Scott, *Prerogative Court of Canterbury Wills and Other Probate Records* (PRO, 1997), a copy of which is on the shelves in the General Reference area. A PRO leaflet on probate records is available near the General Reference area and can be downloaded from **www.familyrecords.gov.uk** or from **www.pro.gov.uk**.

How to find a PCC will

You will need an approximate year of death, but there are printed and typescript indexes to PCC wills proved between 1384 and 1800 available in the General Reference area. You can also access the PCC personal-name indexes gradually being offered by **www.pro-online.pro.gov.uk** (*see* pp. 81–2). The indexes give you only the film and quire number range, so you still have to use the yearly cream-bound Register Books in PROB 12, on the open shelves in the General Reference area, to obtain the specific quire number of a will proved after 1801. The *Index to the Bank of England Will Extracts* (in print for 1807–45, and online on **www.englishorigins.com** for 1717–1845) can also help pinpoint wills and administration grants, but does not give their PRO film and quire reference numbers.

The indexes and Register Books are arranged by the date when a will was proved, not when it was made – which may have been many years earlier, and since then a number of codicils (dated additions or modifications) might have been incorporated. Wills were not necessarily proved immediately upon death, so be prepared to search the indexes and Register Books for anything up to 15 years afterwards.

Consult the indexes covering the years you want to search. When you have found the correct entry, make a note of the year and quire number against the testator's name. (In this context, a quire is a section of 16 pages. In the published indexes for 1701–49, it is referred to as '*sig*'.) Now find the burgundy binders, nearby, labelled 'PCC Wills Reference Book PROB 11' on the spine. Look for the year and for the range of numbers, to the right of it, that includes your quire number. In the left-hand margin, alongside the year, you will find another number, indicating the microfilm on which you will find the quire or *sig*. The typescript indexes for 1701–49 identify the PRO microfilm number for you.

For wills proved between 1801 and 1849, look on the probate finding aids shelves in the General Reference area for the annual Register Books labelled PROB 12 on the spine. These are not strict alphabetical indexes of names, but are chronological lists of people with surnames beginning with a particular letter of the alphabet (initial index), whose wills were proved during the course of the year from January until the end of December. There are usually two volumes per year, labelled A–K and L–Z. Each entry will reveal the deceased's surname, forename, county of residence, month of probate and quire number. 'Ser' or 'serv' means that the testator was in the service of the Crown, in the Army or Royal Navy; 'Pts' means that the person died abroad; 'North Britain' is Scotland. There are separate lists at the end of each initial letter for non-commissioned soldiers' and seamen's wills, but from 1820 until 1852 they are located at the end of the yearly list. Once you have located your entry, follow the steps described above, using the PCC Wills Reference Book.

The typescript and microfiche indexes (1701–49) and Register Books (1801–49) in series PROB 12 include lists of administration grants ('admons'). So, when tying up your references with the microfilm numbers, make sure you look in the right Reference Book – in PROB 11 for a will, or in PROB 6 (*see* pp. 110–13) for an administration grant.

For 1853–7 and January 1858, there are printed consolidated *Calendars of the grants of probate and letters of administration made in the Prerogative Court of Canterbury*, which are also widely available on microfiche (see J. Gibson, *Probate Jurisdictions: Where to Look for Wills*).

You may find a reference to 'A with W annexed'. This indicates that the court had made a grant of letters of administration – usually to the residuary legatee (often the person with the largest interest in the estate) – with the will attached, as the testator had failed to appoint an executor, or his or her chosen executors had already died or renounced their right to act. Such acts were written up in the Probate Act Books in PROB 8 and PROB 9 (only available as documents at the PRO, Kew); and the will was registered in PROB 11, which you can search on microfilm at the FRC and at Kew.

Sometimes, the index or Register Book refers to a will proved and registered in an earlier year but the present entry refers to the year of a later probate grant. Look for this later grant in the finding aid for PROB 8. Unfortunately, at present, you will only be able to search PROB 8 volumes by visiting the PRO, Kew. The index or Register Book will disclose the name of the earlier PROB 11 volume and the quire number where the will has been copied, but not the year. However, at the front of the PROB 11

PCC Wills Reference Book there is a complete alphabetical list of yearly volume names, years and film numbers. These enable you to identify the film you want in the usual way and then read the will.

Taking one of the seat boxes, find the film in the cabinets marked PROB 11, in the search area, and replace it with your seat box. Go to the appropriate seat and load the film onto the microfilm machine. You will see that every other page has a number stamped or written on it at the top right-hand corner. This is the folio number. Make a note of it, as you will have to cite it if you want the staff to make a photocopy; similarly, you will need it if you decide to use one of the self-service photocopiers. Every 16 pages, a new quire number is written in large figures at the top right-hand corner. Somewhere between this quire number and the next will be the entry you want. The name of each testator is written in the margin next to where the registered copy of his or her will begins.

Understanding the will

Wills can be complex documents, using unfamiliar archaic and legal terms, and may run to many pages. There is a glossary of terms in Scott's book cited above (*see* p. 105). You may prefer to take a photocopy of the will home with you to pore over later, when you have more time to decipher and understand its contents.

The document is usually prefaced by 'In the Name of God Amen This is the last will and testament of me . . .' Strictly, the 'will' related to real estate (realty), such as freehold land; the 'testament' to a person's personal possessions, cash, bonds, tools, and leases. Ecclesiastical courts had control over the disposal of personal property but not of realty, which was under the jurisdiction of civil law courts. For convenience, however, both documents were combined.

If you discover a will starting with *'Memorandam quod . . .'*, this is a written copy of a nuncupative (spoken) will, to which there had to be at least two credible witnesses, who then reported the deceased's spoken intentions to the court. These were usually dictated when the person was at death's door.

Look for the date when the will was made, either near the beginning of the will or at the end. Any additional clauses would be clearly tied to this dated will, expressed in a codicil, or series of codicils, dated, signed and witnessed in the usual way.

The probate act, at the conclusion of the will, records the date when it was proved, the names and abodes of the executors, and frequently their relationship to the deceased. If the executor was the widow and she had remarried, then this provides an important clue to the time period within which she had taken a new husband.

68
388

of me George Hume Yeats" ending thus "I have set my hand this eleventh day of February 1810" & thus subscribed "Geo: H: Yeats" these deponents say that they do verily & in their consciences believe the whole body series & contents of the said Will & the subscription thereto to be of the proper handwriting & subscription of the said deceased. Robert Chenocke Smith — Geo: H: King — On the 1st day of February 1811 the above Robert Chenocke Smith & George Hillyard King were duly sworn to this Affidavit Before me J. Parson Surr: pres: Thos Ecott N.P.

Proved at London 24th January 1811 before the Worshipful Samuel Pearce Parson Dr of Laws & by the Oath of Jane Fitzhugh Yeats Widow the Relict & Executrix according to the tenor of the Will she being first sworn duly to administer.

In the Name of God Amen — *William Young*

I William Young living in Cumberstone Street in the parish of Saint George in the East in the County of Middlesex being through Divine mercy in good bodily health & of a perfect sound & composing mind & memory do make this my last Will & Testament in manner & form following that is to say Imprimis First I give & bequeath unto my Sister Sarah Young Widow the sum of Ten pounds per year during her natural life [illegible] arising from the Interest of Eight hundred pounds in the four per Cents Item I also give & bequeath unto my Sister Elizabeth Flack Widow the sum of Ten pounds during her natural life arising as aforesaid Item I also give and bequeath unto my Sister Grace Young Spinster the sum of ten pounds per year during her natural life arising as aforesaid Item Also after the death of my three Sisters aforesaid I give & bequeath of the sum of the Eight hundred pounds in the four per Cents aforesaid in manner & form following that is to say I give & bequeath unto my Nephew John Young Blacksmith of Rumford in Essex one Eighth part of the money aforesaid Item I also give & bequeath unto John Young Harry Young & Grace Young Children of Henry Young deceased one eighth part of the money aforesaid Item I also give unto Grace Wright Wife of Daniel Wright of Essex one eighth part of the money aforesaid Item I also give unto Martha Martrouett Wife of Martrouett one eighth part of the money aforesaid Item I also give unto my Nephew John Young of Woodford in Essex one eighth part of the money aforesaid Item I also give unto my Nephew James Flack Son of Elizabeth Flack of London in Essex one eighth part of the money aforesaid Item I also give unto Elizabeth Flack Daughter of Elizabeth Flack aforesaid one eighth part of the money aforesaid Lastly I give & bequeath unto my Nephew Henry Young Poulterer at Woodford in Essex one eighth part of the money aforesaid And I also hereby nominate & appoint the said Henry Young Executor of this my last Will & Testament with full power & authority after the decease of my three Sisters aforesaid to sell & dispose of the said Eight hundred pounds in the four per Cents & to divide the same equally between the several persons mentioned as aforesaid in this my last Will & Testament In witness whereof I have hereunto set my hand unto the first sheet & my hand & seal unto this last this twenty seventh day of November in the year of our Lord 1802. William Young — Signed sealed & delivered by William Young the Testator as his last Will & Testament in the presence of us who subscribed our names in presence of the said Testator & of each other. John Gray — Richard Wade — Charles Evans.

Proved at London 31st January 1811 before the Worshipful Samuel Pearce Parson Dr of Laws & by the Oath of Henry Young the sole Exor he having been first sworn duly to administer.

This is the last Will and Testament of me Johan Zoffany of Chiswick in the County of Middlesex — *Johan Zoffany Esqr*

117

Esquire Whereas on the Marriage of my Daughter Cecilia Clementina Eliza with the Revd Thomas Horne the younger of Chiswick aforesaid I advanced to him the sum of Three hundred pounds & transferred to Trustees the sum of Two thousand pounds Bank three per Cent Consolidated Annuities In Trust for my Daughter for life & then for the Issue of the said Marriage & in default of such Issue to revert back to me or my Estate Now in case my said Daughter Cecilia Clementina Eliza shall die [illegible] without Issue by the said Thomas Horne or if there shall be any such Issue & they shall all die before their respective shares of and in the said two thousand pounds three per Cent Annuities shall become vested then I hereby give unto the said Thomas Horne the Dividends & annual proceed of the said Two thousand pounds Bank three pounds per Cent Annuities for & during the term of his natural life And Whereas on the Marriage of my Daughter Maria Theresa Louisa with John Doratt of Bruton Street [illegible] I transferred to Trustees the sum of two thousand pounds Bank three pounds per Cent Consolidated Annuities In Trust for my said last mentioned Daughter for life & after her decease In Trust for her Issue by the said John Doratt And in default of such Issue then the Capital of the said last mentioned Annuities was to revert back to me or my Estate Now in case my said Daughter Maria Theresa Louisa shall die without Issue by the said John Doratt or if there shall be any such Issue & they shall all die before their respective shares of & in the said last mentioned sum of Two thousand pounds Bank three pounds per Cent Annuities shall become vested Then I hereby give unto the said John Doratt the Dividends & annual proceed of the said last mentioned sum of Two thousand pounds Bank three pounds per Cent Annuities for the term of his natural life And Whereas since the Marriage of my said Daughter Maria Theresa Louisa I have paid or secured to be paid to the said John Doratt the sum of three hundred pounds to make my last mentioned Daughters fortune equal with that of her Sister Cecilia Clementina Eliza And I give & devise unto my dear Wife Mary Zoffany All that my Messuage or Tenement in which I now dwell situate at Chiswick aforesaid with the Coachhouse Stable Garden & appurts thereto belonging for & during the term of her natural life if she shall so long continue my Widow but not otherwise I likewise give unto my said dear Wife Mary Zoffany the use of all my Household Furniture Plate Linen China Earthen Ware & Household Utensils for & during the term of her natural life if she shall so long continue my Widow but not otherwise & from & after her decease or marriage again of my said Wife which shall first happen then I hereby declare my Will to be & direct that the said Messuage or Tenement Coachhouse & Stable with the Appurts & the said Household furniture Plate Linen China Earthen Ware & Household Utensils shall sink into & be considered as part of the residue of my Estate & Effects & be transferred & disposed of accordingly I give & bequeath unto Anthony Angelo Tremamondo of Howland Street in the Parish of Saint Pancras in the County of Middlesex Esquire & Charles Dumergue of Piccadilly in the said County of Middx Esquire my Trustees and Exors hereinafter named the sum of twenty five Guineas each for a Ring which I request they will accept as a small token of my regard & friendship for them And as to all the rest residue & remainder of my Estate & Effects

Figure 22 Part of the registered office copy of the will of Johan Zoffany, whose state portraits of King George III and the Royal Family form part of the Royal Collection. Made in 1805, it set up a series of complex trusts for his wife and four daughters, and was proved on 24 January 1811 in the Prerogative Court of Canterbury. The will preceding it in the register commences with the customary preamble 'In the Name of God Amen'. (PROB 11/1518, q. 49)

Some of the very early wills are in Latin, and you may need to consult a dictionary to gain an idea of their content. There are copies of Latin dictionaries in the General Reference area. The probate acts appended at the bottom of the registered wills were invariably written in Latin until 1733. You may also find marginal notes in Latin, which will probably relate to a verdict ('sentence') or judgment ('by decree') after a lawsuit. Records of PCC disputes are held by the PRO, Kew, as are those of cases brought to the Court of Chancery for a decree.

You may find it helpful when reading old handwriting to refer to H. E. P. Grieve, *Examples of English Handwriting 1150–1750* (Essex Record Office Publications, 1954, 5th impression, 1981) or L. Munby, *Reading Tudor and Stuart Handwriting* (Chichester, 1988). Copies of these are in the General Reference area. For explanations of Latin terms, consult D. Stuart, *Latin for Local and Family Historians* (Chichester, 1995). Staff will help if you have a problem reading a particular word or phrase.

If you are totally stuck, ask at the Research Enquiries Desk for the names and addresses of palaeography specialists who might be prepared, for a fee, to transcribe or explain the document to you.

Wills express the private wishes and emotional life of the testator in ways that remain undetectable in any other source. They offer the opportunity of settling old scores, as well as returning favours and providing for the future prosperity of immediate family, other kinsfolk and friends. However, landed property was often disposed of by other means, such as a marriage settlement or trust deed, or might be inherited in a predestined way from generation to generation, and so may not feature in a will. Children might have their inheritance settled on them on attaining 21 or at marriage, so not all of them may be mentioned, or they may be given only a token legacy.

There is an incomplete collection of original wills, 1484–1858, in PRO series PROB 10, which are often easier to read than the court copies described above. You have to give five days' notice to read these at Kew, as they are stored elsewhere. They are arranged by year and then by month, so you will need to cite these to identify the will you want. A copy of the PROB 10 finding aid is in the General Reference area at the FRC.

Other probate records

Supporting documents, such as probate inventories, can tell you much more about the living conditions and lifestyles of our ancestors, because they list household items (often room by room), cash, debts, stock, crops and animals, each with their approximate sale value. Indexed surviving PCC probate inventories can be inspected at the PRO, Kew; for details, consult Scott's book cited on p. 105. Indexes to the inventories in PROB 3 and PROB 4 are in the General Reference area.

Death Duty registers, running between 1796 and 1903, add a great deal of information about changing estate values and beneficiaries, since they were kept open by the Board of Stamps for 50 years to allow contingent interests to vest (*see* p. 117–19).

Records of lawsuits

If the will indexes indicate that a will was proved 'by sentence' or 'by decree' (abbreviated to 'sent' and 'decr'), it means there was a dispute. In which case, you may be able to glean much more information about the circumstances under which the will was made, and the subsequent fallout, by exploring the records held at Kew. Disputes handled by the PCC relate only to the authenticity of wills, not the contents – for example, the court might have to decide whether a man was sober and/or sane at the time the will was dictated. If the family or others wished to challenge the way in which the property was disposed of, then the equity Court of Chancery was normally used, since it had jurisdiction over trusts and real estate. Chancery proceedings and decrees can be researched at the PRO, Kew. These are described in *Tracing Your Ancestors in the Public Record Office*, and in a series of leaflets available on **www.pro.gov.uk** and at the PRO itself.

The PCC was very thorough in its proceedings, and a large number of witnesses (on occasion, even an entire village) might be called to give evidence before sentence was passed. Some wills were 'propounded' (that is, proved by witnesses) and there may be surviving documents about this, though the will indexes will not necessarily indicate it.

The only certain way of checking if there was a suit or propounding is to examine the fairly complete series of Act of Court Books in series PROB 29, covering 1536 to 1819, which contains integral indexes; and/or the loose Acts of Court, in PROB 30, 1740–1858, which are arranged in monthly bundles and then alphabetically under the name of the deceased. This may be time-consuming.

How to find a PCC administration grant

Where a person died intestate (i.e. without leaving a valid will) and had personal possessions, leases and cash (personalty) amounting to £5 (£10 for London residents) or more, the court could make a grant of letters of administration relating to his or her personal estate if:

- the widow or next of kin thought someone else might make a claim on the estate
- there was a need for legal title to be established (for instance, when a creditor owed money by the deceased sought to secure payment of the debt).

A 'special' or 'limited' grant meant that it was confined to a particular part of the deceased's estate.

A person's real estate (freehold property or realty) lay outside the court's jurisdiction and passed by inheritance on intestacy to the nearest blood relative (the heir at law).

The records of PCC grants of administration from 1559 until 9 January 1858 are in the Administration Act Books in PROB 6, including special and limited grants up to 1809. Special and limited grants from 1810 until 1858 are in the Limited Administration Act Books in PROB 7. Both series are available on microfilm at the FRC and at Kew.

There are printed indexes to PCC administration grants for 1559–1660, 1661 (A–Sweetinge only) and 1663–4; and typescript indexes for 1701–49. Copies of these are in the General Reference area. The Society of Genealogists plans to publish its index of PCC administrations for 1750–1800. Some of the indexes provide the folio references to administration grants, others merely record the month and year.

Otherwise, you will have to search the yearly Register Books for 1661, 1665–1700 and 1750 onwards, in the PROB 12 volumes, which are on the open shelves in the General Reference area. There are no Act Books for 1662. From 1853 until 1857, there is a printed consolidated *Calendar* of wills and administration grants – in the same area, next to the *Calendar* for 1–9 January 1858. Like the yearly entries for wills, the administrations ('admons') are listed chronologically in initial-alphabetical order of each surname, followed by forename, county of death, and the month when the grant was made. 'Pts' indicates that the person died overseas. Grants relating to the personal property of serving non-commissioned soldiers and sailors between 1801 and 1819 are located in a separate section at the end of each letter, but for 1820–52 you will need to look right at the end of the annual list. The places identified in the indexes and *Calendars* relate to the deceased.

Having found the person you want, note the county and month and then locate the burgundy binders, nearby, labelled 'PCC Administrations Reference Book PROB 6' on the spine. Find the year and month in question, and you will see the number of the microfilm written alongside in the left-hand margin. Starting in 1719, the administration grants are registered in geographical areas called 'Seats': The Registrar's Seat (**1**) covers grants relating to property of people dying overseas – unless the grant was to the widow (in which case, the Seat would be the one where she lived) or to intestates living outside the province of Canterbury, or was disputed. The others are Surrey (**2**), Wales (**3**), Middlesex (**4**) and London (**5**). The Act Books are set out in month by month order and then by Seat, but not always consistently. The entries for each Seat are recorded under the name of its clerk. To find their names, look at the front of the Reference Book.

From 1744, the Act Books are organized in five Seats, four of which are county Seats, and then in month order. At the front of the PCC Administrations Reference Book PROB 6 is a key indicating which counties belong to each of the Seats. The county is the one where the death occurred, which would not necessarily have been the deceased's place of residence. The entries are usually in initial-alphabetical order of surname. The first section (the 'Registrar's Seat', abbreviated in the Act Books to 'Regrs') should always be checked – as it contains, amongst other things, all grants made after litigation and therefore includes people who died in any part of the country.

The Seat arrangement is given below:

Bedfordshire	4	Norfolk	4
Berkshire	4	Northamptonshire	3
Bristol	2, 3	North Britain (Scotland)	1
Buckinghamshire	4	Northumberland	1
Cambridgeshire	4	Nottinghamshire	1
Carlisle	1	Oxford	3
Chester	1	Pts (Abroad)	3
City of London	5	Rutland	3
Cornwall	2	Shropshire	3
Cumberland	1	Sunderland	2
Derbyshire	3	Somerset	2
Devon	2	Southampton	2
Dorset	2	Staffordshire	3
Durham	1	Suffolk	4
Essex	4	Surrey	2
Gloucestershire	3	Sussex	2
Herefordshire	3	Wales	3
Hertfordshire	4	Warwickshire	2
Huntingdonshire	4	Wiltshire	2
Ireland	1	Worcestershire	3
Kent	1	York (the county, and entire Province)	1
Lancashire	1	Grants on Litigated Estates (by decree)	1
Leicestershire	3	Outlying London parishes (Middlesex)	4
Lincolnshire	4		
London	5		
Middlesex	4, 5		

When you have identified the relevant Seat, look for the year in PROB 6, find the Seat, and the Clerk's name from the front of the Reference Book, and this will tell you on which film and folios it will appear.

If you find 'special' or 'limited admon' under the name of the intestate in the Register Books, it will be 'entered at length' in PROB 6 up to 1809, at the beginning of the relevant month, under the appropriate Seat from 1719; and as part of a group at the beginning or end of each Seat, or at the beginning of the appropriate month for that Seat, from 1744 onwards. The entry in PROB 6 between 1810 and 1858 serves as a cross-reference to special or limited administration grants recorded in PROB 7.

From 1810 until 1858, for special and limited administration grants, you will need to find the microfilm reference in PROB 7, using the year, county and month as your key, as with PROB 6. Again, each Act Book is divided into five discrete sections according to the Seats described above, and then into monthly segments. As with the PROB 6 volumes, the different Seats, apart from the Registrar's ('Regrs'), are identified by the name of the Clerk.

Once you have located the correct film number, help yourself to a seat-number box and use this as a marker when you remove each film from the cabinets marked PROB 6 or PROB 7, as appropriate, and then find your chosen numbered microfilm machine.

When you wind the reel onto the machine's spool, you will see that there are sub-sections within each month. If a folio number was given in an index, then locating the entry should be easy; otherwise, you will need to check the entries for the relevant month carefully, under the name of the appropriate clerk. Names are written in the margin, but they are all in Latin until 1733 and the handwriting may be difficult to decipher, so you may have to follow the advice given above (*see* p. 109) and make a photocopy once you have identified the correct entry.

Understanding the grant

Even though they are composed in Latin before 1733, the wording of administration grants follows a pattern, so it is simple to extract the information you want.

The name in the margin is that of the deceased. From 1792 onwards, you will also find a valuation figure for the personal estate. In the body of the entry you will find the date of the grant, the name of the intestate, his or her place of abode, and the particulars of the administrator or administrators (name, address and relationship to the deceased). The entry is endorsed with the date by which a probate inventory of the deceased's personal assets had to be filed with the court by the administrator(s), which was usually within six months of the grant of letters of administration.

Because letters of administration were granted to the next of kin in strict order of affinity to the deceased, you can discover who was the nearest living relative at the time when the grant was made – so these records may prove invaluable. The spouse came first, then the children equally (grandchildren taking any deceased children's place), then the parents, then the brothers and sisters equally (their children or grandchildren stepping into their shoes if they had predeceased the intestate), then half-brothers and half-sisters equally (or their children or grandchildren if they themselves were already dead), then the grandparents, then uncles and aunts equally (or their children or grandchildren, as before), and then the chief creditor. For want of any of these, the estate passed as *bona vacantia* to the Crown. Any renunciations or failures to appear by individuals with a prior right to the grant will be cited, so you can discover who was the living next of kin and the proximity of the blood relationship. For an illustration of this, look at the admon of John Constable, the famous artist, reproduced below.

Occasionally you may find that an administration grant was made *'de bonis non'*. This means that the court had to appoint another administrator to replace a previous one who had renounced the right to act, or who had died leaving part or all of the personal estate undisposed of.

Problems and solutions

1. *There is not much information in the Act Book entry. Is there anything else I can look at?*

   There may be an inventory (list of possessions) or an administration bond or warrant to administrators to dispose of the personal estate, mentioning the date and place of death. These records are held by the PRO, Kew. For details about them, look at Scott's book cited above (*see* p. 105).

John Constable Esqr. £25,000. On the first day Admon of the Goods Chattels and Credits of John Constable late of Charlotte Street Fitzroy Square in the County of Middlesex Esquire Royal Academician Widower deceased was granted to Golding Constable Esquire the lawful Uncle and one of the next of Kin and Lancelot Archer Burton Esquire the Curators or Guardians lawfully assigned to John Charles Constable, Maria Louisa Constable Spinster, Isabel Constable Spinster, Emily Constable Spinster Alfred Abram Constable and Lionel Bicknell Constable (Minors) six of the natural and lawful Children of the said Deceased for the use and benefit of the said Minors and also of Charles Golding Constable, a Minor also the only other natural and lawful Child of the said Deceased now

This Admon ceased & expired & another Admon granted Decr. 1838. —

Death Duty registers, 1796–1903, may supply extra details of what became of a person's estate. You can search the yearly indexes to these on microfilm at the FRC and the registers (also on microfilm) up to 1857. Later registers, 1858–1903, are held off-site, so you need to give three days' notice to search them at Kew.

Like wills, an intestate's personal assets might form the subject of litigation (for possible sources, *see* p. 110 above). The most common suits were 'interest causes', concerning who was related, and in what way, to the deceased.

2. *There is an administration in the indexes for my ancestor, but I can find no trace of it on the PROB 6 film. Why not?*

   Either you are looking in the wrong Seat (*see* p. 112) or your grant is 'special' or 'limited' (*see* pp. 111 and 113).

3. *My will/administration search has been unsuccessful. What shall I do now?*

   There are three main reasons why you have not found what you are looking for:

   - You have not searched a long enough period. When that person's heir died, unadministered estate might come to light and so a late grant might be made. Try searching a few years after the year of the heir's death as well.
   - You are hunting in the wrong probate court. Maybe the deceased's property was in one of the Northern dioceses, so came under the jurisdiction of the Prerogative Court of York? Or perhaps probate was dealt with by one of the diocesan or archdeaconry courts? *The Phillimore Atlas and Index of Parish Registers* or *Probate*

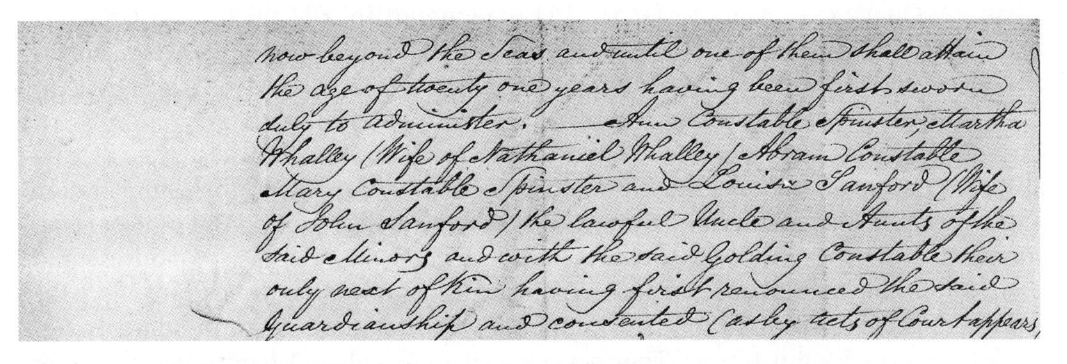

now beyond the Seas and until one of them shall attain
the age of twenty one years having been first sworn
duly to administer. — Ann Constable Spinster Martha
Whalley (Wife of Nathaniel Whalley) Abram Constable
Mary Constable Spinster and Louisa Sanford (Wife
of John Sanford) the lawful Uncle and Aunts of the
said Minors and with the said Golding Constable their
only next of Kin having first renounced the said
Guardianship and consented (as by Acts of Court appears,

Figure 23 PCC grant of letters of administration, 1 June 1837, for the personal estate of painter John Constable, which was valued at £25,000. Constable's wife was already dead, and his seven named children were still under 21. Three of their uncles and aunts had renounced the right, as next of kin, to act as their guardians, but another uncle, Golding Constable, was appointed to administer the estate until they came of age. The marginal note refers to a further grant, dated 20 December 1838, which superseded this one when one of the sons, John Charles Constable, reached maturity. Alas, he died within three years, and yet another grant relating to the estate was made, to his sister Maria Louisa, on 7 April 1841. (PROB 6/213, ff. 39 and 240)

Jurisdictions: Where to Look for Wills may provide guidance. Try also the yearly indexes to the Death Duty registers, 1796–1903, to see if the will was proved elsewhere. These are in series IR 27; for how to search them, *see* pp. 119–21.

- No grant was ever made. Probate was a matter of conscience on the part of executors, and an administration grant might have been thought unnecessary if the surviving family agreed about the distribution of the personal estate.

Finding wills and administrations from 1858 onwards

Since 9 January 1858, the ecclesiastical courts have ceased to function over probate matters. In England and Wales, wills are now proved by District Probate Registries and Sub-Registries, where administration grants are also made. These operate under the aegis of the Principal Registry of the Family Division, First Avenue House, 42–49 High Holborn, London WC1V 6NP (telephone 020 7947 7022, website **www.courtservice.gov.uk**). The website sets out the titles, addresses and contact details of each of the Registries. Many of these hold copies of the countrywide annual union indexes, the dates of which are given on the above website. Although most Registries will have had indexes dating back to 1858, they are only obliged to keep them for 50 years. However, you may find that they have passed them on to the local record office.

Microfiche copies of the indexes from 1993 to 1998 and computerized indexes to wills and administrations since 1996 can be searched on the Probate Service database, at present available both at the Probate Searchroom, First Avenue House, in London (*address above*) and at the Manchester District Probate Registry, 9th Floor, Astley House, 23 Quay Street, Manchester M3 4AT (telephone 0161 834 4319). It is planned to make these indexes available online at all District Probate Registries (listed in the *Family and Local History Handbook*).

Consolidated yearly personal-name indexes are available on microfiche at the FRC and at Kew. They span 1858 to 1943. Up to 1870, inclusive, the indexes to administration grants follow those to wills and administrations with will annexed. The index entries summarize the date (and, up to 1891, place) of death, the deceased's address and occupation, the date, place and type of probate or administration grant, and the names and (up to 1891) addresses, occupations and relationship to the deceased of the executors or administrators. They also give an estate value. A handwritten number adjacent to entries of Principal Probate Registry (London) wills up to 1930 refers to the relevant folio number in the registered office copies, so make a note of this.

In order to examine a will, you will need to visit the Probate Searchroom at First Avenue House or a District Probate Registry. For details of the Probate Registry's search services and how to obtain copies of wills and letters of administration, *see* p. 27.

Scottish wills and testaments

It is planned to make the personal-name indexes to these available via the internet. Visit **www.familyrecords.gov.uk** or **www.nas.gov.uk**, the website of the National Archives of Scotland (NAS), for up-to-date information and a fact sheet on Scottish wills and testaments.

Irish wills and administration grants

At the FRC, in the library in the General Reference area, there is a published *Index to the Prerogative Wills of Ireland, 1536–1810*, edited by Sir Arthur Vicars (1897, reprinted Baltimore, 1967). These relate to the Prerogative Court of Armagh, which had overriding jurisdiction over wills in Ireland up to the end of 1857. All the original wills and the vast majority of the registered copies were consumed by fire in 1922, but look at J. Grenham, *Tracing Your Irish Ancestors* (Dublin, 2nd edn 1999) for information about what survives (a copy is in the library in the General Reference area). Also, visit **http://proni.nics.gov.uk**, the website of the Public Record Office of Northern Ireland, which can be accessed direct or via **www.familyrecords.gov.uk**.

Death Duty registers and indexes

These records, in PRO series IR 26, complement and add to information in many English and Welsh wills and administrations that took effect between 1796 and 1903. For the period 1796–1857 they can be read on microfilm both at the FRC and at the PRO, Kew; and for 1858–1903 as original documents at Kew. A minimum of three days' notice is necessary to see the later records, because the registers are stored off-site. There are annual indexes from 1796 until 1903, in series IR 27, available on microfilm at both sites.

The Death Duty records are a prime nineteenth-century genealogical source, and yet they are largely underused. Approximately 9,000 registers and indexes track the levying of a series of different taxes, and provide:

- A countrywide probate index for the crucial period of 1796–1858 (though not fully comprehensive, since the taxes did not reach down to everyone's will or administration grant). During these years, as already mentioned, England and Wales were served by hundreds of local church and other courts, presided over by the Prerogative Courts of York and Canterbury. If you have no idea where a person's will was proved, then you may have to search the indexes to records of a variety of courts, not all of which have been published. From 1858 this ceases to be a problem, since there are annual National Probate Indexes (*see* pp 26 and 116) covering the whole country.

- Details not otherwise available for much of Devon and Somerset. In many cases, the Death Duty registers and indexes for the dioceses of Exeter and Bath and Wells may be all that survives of local records which have been largely destroyed. You will find an *Index to Somerset Estate Duty Office Wills and Letters of Administration, 1805–1811*, edited by D. T. Hawkings (Weston-super-Mare, 1995), and an *Index to Somerset Estate Duty Office Wills, 1812–1857* by the same editor (2 vols, Weston-super-Mare, 1995) in the General Reference area, relating to copy wills sent to the county record office in Taunton.

- Information about thousands of families and their current wealth, both at the time when a will was proved and at a later date when the Board of Stamps extracted its dues as contingent interests fell in during the 50 years that the registers were kept open. Typically, a will might provide money or other property for the spouse during widowhood or for life, after which what remained was to be sold off and the sale proceeds distributed according to the testator's instructions. A note was made in the Death Duty register of the sale price, and the tax owed was then calculated, based on the proximity of blood or other relationship of each beneficiary. Basically, the closer the relationship was, the lower the tax. These relationships can be crucial in establishing illegitimate issue. Gifts to spouses were exempt from Death Duty, so the Board of Stamps bided its time until a liable beneficiary received his or her share.

The registers record a series of taxes. Legacy Duty was introduced in 1796, and was payable on legacies worth £20 or more and on the residue of personal estates left by will or on intestacy. Gifts to spouses, children, grandchildren, parents and grandparents were exempt from this duty. The Legacy Duty Act of 1805 exempted only legacies to spouses and direct ancestors, whilst the Stamp Act of 1815 excluded only gifts to wives. These later Acts also broadened the range of the duty to embrace legacies and estate residues raised from the sale of real estate (freehold property) as directed by wills. Under a further Act of 1853, Succession Duty became payable on all gratuitous acquisitions of property worth £20 or more at death from estates of a total value of £100 and upwards. This included real and personal estate, and leases were now deemed to be realty rather than personalty. Where there was an existing liability to Legacy Duty, that part of the estate was not taken into account in calculating Succession Duty. Rather, it extended its reach to inheritance under trust deeds and settlements. Probate Duty, which was introduced in 1881, was a tax on all personal property passing at death. In 1894, with Legacy Duty, it was merged into Estate Duty, relating to all property transfers at death. There are no surviving registers at the PRO after 1903 (*see* p. 125).

The gradual extension of the scope of the taxes as the century progressed means that you have more chance of finding details about your ancestor's estate as the years pass. The Board of Stamps, which originally administered the taxes, did not usually bother to pursue collection unless the assets were valued at £1,500 or more, so many entries may just record a total valuation without any further information. 'N.E.' against a person's name in the index means there was no entry in the register. If you find the annotation 'Upper Limit', that indicates your ancestor was worth over £1,000,000, because under the Stamp Act 1815 such estates were exempt.

The coverage of the registers

There are five series of registers:

- Legacy Duty registers, 1796–1893
- Succession Duty registers, 1853–93 (Probate Duty from 1881)
- Estate Duty registers, 1894–1903 (incorporating the two other taxes)
- Succession Arrears registers, opened in 1885 and 1889 to cope with outstanding claims for duty from 1853 to 1865 and from 1866 to 1878 respectively
- Reversionary registers, created in 1899 to deal with outstanding claims from 1812 to 1852

All registers from 1858 onwards and the Succession Duty and Reversionary registers are available only at the PRO, Kew; a minimum of three days' notice is required to inspect them. See p. 120 for details about the indexes in IR 27 and registers in IR 26. About 500 Estate Duty registers and 11 Succession Duty registers are missing.

Using the indexes

To try and locate an ancestor's will or administration grant, check through the films of the annual Death Duty indexes in IR 27. They do not relate to every probate or grant, as the tax did not ever extend to estates or legacies under the value of £20, but you may be able to pick up other members of the family whose wills were proved in the diocesan or Prerogative Courts serving the area where your ancestors lived. From about 1815, because of the increasing scope of the tax and because only a single group of beneficiaries (spouses) were exempted, most probates and administration grants should be traceable in the indexes. In 1854, it was said that there was a Death Duty entry for one of every 16 people dying in this country. The estates of servicemen killed in action were exempted after 1837, and the UK estates of British people resident abroad from 1853. The indexes are arranged under the names of testators and intestates. Look at the binders labelled 'Death Duty Registers Indexes IR 27' in the General Reference area and you will see that the indexes are in various series, as shown in the following table.

Dates	Legacy Duty	Annual indexes	Registers
1796–1811	PCC wills	IR 27/1–16	IR 26/1–178
1796–1857	PCC administrations (admons)	IR 27/17–66	IR 26/179–286
1796–1811	Country courts wills and admons	IR 27/67–93	IR 26/287–437
1812–57	Country courts admons	IR 27/94–139	IR 26/438–534
1812–81	All courts: wills	IR 27/140–419	IR 26/535–3292
1858–63	All courts: admons	IR 27/420–9	IR 26/3293–3316
1864–81	All courts: admons	no indexes	IR 26/3317–3433
1882–94	All courts: wills and admons	IR 27/430–531	IR 26/3434–4855
1812–52	Reversionary registers (outstanding claims)	no indexes	IR 26/4856–67
Dates	**Succession Duty**	**Annual indexes**	**Registers**
1853–94	All wills and admons	no indexes	IR 26/4868–6262
1853–78	Registers of arrears (outstanding claims 1853–65)	no indexes	IR 26/6263–70
	(outstanding claims 1866–78)	no indexes	IR 26/6271–82
Dates	**Estate Duty**	**Annual indexes**	**Registers**
1894–1903	All wills and admons	IR 27/532–605	IR 26/6283–8743

There is a card index to IR 26/287–321, covering abstracts of wills and administration grants in the Consistory (Bishops') Courts of Bangor, Bath and Wells, Bristol, Canterbury, Carlisle, Chester, and Chichester, between 1796 and 1811; and a series of burgundy-bound Death Duty Surname Indexes for the dioceses of Durham, Exeter, Ely and Oxford, for the same period. This card index will eventually become a new PRO database.

Remember that registers covering the years up to and including 1857 can be seen on microfilm at the FRC and the PRO, but items from IR 26/2086 onwards can be searched only at Kew. A minimum of three days' notice is required before you can see these, as many of the volumes are stored off-site.

The indexes in IR 27 are not strictly alphabetical, but later ones group surnames according to their first three letters – for instance, all names beginning with 'Tur...' will be listed together, chronologically by date of probate or administration grant. The indexes record the surname and forename of the testator or intestate, residence at death ('SP' means of the same place), names of executors or administrators ('& ors' means 'and others', '& anor' means 'and another') and the name of the court. This is sometimes abbreviated – for instance, 'PC' or 'PreC' stands for Prerogative Court of Canterbury; 'PCY' indicates Prerogative Court of York; 'Arch.', 'Arch.CL', 'A', 'Ady' or 'Ay' means an archdeaconry court; 'C' or 'Const.' is a bishop's consistory court; and, from 1858 onwards, 'PR' represents the Principal Probate Registry in London. Also included are the register number and folio or entry number where extracted details will be found. Only those parts of a will or administration grant that were of financial interest to the Board of Stamps will have been extracted, so you will still need to read the original or a registered copy of it. Look in Gibson's *Probate Jurisdictions: Where to Look for Wills* to discover their whereabouts.

The year and folio or entry number are your keys to the Death Duty registers themselves, in IR 26.

Finding an entry in a Death Duty register

Use the microfilm indexes in IR 27, as explained on pp. 119–20. Note the year you have just searched, and the folio or entry number given in the far right-hand column under the appropriate heading. Then go to 'Death Duty Registers Reference Book IR 26' in the General Reference area. Find the correct series – Country Wills, PCC Wills, Administrations (*see* list on p. 120 above) – and the year, then the part of the alphabet covering your surname. Trawl down the number ranges on the right-hand side of the page until you find the one that includes your folio or entry, and write down the microfilm number given in the left-hand column. Remember that IR 26 references from number 2086 onwards can be read only as documents at the PRO, Kew.

Now take a seat box (*see* pp. 71–2), and help yourself to the IR 26 microfilm in the labelled cabinets in the search area, using the seat box as a marker. Find that seat and wind on the film until you come to the correct folio or entry number. Now your problems start! What on earth do all the abbreviations mean? The example reproduced on p. 122 and the key below will help you to sort out much of the entry, but Death Duty registers can be complex and difficult to understand. It is a good idea to make a photocopy and then try to untangle the various coded references. Ask at the Research Enquiries Desk if you need to seek the help of a professional researcher. There is also a PRO information leaflet to help unravel the language used. You can download this from **www.pro.gov.uk**, and there are copies available near the General Reference area.

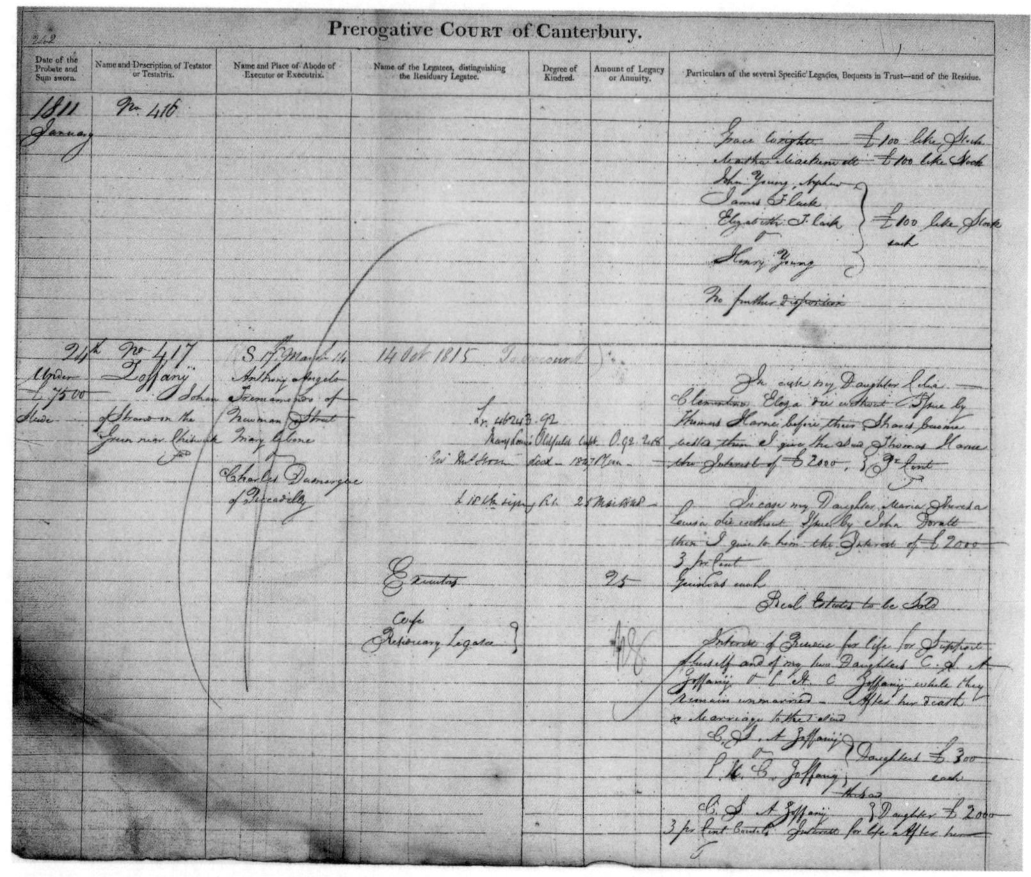

Prerogative Court of Canterbury.

Date of the Probate and Sum sworn.	Name and Description of Testator or Testatrix.	Name and Place of Abode of Executor or Executrix.	Name of the Legatees, distinguishing the Residuary Legatee.	Degree of Kindred.	Amount of Legacy or Annuity.	Particulars of the several Specific Legacies, Bequests in Trust—and of the Residue.

Figure 24 Part of the Death Duty register entry for Johan Zoffany. When his will (see Figure 22) was proved in the PCC on 24 January 1811, his estate was worth under £7,500. Altogether, 25 of his direct descendants and their husbands can be identified, as a result of the trusts set up in his will. The final entry relates to the death of his grandchild, Mrs Mary Louisa Oldfield, on 26 October 1922. (IR 26/167, number 417)

How to interpret Death Duty registers

Consanguinity

BF	= brother of a father (uncle)
BM	= brother of a mother (uncle)
Ch	= child of deceased (legitimate)
Child	= child of deceased (legitimate)
DB	= descendant of a brother (nephew, niece etc.)
DS	= descendant of a sister (nephew, niece etc.)
DBF	= descendant of a brother of a father (cousin)
DBM	= descendant of a brother of a mother (cousin)
DSF	= descendant of a sister of a father (cousin)

DSM	= descendant of a sister of a mother (cousin)
DBGF	= descendant of a brother of a grandfather
DMGM	= descendant of a brother of a grandmother
DSGF	= descendant of a sister of a grandfather
DSGM	= descendant of a sister of a grandmother
G child	= grandchild
GG child	= great-grandchild
G daughter	= granddaughter
G son	= grandson
SF	= sister of a father (aunt)
SM	= sister of a mother (aunt)
Str	= stranger in blood
Stra	= stranger in blood
Strag	= stranger in blood
Stra BL	= stranger, brother-in-law
Stra DL	= stranger, daughter-in-law
Stra NC	= stranger, natural child (illegitimate)
Stra ND	= stranger, natural daughter (illegitimate)
Stra NS	= stranger, natural son (illegitimate)
Stra NC (of a daughter)	= stranger, illegitimate child of a daughter
Stra NC (of a son)	= stranger, illegitimate child of a son
Stra (sent)	= stranger, servant of the deceased
Stra SL	= stranger, sister-in-law or stranger, son-in-law
Stra or 'son'	= stranger, natural son (illegitimate)
Stra or 'daughter'	= stranger, natural daughter (illegitimate)

What deemed

abs	= absolute legacy, without any conditions attached to it
abs & int	= absolute legacy with interest attached to it
abswp	= absolute legacy with a proviso (legacy conditional on something)
anny	= annuity
annywp	= annuity with a proviso (annual sum with a condition attached to it)
dwp	= ditto (usually absolute) with proviso
in deft of appt eq'y am'g them	= in default of appointment equally amongst them

There is an excellent PRO information leaflet, *Death Duty Registers – How to Interpret Them*, available on **www.pro.gov.uk** and near the General Reference area.

How Death Duty registers can supplement information in wills and administration grants

Because the registers remained open for 50 years (*see* p. 118), they are an invaluable source for family historians. They usually provide the date of death of the testator, as well as the testator's last known address and occupation, the date the will was made, and the date and name of the court where it was proved, or the name of the court issuing a grant of letters of administration and the date of the grant. And they also give the names, addresses, occupations and blood relationships of executors or administrators to the deceased, and the probate value under which the estate was sworn. Headed columns set out details of cash legacies, stock, houses and other property, the names of the legatees or trustees who were to receive them, and for what purpose. Contingencies such as an instruction for an equal division of the estate or a gift for a person's lifetime only were recorded, as were any annuity values and, finally, the date when the specified duty was paid.

Within each entry you will come across changes of address of spouses and their dates of death or remarriage, and names and exact relationships to the deceased of beneficiaries (which may be unstated or unclear in the will itself), plus the dates (if appropriate) of their marriage, death or migration abroad. If the will provided for children as yet unborn when it was made, any posthumous issue will be named in the registers. Ages of recipients of annuities are frequently given, too.

A comparison between an estate's value at the time of the original probate and the sale proceeds at the time of the final distribution after the death of the spouse will reveal how property prices increased or became worth less. Remember, though, that before 1853, no account was made of real estate unless it had been sold to pay legacies or to form part of the residual estate. After 1853, there is information in the registers about descent of landed property passing outside the will and thus not mentioned in it. The registers contain references to any lawsuits connected with the estate and include cross-references to other register entries – for example, to estates left in trust before 1852. The last will be mentioned with a Reversionary Register reference.

The Reversionary Registers (which can be searched only as documents at the PRO, Kew) are especially useful, because they concern trusts set up in wills and these were usually administered over a long period. From 1853, Succession Duty became payable as each property transfer occurred, and so entries may span several generations in a family, again supplying details about marriages, deaths and changes of address. From the main registers you will be able to identify where there is a Reversionary Register entry, since it will be cited as 'RR'.

Death Duty records after 1903

The PRO does not have any Death Duty registers after 1903. But if you are a direct descendant of the subject of your enquiry, it is possible that the Capital Taxes Office might be prepared to release some information to you. Write to the Capital Taxes Office, Ferrers House, PO Box 38, Castle Meadow Road, Nottingham NG2 1BB.

Divorce indexes for England and Wales

Until 1858, divorce – which, as well as terminating a marriage, granted both parties the right to remarry – could only be obtained by a private act of Parliament and on the grounds of adultery. To prove this, the husband might first pursue a civil action for damages, in the Court of King's Bench sitting in Westminster, alleging criminal conversation ('Crim. con.') against his wife's lover. It was rare for a woman to petition for divorce, since she had to prove her husband's violence towards her as well as his adultery. The House of Lords Record Office, House of Lords, London SW1A 0PW (telephone 020 7219 3074, email **hlro@parliament.uk**) holds the private acts, whilst the records of the King's Bench are held by the PRO, Kew. Because of their unwieldiness and the lack of convenient catalogues, the Court of King's Bench records have remained largely untouched by family historians; to consult them you will need a reader's ticket. For either party, divorce was a very expensive process.

The alternatives were to apply to a church court for an annulment of the marriage on the grounds that it had never been valid in the first place, or for the issue of a decree of separation '*a mensa et thoro*' ('from bed and board'). This second option did not permit remarriage while the other party remained alive. These ecclesiastical records are kept in diocesan or county record offices. Appeals against church court decisions could be made to the Archbishop of Canterbury's Court of Arches, and many matrimonial causes feature in the *Index of cases in the records of the Court of Arches in Lambeth Palace Library, 1660–1913*, edited by J. Houston (Chichester, 1972). The Court of King's Bench could hear appeals against decisions by ecclesiastical courts, too.

The most usual remedy, however, was to desert or to reach a private settlement, which was then enshrined in a separation deed. This exonerated each party from liability for the other's debts, and so deeds of this kind sometimes surface among family and estate papers. Wife selling was another resort, often with the collusion of the wife and her lover, and was done in a public place before witnesses. The local newspapers, always on the look-out for a sensational story, might contain a piece about such an event. You can often read these on microfilm in local reference libraries.

On 11 January 1858 a more potent court was established to deal with divorce petitions. Named the Court for Divorce and Matrimonial Causes, it removed all ecclesiastical jurisdiction over marital matters, except for the issue of marriage licences. Then in 1873 it was, in turn, superseded by the Probate, Divorce and Admiralty Division of the High Court of Justice. From 1922, some assize courts could hear certain divorce cases; and in 1927, 23 district registries began to receive divorce petitions. In 1967 county courts were authorized to grant divorces in undefended cases, making the process quicker, cheaper and more convenient.

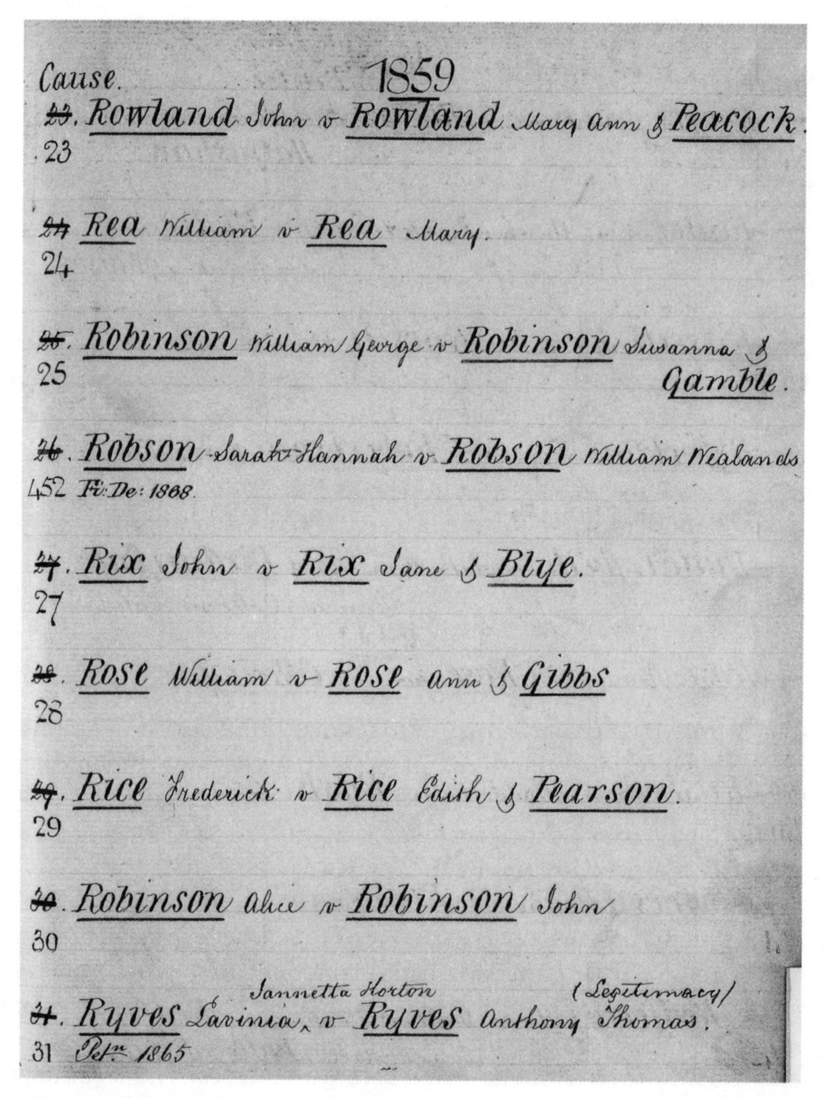
Cause. 1859

23. Rowland John v Rowland Mary Ann & Peacock.
23

24 Rea William v Rea Mary.
24

25. Robinson William George v Robinson Susanna & Gamble.
25

26. Robson Sarah Hannah v Robson William Wealands
452 Fi: De: 1868.

27. Rix John v Rix Jane & Blye.
27

28. Rose William v Rose Ann & Gibbs
28

29. Rice Frederick v Rice Edith & Pearson.
29

30. Robinson Alice v Robinson John
30

31. Ryves Lavinia Jannetta Horton v Ryves Anthony Thomas. (Legitimacy)
31 Petn 1865

Figure 25 Divorce index entry (in J 78/1) for the 1859 and later petitions of Lavinia Jannetta Horton Ryves against Anthony Thomas Ryves, seeking decrees declaring her own legitimacy and that of her mother Olive Serres, claimed to be the legitimate daughter of Prince Henry Frederick, Duke of Cumberland, brother of King George III, by his alleged wife, Olive Wilmot. The judge ordered that all the papers put in evidence by the petitioner be returned to her except 'the alleged forged documents', which are today in PRO series J 77/44 R31.

You can search microfilm copies of the indexes to the files and papers containing the petitions for divorce, declarations of nullity, judicial separations, declarations of legitimacy and petitions for restitution of conjugal rights, between 1858 and 1958, in PRO series J 78, both at the FRC and at the PRO, Kew. There is a gap between 1946 and 1949, which can be bridged by searching the strictly chronological list of received petitions in the Divorce Receipt Books in J 78/28–32.

The other index entries in J 78 are arranged initial-alphabetically by surname and chronologically by date during each year. There is some overlap, as it seems that when the allocated pages for one letter of the alphabet were filled up, the rest of the year's entries were written into a new volume, but the old book continued until completely full. In 1876, a new series of indexes was introduced, probably reflecting the setting up of the new Probate, Divorce and Admiralty Division, but there is some duplication. As a result, you may have to search three different indexes during the years around 1876 to be sure your search is complete.

You will find the surnames of both parties in the indexes, plus that of any co-respondent, the year of registration of the petition, and the case or file number. From 1906, these numbers are prefixed by letters identifying the type of cause:

HD	= petition by husband for decree of divorce
WD	= petition by wife for decree of divorce
HN	= petition by husband for decree of nullity
WN	= petition by wife for decree of nullity
HJS	= petition by husband for decree of judicial separation
WJS	= petition by husband for decree of restitution of conjugal rights
WRCR	= petition by wife for decree of restitution of conjugal rights
Legit	= petition for declaration of legitimacy
Div Ct	= appeal to Divisional Court from Justices
Prot	= application for order for protection of wife's earnings and property

Armed with details of the name of the case, the year and number, you can then go to the Decree Absolute Search Section of the Principal Registry of the Family Division, First Avenue House, 42–49 High Holborn, London WC1V 6NP (telephone 020 7947 7017) – generally referred to as the Divorce Registry – and order a copy of the decree absolute (or decree nisi, if applicable) for £1. The Registry is open Monday to Friday, between 10 a.m. and 4.30 p.m. A decree nisi is the first stage in the final dissolution of a marriage; unless the court rules otherwise, it is followed by a decree absolute, which is now issued, at the petitioner's request, at least six weeks after the first decree. Both parties are then free to remarry.

As mentioned earlier, searches of the Registry's centralized indexes to all the divorces granted in England and Wales after 1958, including those granted by assize courts, district registries and county courts, can be conducted for you for a fee. It will cost you £20 for each 10 years searched, which covers the charge of posting you a copy of the decree itself. These are dispatched to you within 10 days of receipt of the enquiry, but if no decree is found there is no refund. Cheques and postal orders should be made payable to HM Paymaster General, and you are advised to write your name and address, plus the name of the divorce case, on the back.

If you are able to visit the Divorce Registry yourself, a three-year search will be done for you while you wait, and if successful a copy of the decree will then be issued to you. If not, then the remaining seven years will be searched and you will be notified by post. The cost of this service is still £20 for the full 10 years or part of it. In all cases, you will need to supply the full names of both parties, their date of marriage and likely year of divorce.

For divorces within the last five years, you are strongly advised to contact the relevant county court, since these local searches cost only £5. County courts are listed on **www.courtservice.gov.uk**.

The indexes in J 78 are therefore the key to obtaining a copy of the decree itself, but they also serve as the link to the numbered files and papers, 1858–1954, in J 77 at the PRO, Kew. Up to 1937, the papers are preserved almost in their entirety (though there are some gaps, as indicated in the catalogue). From 1938 onwards, only a small representative sample has been kept, and these are listed by year, file number and case name. Most files consist of the petitions, minutes, pleadings and evidence, which may include the marriage certificate and the birth certificates of any children. Only a few files after 1954 have been selected for permanent preservation. Contact the Principal Registry of the Family Division (*address above*) for advice about this.

Non-parochial registers

The FRC has microfilm copies of about 6,000 authenticated and other registers of births, baptisms and burials from nonconformist and Roman Catholic congregations in England and Wales. They are in PRO series RG 4 and RG 8, and can also be searched on microfilm at the PRO, Kew. They mainly cover the period 1775–1837, and most birth and baptism entries in RG 4 registers are included in the *IGI*. RG 4 also includes registers of birth, baptism, marriage and burial from some Scottish, Dutch, French, German and other foreign Protestant churches in England, from the English church in St Petersburg, in Russia, from Chelsea and Greenwich Hospitals, and from Bunhill Fields Burial Ground. Of these, the registers of foreign Protestant churches have been published by the Huguenot Society, and copies can be found in the library in the General Reference area on the first floor of the FRC. Extracts of the births, baptisms and marriages of these foreign congregations are included in the *IGI*, too.

Whilst RG 4 contains registers collected and authenticated as legal documents by the Non-Parochial Registers Commissioners in 1840, series RG 8 consists of a rich assortment of deposits made in 1857. Among the more extensive registers are those of admissions to and births in the British Lying-In Hospital, in Holborn, interments in Victoria Park Cemetery, Bunhill Fields Burial Ground and Bethnal Green Protestant Dissenters' Burying Ground (also called the Gibraltar Burying Ground), and the registers of the Chapels Royal in St James's Palace, Whitehall and Windsor Castle, and of the Russian Orthodox Church in London.

However, many nonconformist and Roman Catholic registers were never handed over to the authorities, and are now in local record offices or denominational archives or remain with the congregation. A number of Welsh nonconformist chapel registers are now held by the National Library of Wales (NLW), in Aberystwyth, for which there is a published list that you can consult in the library in the General Reference area on the first floor of the FRC. The Society of Genealogists is publishing a series of *National Index of Parish Registers* county volumes, copies of which are on the open shelves in the General Reference area. These often tell you the dates and known whereabouts of nonconformist congregation registers. M. Gandy has produced a set of regional booklets on *Catholic Missions and Registers, 1700–1880* (London, 1993), all of which are in the library at the FRC.

Sometimes local family history societies can help, and there are some devoted solely to specific denominations. For details about these, plus links to their websites, visit **www.genuki.org.uk**.

From the mid sixteenth century, numerous groups of people began to break away from the established Church of England and worship in small autonomous congregations. In the mid nineteenth century, about a quarter of the population is thought to have been Protestant nonconformist, an impression supported by chapel attendance figures logged on census Sunday, 30 March 1851. Your Welsh ancestors are more than likely to have been 'chapel', and certain parts of the country were renowned for their pockets of Protestant nonconformity, such as Cornwall and Westmorland, or for Roman Catholic dissent (most notably Lancashire). Their registers are a vital source for births, baptisms and burials of a large percentage of the populace before civil registration began in 1837. Unfortunately, because of political and religious intolerance, many of the records were not well kept or have been lost to us, especially before the late eighteenth century. Marriages were conducted in nonconformist chapels until 24 March 1754; after which, until 30 June 1837, they had, by law, to be performed in the established Anglican Church, except in the case of Quakers and Jews. Burials of nonconformists may frequently be found in parish church registers, but many had their own separate burial grounds. The registers of some of these, and particularly those of London dissenters' burial grounds, are on microfilm in RG 4 and RG 8.

How to find nonconformist ancestors at the FRC

It may be that you know or suspect your family were Congregationalists, Presbyterians or Methodists, but have failed to find any baptisms or burials in parish registers. If you have traced a marriage entry in a church register, particularly after 25 March 1754, and there are no subsequent baptisms of children in the records, this may indicate nonconformity.

First look at the *IGI*, on one of the Family History Databases terminals (*see* pp. 73–5) or on microfiche, to see if you can spot your family and the relevant PRO reference. If you are successful, check the filmed chapel registers themselves to confirm the entry, and write down any additional information.

If you already know the name of the chapel, you can find the RG 4 reference using PROCAT, the PRO's online catalogue (*see* p. 80), or look for it in the RG 4 binders in the General Reference area. The RG 4 catalogues are arranged in several ways. The 'Nonconformist Registers Reference Book Index' lists the chapels, denominations and deposited registers for specific places alphabetically under each county. The 'Nonconformist Registers Reference Book English Counties' identifies in which chapel registers a particular local congregation may be found (as some volumes were shared or taken away by itinerant ministers). The 'Nonconformist Registers Reference Book List of Chapels by Denomination and Miscellaneous' tells you the whereabouts of the various chapels; and the 'Nonconformist Registers Numerical Order' runs sequentially by number of each item. Whichever catalogue you choose, the result will be the same, as the film number will not vary.

Some of the above registers have been copied and/or indexed. Those available at the FRC are arranged alphabetically by county on the shelves in the General Reference area, where you will also find an alphabetical place-name list.

Why are there no registers for my chapel/area in the binder labelled RG 4?

- Some registers are in series RG 8. Check the online PRO catalogue for the chapel you want, or the binder labelled RG 8 in the General Reference area.
- Some registers are still kept locally. To find out what is available where, look at the relevant county volume of *National Index of Parish Registers* in the General Reference area; or phone the county record office, using the telephone number given in *Record Repositories in Great Britain* (PRO, 11th edn, 1999), or visit its website (accessible via **www.hmc.gov.uk/archon**).
- Your ancestors were Quakers. See pp. 134–5.

Two dissenters' birth registries

In 1742 a central birth registry was established for members of the Old Dissent (Baptists, Congregationalists, Independents/Presbyterians) at Dr Williams's Library, in London. If you are unsuccessful in tracking down the register of a congregation or cannot find a recorded birth or baptism, it is worth searching these registers. About 50,000 births from 1716 until 1837 were registered there, and the entries include children born in London, the provinces, and overseas.

Registration was voluntary, and the registry closed soon after civil registration began on 1 July 1837. Parents brought with them two completed and signed parchment certificates, obtainable from their local chapel. On these were written the name and sex of the child, its parents' names, the name of the mother's father, and the date and place (parish) of birth. These were signed by the minister, the midwife and other witnesses of the birth. From 1828, paper certificates were substituted and the signatures of the parents were appended, too. The details (except the birthplace) were copied in the register, and the two certificates endorsed with a number corresponding to the entry in the book. One of the certificates was handed back to the parents, and the other was retained by the registrar. The numbered entries in the microfilm copies of the office registers in RG 4/4658–65 are indexed for the period 1742–1837 (parchment certificates) in brown books labelled RG 4/4666–73, on the shelves of the General Reference area; and for 1828–37 (paper certificates) in brown books labelled RG 4/4674 and RG 4/4675. A further index, for paper certificate entries in 1837 only, is in RG 4/4676, on microfilm. The indexes in RG 4/4674–76 serve as registers as well. You can also search copies in the Microfilm Reading Room of the PRO, Kew.

Each index covers a tranche of years, the surnames being arranged by their initial letter and then chronologically by date, rather than strictly alphabetically, with the registered entry number alongside. Parents might register all their children at once, so their certificates would be allocated sequential numbers. Births were therefore not necessarily registered immediately after the event. Make a note of the letter at the front of each index – you will need it when selecting the filmed registers themselves.

The registers are listed under Middlesex in the catalogue for RG 4. Once you have identified the one you want, take a seat box (*see* pp. 71–2); and when you remove the microfilm from the labelled cabinet in the search area, leave the seat box in its place. Find the right seat, wind on the film until you see the numbered entry, and you should discover the child's name, those of its parents, the names of at least two witnesses, the date and parish of birth, and the date of registration.

Figure 26 Key to the parchment series of indexes, certificates and registered office copies of births recorded at Dr Williams's Library between 1742 and 1837. Your search may have to cover several years after a birth occurred, since many were registered retrospectively, frequently with those of other siblings.

Births registered 1742–1837: Parchment Series			
Dates of Registrations	Indexes RG4/	Registers RG4/	Certificate Numbers
1742–1758	4666	4658	A1–181, 1–112
1759–1792	4667	4659	B 1–3507
1792–1805	4668	4660	C 1–3800
1805–1812	4669	4661	D 1–4429
1812–1817	4670	4662	E 1–4365
1817–1820	4671	4663	F 1–4217
1820–1824	4672	4664	G 1–5089
1824–1837	4673	4665	H 1–4627

Naylor Maria 3293
Newsham William 3502 29
— Eliza 3
— Jecks 4
Nightingale Frances Parthenope — 50
Nunn Benjamin Hitchcock .. 405
Nash Ebenezer Michael 30
Noble Thomas 746
Nicholson Elizabeth 79
— Anne 80
— William 1
— James 2
Nightingale Florence 4050
Newson Henry 102
Noville Ann 53

Figure 27 Index reference to Florence Nightingale's birth in 1820, showing the registration number of the certificate, which matches that in the office register. The name and number (3350) of the earlier registration of the birth of her sister, Frances Parthenope Nightingale, is in the same column. (RG 4/4671)

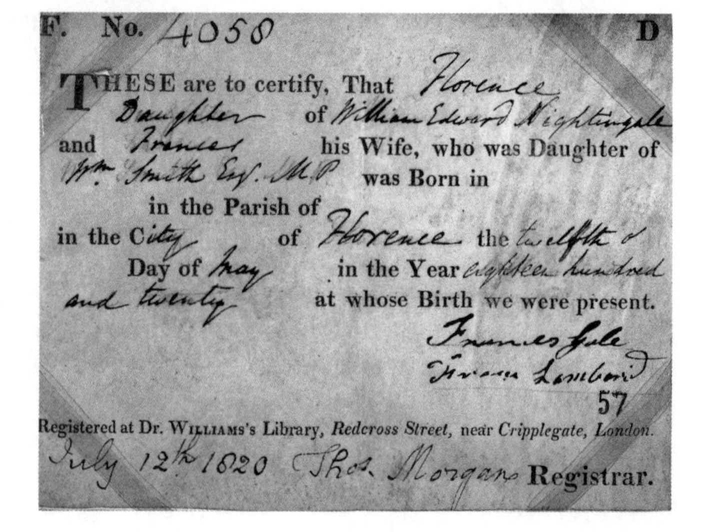
F. No. 4050 D

THESE are to certify, That Florence Daughter of William Edward Nightingale and Frances his Wife, who was Daughter of Wm. Smith Esq. M.P. was Born in in the Parish of in the City of Florence the twelfth of Day of May in the Year eighteen hundred and twenty at whose Birth we were present.

Frances Gale
[illegible] Lombard

57

Registered at Dr. Williams's Library, *Redcross Street*, near *Cripplegate, London.*
July 12th 1820 Thos. Morgan Registrar.

Figure 28 One of the duplicate birth certificates presented by Florence Nightingale's parents at Dr Williams's Library on 12 July 1820, for copying into the register. Each registered entry was assigned a sequential number, which was then written on each of the two certificates. One was handed back to the parents, and the other kept by the Registry. (RG 5/83, number 4058)

RG 5	Date	Description
		DR WILLIAMS'S LIBRARY: PARCHMENT SERIES (Pieces 1–124)
		NOTE – indexes to this series are preserved in RG 4/4666–4673
		Certificate nos:
75	1818 Nov 10–1819 Jan 26	F 2001–2250
76	1819 Jan 26–Apr 7	F 2251–2500
77	1819 Apr 7–June 23	F 2501–2750
78	1819 June 23–Sept 15	F 2751–3000
79	1819 Sept 15–Nov 18	F 3001–3250
80	1819 Nov 18–1820 Feb 9	F 3251–3500
81	1820 Feb 9–May 2	F 3501–3750
82	1820 May 2–June 30	F 3751–4000
83	1820 June 30–Sept 29	F 4001–4217
84	1820 Oct 3–Nov 22	G 1–250
85	1820 Nov 22–1821 Jan 25	G 251–500
86	1821 Jan 25–Apr 3	G 501–750
87	1821 Apr 3–June 5	G 751–1000
88	1821 June 5–Sept 28	G 1001–1250
89	1821 Oct 2–Dec 6	G 1251–1500
90	1821 Dec 6–1822 Feb 12	G 1501–1750
91	1822 Feb 12–Apr 10	G 1751–2000
92	1822 Apr 10–June 11	G 2001–2250

Figure 29 Page from the series list for the numbered birth certificates filed in Dr Williams's Library. RG 5/83 covers births registered between 30 June and 29 September 1820 (numbered 4001 to 4271). Florence Nightingale's birth certificate is number 4085.

No.	Names of Children.	Names of Parents.	Witnesses.	Time when born. Day.	Month.	Year.
4058	Florence Nightingale City of Florence Italy Regd. July 12th 1820 Thos. Morgan	William Edward Nightingale & Frances, Daughter of William Smith M.P.	Frances Gale Frances Lambird	12th	May	1820

Figure 30 Registered office copy of the details of Florence Nightingale's birth in Florence, Italy, on 12 May 1820, extracted from the certificate produced by her parents. Her maternal grandfather's name and occupation are included, making it a record of three generations. (RG 4/4663, number 4058)

Births registered 1828–1837: Paper Series		
Dates of Registrations	**Alphabetical/Registers RG4/**	**Certificate Numbers**
1828–1837	4674	1–8000
1837	4675	8001–17116
1837	4676	1–2060

Figure 31 Key to the paper series of births registered at Dr Williams's Library between 1828 and 1837. The entries are not in strict alphabetical order, but the certificate numbers will take you to the registered office copies in series RG 4, and to the original certificates in series RG 5.

Duplicate numbered certificates may be more informative about maternal grandfathers and their abodes and occupations, as well as those of the fathers, and they will of course bear the signatures of the parents and witnesses to the registered births. These are in series RG 5, and 80 per cent of them have been extracted and included in the *British Isles Vital Records Index* (*see* p. 77). It is also widely available on CD-ROM, but has not yet been incorporated into **www.familysearch.org**.

Look in the RG 5 labelled catalogue for the pages headed 'Dr Williams's Library: Parchment Series' or 'Dr Williams's Library: Paper Series', as appropriate, and then use the same means of reference as for RG 4.

A similar Wesleyan Methodist Metropolitan Registry of births was set up in Paternoster Row, London, in 1818, and about 10,000 Methodist births and baptisms were registered there before it closed in 1838. It also contains retrospective entries of births going back to 1773. These disclose the child's name and sex, the father's name and residence, the mother's name and the names of both her parents, as well as the date of birth, the name of the Wesleyan circuit, the parents' signatures, those of witnesses to the birth, and that of the baptizing minister. There is a microfilm index in RG 4/4680, in which the children's names are recorded, with the certificate number and registered folio number written alongside. Note these down. If you want to inspect the microfilm copy of the register, in RG 4/4677–79, look in the catalogue under Middlesex, and then under the name of the Registry, and find the range of certificate numbers that includes the one you want. You can then identify the correct microfilm number in the left-hand margin. Take a seat box, and when you remove the film from the labelled cabinet in the search area, put this in its place as a marker. On the microfilm reader at the appropriate seat, wind the film until you spot the relevant folio number and then hunt for the certificate number itself. If you want to look at one of the retained duplicate certificates in RG 5/162–207, use the index to the office copies, which is in RG 4/4680, and select the pages headed 'Wesleyan Methodist Metropolitan Registry at Paternoster Row'. Scan the number ranges on the right-hand side until you see the one that includes your certificate number. Note down the microfilm reference in the left-hand margin; and then help yourself to the film in the usual way.

The Religious Society of Friends (Quakers)

The Religious Society of Friends was established in the 1640s and 1650s. A number of registers of Quaker births, deaths, burials and marriages from 1578 until 1841 recorded in the minutes of monthly meetings in England and Wales were deposited in the PRO and can now be searched on microfilm, in series RG 6, both at the FRC and at Kew. Unlike other nonconforming congregations, Quakers were permitted to continue with their own marriage ceremonies after 25 March 1754. The registers of marriages give the names of the relatives and Friends who were present. Many of the volumes contain integral indexes, which makes your task easier if you want to pursue collateral branches of your family or discover the precise relationships between witnesses and bridal couples.

A number of Quaker records of monthly meetings are held elsewhere. The Religious Society of Friends Library, at Friends House, 173–177 Euston Road, London NW1 2BJ, holds microform copies, which you can search for a fee, of county Digests of births, marriages and deaths up to 1837 and countrywide Digests of births, marriages and deaths of members that continue well into the twentieth century. These serve as a key to the minutes of the relevant monthly meetings, and staff can usually advise you about the present whereabouts of these, if not held by the PRO. For details of opening hours and regulations, either phone 020 7663 1135 or visit the Religious Society of Friends website (**www.quaker.org.uk**), or email **library@quaker.org.uk**. The Digests almost replicate the original registered entries of births, deaths and burials, but do not contain the names of relatives and Friends who were witnesses to the marriages. You would need to consult the minutes themselves for this information. Quaker record-keeping of vital events was superb, so you will find that from an early period details about ages and parentage were recorded, as were dates and places of death and burial of adherents, and will learn the names, places of residence and occupations of the parents of bridal couples, enabling you to jump to birth entries with ease. Using the Digests, it is often possible to trace Quaker ancestry over several generations and counties in an afternoon.

Roman Catholics

To profess Roman Catholicism was illegal for most of the time from the mid sixteenth century until 1779. Consequently records of births and baptisms were kept privately and secretly, and Catholics were frequently married and buried following the rites of the established Church of England. In any case, from 25 March 1754 until 30 June 1837 everyone except Quakers and Jews was obliged by law to marry in an Anglican parish church.

There are only 44 Roman Catholic registers in the PRO, and these are on microfilm in series RG 4. Look for them in the PRO's online catalogue (*see* p. 80), or in the list of chapels in the denominational catalogue for RG 4 in the General Reference area. Most surviving registers have been retained by the parish priests. For full details of known English, Welsh and Scottish Catholic records, consult M. Gandy's series of six volumes listing regional *Catholic Missions and Registers, 1700–1880*. Copies of this series and of *Catholic Parishes in England, Wales and Scotland, An Atlas* by the same author (London, 1993) are in the library in the General Reference area.

Huguenots and other foreign Protestant congregations

If you have a French-sounding name, you may have Huguenot ancestry, particularly if the family came from Spitalfields or Bethnal Green, in the East End of London. 'Huguenot' was the nickname bestowed on continental Protestants (mainly French) who took refuge in this country during the sixteenth and seventeenth centuries. The main influx came in the aftermath of the Revocation of the Edict of Nantes in 1685, when religious persecution recommenced. Some 40,000 refugees are said to have arrived here as a result.

The foreigners set up their own chapels and wrote their records in their native language. All of the Huguenot registers of births, baptisms, marriages, deaths and burials have been published by the Huguenot Society. You will find copies on the library shelves in the General Reference area, and they are widely available elsewhere. The original records, in RG 4, have been microfilmed and you can search these at the FRC or at the PRO, Kew. The entries are also included in the *IGI*. For information about additional PRO and other sources, read R. Kershaw and M. Pearsall, *Immigrants and Aliens* (PRO, 2000).

A quick way of investigating which part of France your family hailed from is to search the French section of the *IGI*, either on the internet (at **www.familysearch.org**) or on one of the Family History Databases terminals at the FRC.

There is a fine collection of material in the Huguenot Society Library, in University College, Gower Street, London WC1E 6BT (telephone 020 7679 7094, email **ucylswm@ucl.ac.uk**). The library catalogue is available on the internet at **www.ucl.ac.uk/UCL-Info/Divisions/Library/huguenot.htm**.

Clandestine and irregular marriages

Before 25 March 1754 it was possible for people to get married in places other than where they were living. Some clergy in country chapels, as well as 'marriage mongers' and obliging tavern landlords, performed ceremonies for non-residents in exchange for money and without the formalities of a licence or the reading of banns. These were clandestine. Without banns or a licence, marriages in the parish where one of the parties lived were condemned as irregular; and, similarly, so were weddings that took place in a church other than where banns had been published; or when a licence was granted for non-residents or for a couple who had not lived in the parish for the mandatory four weeks.

Although such unions were valid in common law, the practice became notorious as a means of exploiting the naïve and vulnerable – especially under-age heirs and heiresses. A law, known as Hardwicke's Marriage Act, was passed suppressing any clandestine and irregular weddings after 24 March 1754. Many of the registers and notebooks kept by these ministers and clerks are now available on microfilm, in series RG 7, both at the FRC and at the PRO, Kew. The entries span the period 1667–1754, with some later annotated entries of baptisms up to about 1777. Altogether, some 400,000 marriages are recorded, included those that took place in the Fleet Prison, Mayfair Chapel and the King's Bench Prison.

A few of the registers are available in printed form – for instance, M. Herber, *Clandestine Marriages in the Chapel and Rules of the Fleet Prison, 1680–1754* (3 vols, London, 1998–2001) – and some, particularly for Kent, Surrey and Sussex couples, have been indexed. Copies of these are in the library in the General Reference area. The handwriting in some of the registers is indescribably awful, so it is advisable to peruse these indexes first.

You will see that many couples travelled long distances to London to marry at one of these places, so if you have failed to find a particular marriage in a parish register, these records are well worth exploring.

Dissenters' burial grounds

Burials of nonconformists may often be found recorded in parish registers, many of which are now deposited in county record offices (*see* pp. 22–3 and *The Phillimore Atlas and Index of Parish Registers*). However, congregation members might purchase or donate land for use as a burying ground. A number of non-parochial registers were centrally deposited in 1840 or 1857 and are now available on microfilm, in series RG 4 and RG 8, at the FRC and at Kew. The following records are also on microfilm:

- Bethnal Green Protestant Dissenters' Burying Ground (Gibraltar Row), 1793–1837, in RG 8/305–14, to which there is an index in the General Reference area.
- Bunhill Fields Burial Ground, 1713–1854, in RG 4/3974–4001, 4288–91 and 4633, indexed in RG 4/4652–7.
- Golden Lane Cemetery (Bunhill Burial Ground), 1833–53, in RG 8/35–8, for which an index is in preparation.
- Victoria Park Cemetery, Hackney, 1853–76, in RG 8/42–51. The entries are alphabetical.
- South London Burial Ground, East Street, Walworth, 1819–37, in RG 4/4362.
- Southwark New Burial Ground, London, 1821–54, in RG 8/73–4.
- Spa Fields, Clerkenwell, 1778–1849, in RG 4/4316–22 and 4366–7, for which an index is in preparation.

- Necropolis Burial Ground, Everton, Liverpool, 1825–37, in RG 4/3121, for which there is a partial index.
- Royal Hospital Cemetery, Greenwich, 1705–1864, in series RG 4/1669–76 and in RG 8/16–18.
- Royal Hospital Chelsea Burial Ground, 1692–1856, in RG 4/4330–2 and 4387.

If your ancestor died in Greater London, consult *Greater London Cemeteries and Crematoria* (compiled by P. Wolfston and revised by C. Webb, London, 6th edn, 1999) and H. Meller, *London Cemetries, An Illustrated Guide and Gazetteer* (Brookfield, Vermont, 3rd edn 1994). Outside London, District Council offices should be able to tell you which cemeteries and crematoria serve the area; or look at the list in *The Family and Local History Handbook*. Many cemeteries are run by private companies, which will not grant you access to their records but may be willing to search them for you, usually for a fee.

For background history and further sources for tracing non-Anglican ancestors, read D. Shorney, *Protestant Nonconformity and Roman Catholicism, A guide to sources in the Public Record Office* (PRO, 1996) and D. J. Steel, *National Index of Parish Registers, Vol. 2: Sources for Nonconformist Genealogy and Family History* (Chichester, 1973, reprinted 1980) or *Vol. 3: Sources for Roman Catholic and Jewish Genealogy and Family History* (Chichester, 1974). Both of these are in the library in the General Reference area. Sometimes local family history societies can help, and there are some devoted solely to specific denominations. For links to their websites, visit **www.genuki.org.uk**.

Miscellaneous non-statutory returns of births, marriages and deaths of Britons abroad

Records of births, baptisms, marriages, deaths and burials registered in British embassies and consulates are dispersed in a variety of places, including the Family Records Centre, the Public Record Office, Kew, the Guildhall Library and the Society of Genealogists, to name but a few. A good guide to the known whereabouts of these records is the Guildhall Library Research Guide 2, *The British Overseas* (Guildhall Library, 3rd revised edn, 1995). Copies of this are in the library in the General Reference area.

At the FRC and the PRO, Kew, you can scour the microfilmed personal-name indexes in RG 43, which relate to miscellaneous non-statutory foreign returns sent to the Registrar General in London. They cover the period 1627–1960, but the majority of the registers date from the late eighteenth century. The RG 43 catalogue, in the General Reference area, will help you identify which index is the key to which of the microfilmed registers ranging from 1627 to 1965 in series RG 32–6. These can be viewed both at the PRO and at the FRC.

- RG 32 largely comprises births, baptisms, marriages, deaths and burials abroad, or on British or foreign ships, of British subjects and nationals of British colonies, the Commonwealth and countries under British jurisdiction, between 1831 and 1964. It also includes some notifications of deaths of members of the Armed Services, prisoners of war, civilian internees and deaths on board missing aircraft, so these complement and overlap the GRO indexes to statutory registrations on the ground floor (*see* pp. 50–2).

- RG 33 consists of original registers, notebooks and copies of registers kept by clergy in English churches and missions, British embassies and legations and by political agents overseas, between 1627 and 1958. The earliest entries concern the English congregation at The Hague. This series includes a book of marriages performed on Royal Naval ships between 1842 and 1879, and some consular marriages before 1859. If you are looking for deaths from enemy action in the Far East between 1941 and 1945, this might be the place to find them.

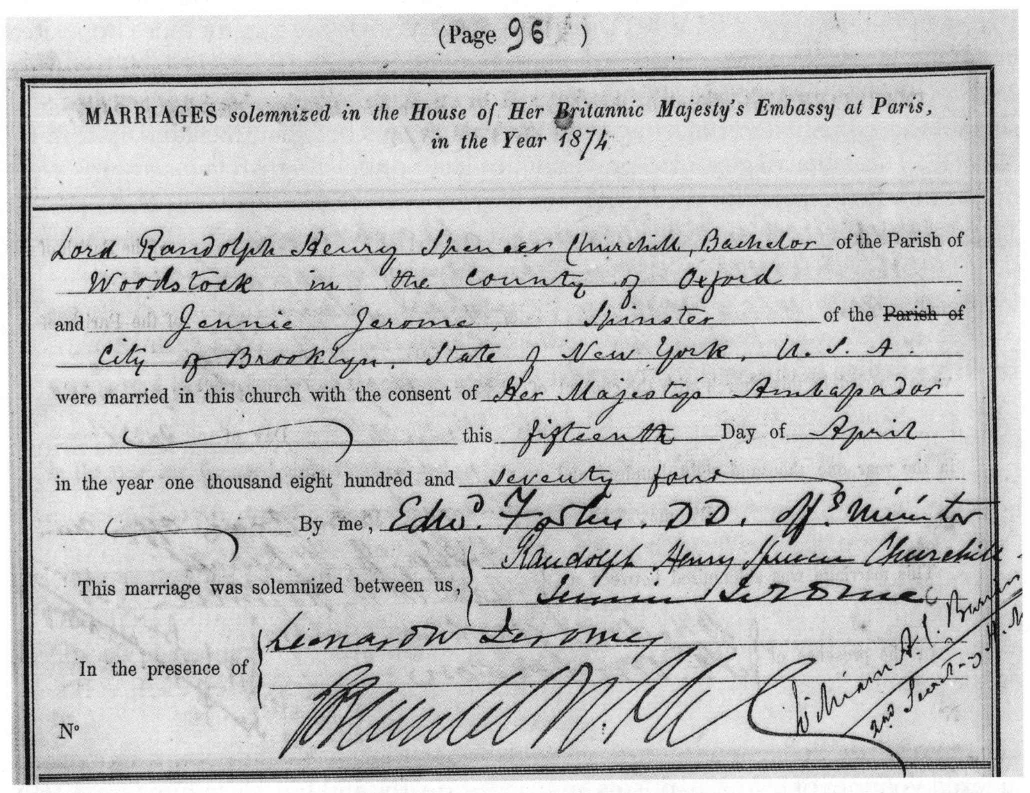
(Page 96)

MARRIAGES *solemnized in the House of Her Britannic Majesty's Embassy at Paris, in the Year* 1874

Lord Randolph Henry Spencer Churchill, Bachelor of the Parish of Woodstock in the County of Oxford
and Jennie Jerome, Spinster of the ~~Parish of~~ City of Brooklyn, State of New York, U.S.A.
were married in this church with the consent of Her Majesty's Ambassador
this fifteenth Day of April
in the year one thousand eight hundred and seventy four
By me, Edwd. Forbes, D.D. Offg. Minister

This marriage was solemnized between us, Randolph Henry Spencer Churchill / Jennie Jerome

In the presence of Leonard W. Jerome

N°

Figure 32 Entry from the marriage register of the British Embassy in Paris, recording the nuptials of the parents of Sir Winston Churchill, in 1874. The bride had moved to Paris with her mother and sisters. In the same year, her husband was elected MP for Woodstock, near Oxford, which included Blenheim Palace, the family seat of his father, the Duke of Marlborough. (RG 33/76, p. 96)

- RG 34 is a set of miscellaneous foreign marriage returns from 1826 until 1921. There are certificates issued by foreign registration authorities and churches, copies of registered entries from British embassies and English churches and chaplaincies, and notifications of marriages of men on active service abroad.
- RG 35 is a series of records similar to those in RG 34, but covering deaths abroad between 1830 and 1921. They include an incomplete set of death certificates of British military personnel in France and Belgium, 1914–21, which complement those recorded in the GRO indexes of Army War Deaths (*see* p. 61).
- RG 36 is a mixture of registers and returns of births, marriages and deaths in British African and Asian Protectorates from 1895 until 1965.

It is well worth trawling the indexes to these as well as the GRO indexes, because it is more than likely you will find overlaps and new entries not statutorily recorded.

If you are trying to trace an ancestor who was born on board a ship or who married or died at sea, download the relevant information leaflet from the PRO website or ask for a copy at the Research Enquiries Desk. The PRO records are mostly those deposited by law with the Registrar General of Shipping and Seamen (RGSS), which run from 1854 to 1960 for births of passengers and from 1854 to 1964 for deaths; there is also a single indexed register of marriages on merchant ships between 1854 and 1972 in BT 334/117. These marriages were probably not legal under English law, as ships were not 'authorized places' for weddings, but they may have been legal for other reasons. There are also records of deaths of merchant seamen, starting in 1852. None of these Board of Trade (BT) series is yet available on microfilm at the FRC.

British Empire and Commonwealth

Births, marriages and deaths registered in countries that were once part of the British Empire or Commonwealth are normally kept locally. Increasingly indexes to these are being made available on the internet (mostly with an online ordering facility, using a credit card) or can be searched on CD-ROM. Otherwise, consult T. J. Kemp's *International Vital Records Handbook* for information about which microfilmed indexes and registers can be hired at LDS Family History Centres. An up-to-date list of addresses of general registrars worldwide is available at the Customer Services Desk on the ground floor of the FRC and at the Research Enquiries Desk on the first floor.

The India Office Collections (*see* p. 26), at the British Library, include about a thousand indexed volumes of births, baptisms, marriages, deaths and burials in India from 1698 until 1947.

4 Case studies

Here are two case studies of typical working families, the Richardsons of Brighton, in Sussex, and the Pearces of Potterne, in Wiltshire, based largely on information gleaned in the Family Records Centre. The resulting family trees demonstrate the use of sources and research methods to construct a pedigree going back to the beginning of civil registration in 1837.

1 The Brighton Line

The starting point of this family history quest was the birth of John William Richardson's daughter in mid December 1931. It was not registered in the sub-district of West Brighton, in Sussex, until over a month later. The birth index for the March quarter of 1932 had to be culled, as well as the index for the December quarter of 1931, because entries are arranged by date of registration not date of birth. The baby was born at home, the youngest of John's four children by his wife, Annie Pearce.

The next step was to find the date of their marriage. Since the date of birth of their eldest child was known, it was logical to use this as the springboard for a search of the GRO quarterly marriage indexes for John and Annie's wedding, working backwards from that date. The couple were married at the Register Office in Brighton in May 1920, and their marriage certificate indicated that the groom resided at the same address in St Mary Magdalene Street where his daughter was born 11 years later. On both occasions, he described himself as a fruit merchant's salesman. He was 23 years old when he married, a year younger than his bride.

John's father, Percy George Richardson, was dead by the time of his son's marriage. According to John's wedding certificate, Percy's occupation was a stoker-engineer at a brewery; but when John was born in 1896, further down the street, Percy was working as a baker journeyman. We do not know when Percy changed his job. *Instructions to the Clerks employed in classifying the occupations and ages of the people* (London, 1881), which is available at the Research Enquiries Desk on the first floor of the FRC, contains information about the main occupations and associated job titles; a look under the headings 'Brewing', 'Engineers' and 'Stokers' revealed that Percy's line of work was probably looking after the brewing equipment.

As John William Richardson was 23 in 1920, he must have been born around 1897. But

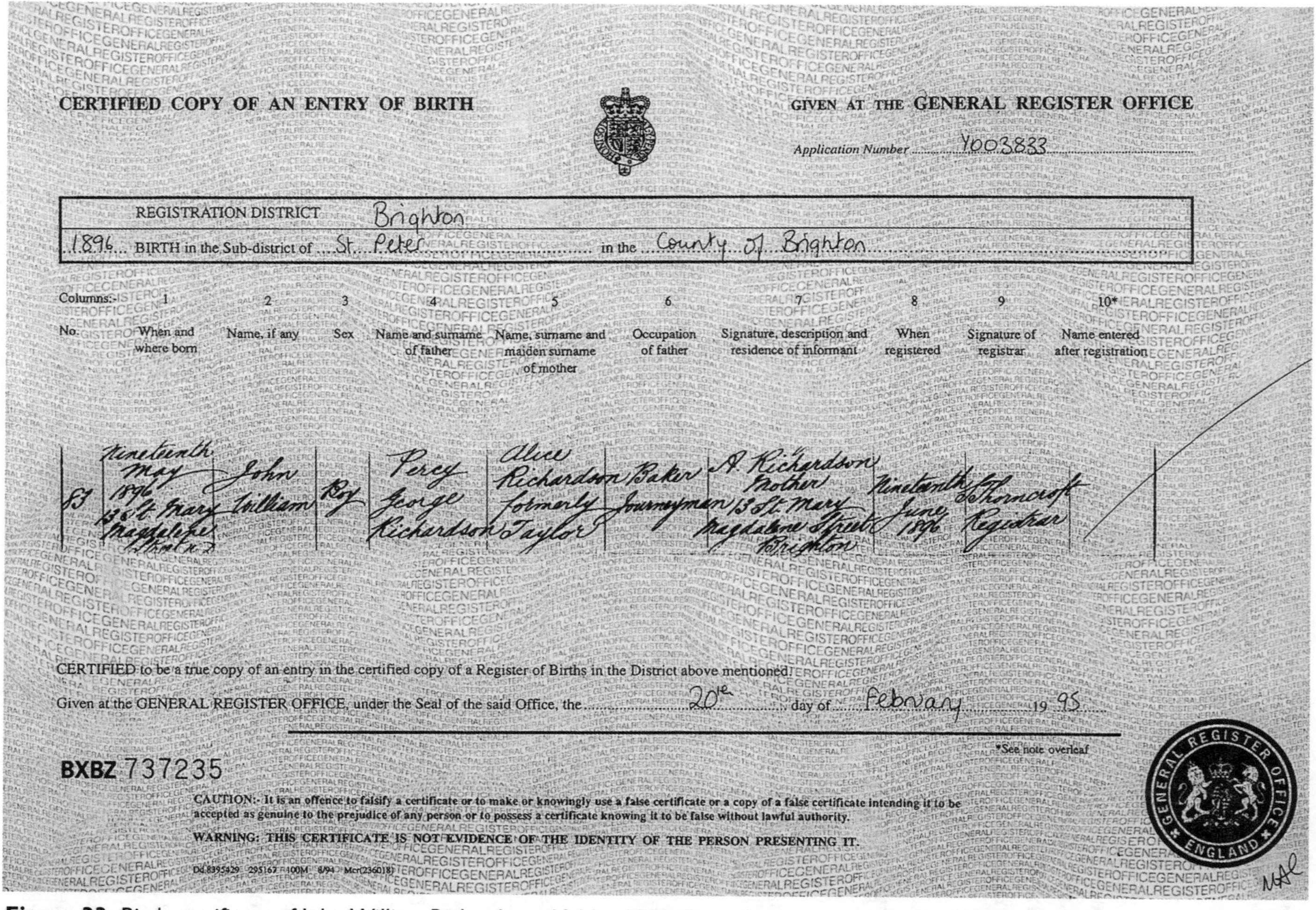

CERTIFIED COPY OF AN ENTRY OF BIRTH

GIVEN AT THE GENERAL REGISTER OFFICE

Application Number Y003833

REGISTRATION DISTRICT Brighton

1896. BIRTH in the Sub-district of St. Peter in the County of Brighton

Columns:– 1	2	3	4	5	6	7	8	9	10*
No. When and where born	Name, if any	Sex	Name and surname of father	Name, surname and maiden surname of mother	Occupation of father	Signature, description and residence of informant	When registered	Signature of registrar	Name entered after registration
83 Nineteenth May 1896 13 St. Mary Magdalene Street	John William	Boy	Percy George Richardson	Alice Richardson formerly Taylor	Baker Journeyman	A. Richardson Mother 13 St. Mary Magdalene Street Brighton	Nineteenth June 1896	[illegible] Thorncroft Registrar	

CERTIFIED to be a true copy of an entry in the certified copy of a Register of Births in the District above mentioned.

Given at the GENERAL REGISTER OFFICE, under the Seal of the said Office, the 20th day of February 1995.

*See note overleaf

BXBZ 737235

CAUTION:– It is an offence to falsify a certificate or to make or knowingly use a false certificate or a copy of a false certificate intending it to be accepted as genuine to the prejudice of any person or to possess a certificate knowing it to be false without lawful authority.

WARNING: THIS CERTIFICATE IS NOT EVIDENCE OF THE IDENTITY OF THE PERSON PRESENTING IT.

Figure 33 Birth certificate of John William Richardson, 19 May 1896. The information supplied by his mother, who registered his birth, reveals that her confinement took place at home.

in fact his birth was registered in the June quarter of 1896. He celebrated his twenty-fourth birthday 11 days after his wedding.

From family information it was believed that John's parents, Percy and Alice, had at least three more children, the eldest of whom was thought to have been born around 1881 and the second about a year later. However, when the quarterly marriage indexes were searched back from John William Richardson's birth registration in 1896, their wedding was found to have taken place in the summer of 1884. The marriage certificate omits Percy's second name, George.

The online personal-name index of the 1901 census returns of England and Wales was searched for Percy Richardson. The digital image of the relevant census page shows that in 1901 Percy and Alice still resided at 13 St Mary Magdalene Street, where they had lived since at least 1896. Charles was the oldest child at home on the night of the census and was working as a newspaper clerk. Young Percy, John and a younger brother, Albert, Percy's widowed mother-in-law, Phoebe Taylor, and a boarder completed the household. By now Percy had found employment as a railway labourer. He was probably an employee of the London Brighton & South Coast Railway Company, which was founded in 1846. Its staff records (*see* the PRO's online

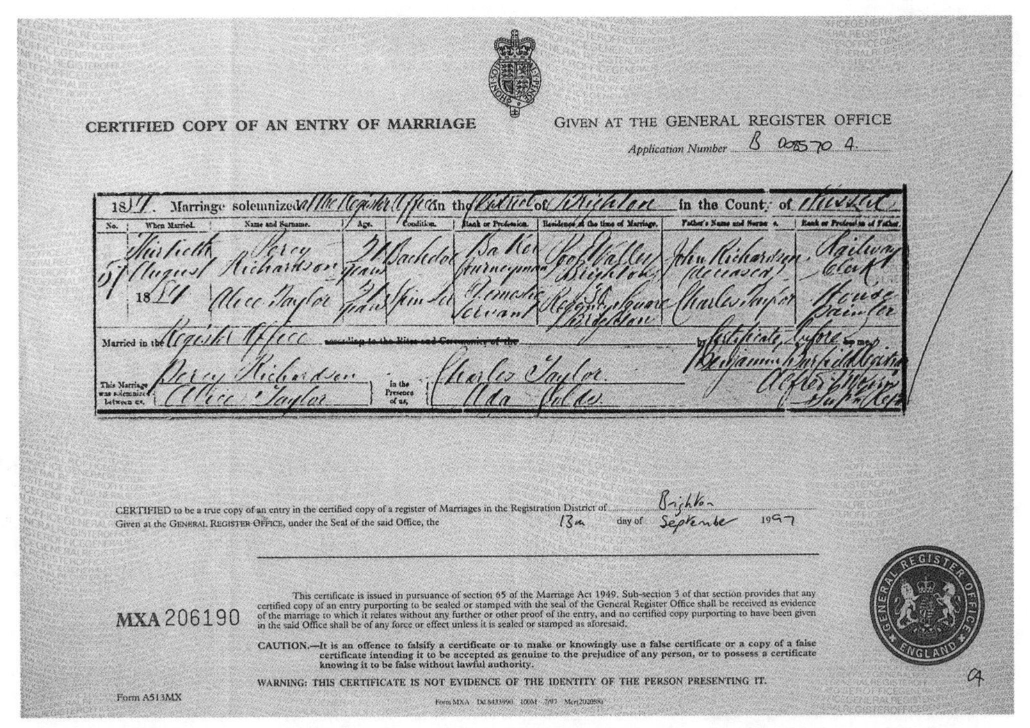
CERTIFIED COPY OF AN ENTRY OF MARRIAGE — GIVEN AT THE GENERAL REGISTER OFFICE

Application Number B 008570 4.

1884. Marriage solemnized at the Register Office in the District of Brighton in the County of Sussex

No.	When Married	Name and Surname	Age	Condition	Rank or Profession	Residence at the time of Marriage	Father's Name and Surname	Rank or Profession of Father
57	Thirtieth August 1884	Percy Richardson	21 years	Bachelor	Baker Journeyman	[illegible] Brighton	John Richardson deceased	Railway Clerk
		Alice Taylor	21 years	Spinster	Domestic Servant	[illegible] Square Brighton	Charles Taylor	House Painter

Married in the Register Office ~~according to the Rites and Ceremonies of the~~ by Certificate before ~~by me~~,

This Marriage was solemnized between us, Percy Richardson, Alice Taylor

in the Presence of us, Charles Taylor, Ada [illegible]

Benjamin [illegible] Registrar, Alfred [illegible] Supt Regr

CERTIFIED to be a true copy of an entry in the certified copy of a register of Marriages in the Registration District of Brighton
Given at the GENERAL REGISTER OFFICE, under the Seal of the said Office, the 13th day of September 1997

MXA 206190

This certificate is issued in pursuance of section 65 of the Marriage Act 1949. Sub-section 3 of that section provides that any certified copy of an entry purporting to be sealed or stamped with the seal of the General Register Office shall be received as evidence of the marriage to which it relates without any further or other proof of the entry, and no certified copy purporting to have been given in the said Office shall be of any force or effect unless it is sealed or stamped as aforesaid.

CAUTION.—It is an offence to falsify a certificate or to make or knowingly use a false certificate or a copy of a false certificate intending it to be accepted as genuine to the prejudice of any person, or to possess a certificate knowing it to be false without lawful authority.

WARNING: THIS CERTIFICATE IS NOT EVIDENCE OF THE IDENTITY OF THE PERSON PRESENTING IT.

Form A513MX

GENERAL REGISTER OFFICE ENGLAND

Figure 34 Certificate recording the marriage of Percy Richardson and Alice Taylor on 30 August 1884, at the Register Office in Brighton. The age of both bride and groom is given as 21.

The Richardsons of London and Brighton

Case study 1

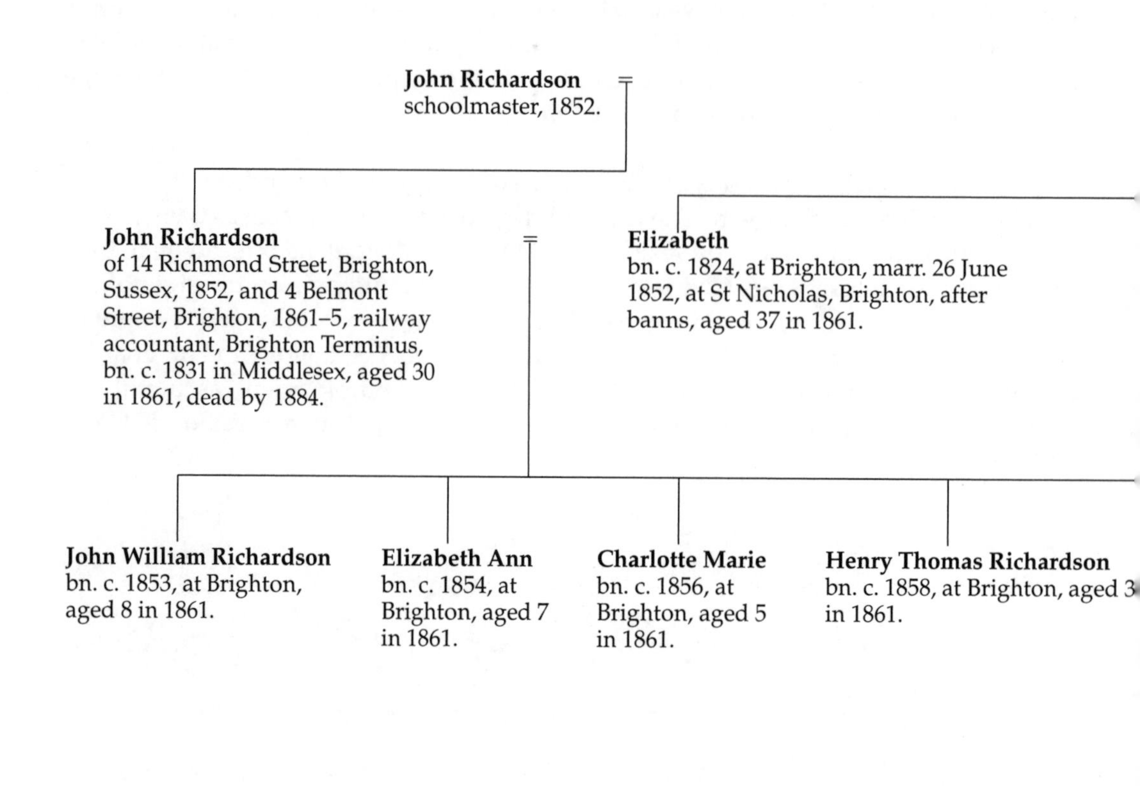

Charles Archer Richardson
newspaper clerk, 1901,
bn. c. 1886, at Brighton,
aged 5 in 1891, 15 in 1901.

Alice Martha
bn. c. 1887 at
Brighton,
aged 4 in 1891.

Percy Richardson
bn. c. Feb/March
1891, aged 1 month
on 5 April 1891,
10 in 1901.

Key:
bn = born
c = circa (about)
marr. = married
.↓. = unnamed children
QV = see PEARCE family tree

Thomas Pocock =
general dealer, 1852.

Charles Taylor =
house painter, journeyman, 1863,
dead by 5 April 1891.

Phoebe Goss
bn. c. 1826–31, at Wrotham, Kent,
aged 65 in 1891, receiving parish pay,
aged 70 in 1901.

Martha
bn. c. 1860, at
Brighton, aged 1
in 1861.

Percy George Richardson =
of 9 Pool Valley, Brighton, 1871
and 1884, 13 St Mary Magdalene
Street, Brighton, 1891–1901, baker,
journeyman, 1871–96, railway
labourer, 1901, stoker-engineer
at a brewery by 1920, bn. 6 Aug
1865, at 4 Belmont Street,
Brighton, aged 36 in 1901,
dead by 8 May 1920.

Alice
bn. 13 Feb 1863,
at 23 Lomax Street,
Brighton, marr.
30 Aug 1884,
aged 37 in 1901.

James Pearce =
coal merchant,
1920.

QV

John William Richardon =
of 7 St Mary Magdalene
Street, Brighton, fruit
merchant's salesman,
1920, bn. 19 May 1896, at
13 St Mary Magdalene
Street, Brighton, aged 6
in 1901.

.↓.

Annie
nurse (domestic),
1920, bn. 1 Feb
1896, at Old Oak
Lane, East Acton,
Middlesex, marr.
8 May 1920, at the
Register Office,
Brighton.

Albert E. Richardson
bn. c. 1897, at Brighton,
aged 4 in 1901.

catalogue, or *Tracing Your Ancestors in the Public Record Office*) can be searched at Kew, so it should be possible to trace his appointment, income and career through the company's ledgers, which encompass the early twentieth century.

Percy was 21 when he married in 1884, and his address was given then as Pool Valley, Brighton, where he had been lodging with Francis Cowley in 1881. His father, John Richardson, was already dead by 1884. Alice Taylor was the same age, and a Brighton resident. When ages are given as 21, it may merely indicate that a person was of full age (21 or over) and so did not need parental consent to marry. This can be misleading if you take the age literally – for instance, if you use it to calculate when to begin looking for a birth. In both cases here, however, the couple's ages were correct.

Percy (George) Richardson's death appears not to have been registered in England or Wales between 1901 and the June quarter of 1920, when his son John married; but according to his marriage certificate he was born in 1865, in which case he would have been 49 at the outbreak of the Great War in 1914. No trace of him was found on the Commonwealth War Grave Commission's website (**www.cwgc.org**), nor on the CD-ROM of *Soldiers Died in the Great War*. The GRO indexes of Army War Deaths, Other Ranks, 1914–21, and of Naval War Deaths for the same years yielded nine entries, in the former, for a man named Percy Richardson. Unfortunately, however, although the name of the regiment, regimental number, rank and year of death are recorded in the index, no ages are given. A reference check was made against each of these entries, using Percy's estimated age and the name of his wife, who would have been his next of kin. None of the entries matched up with the known details. This is a good example of the stumbling blocks you will occasionally come up against and it remains a loose end – but it is possible that the railway company's staff records will reveal when he left its employ, thus narrowing the gap.

Percy's birth occurred at his parents' home, 4 Belmont Street, Brighton, on 6 August 1865. His birth certificate confirms that he was given the second name of George. His father, John Richardson, was a railway accountant at Brighton Terminus. His career as a railway employee should be traceable, like Percy's after him, in the staff records of the London Brighton & South Coast Railway Company.

Three generations of Richardsons were born at home, which would have been the norm during this period. Sometimes, though, a young mother would return to her own mother's house for her confinement, or the birth might take place in temporary lodgings. It is important to look on the birth certificate for the address of the informant, who was generally one of the parents, for the family's usual domicile.

From the data gathered from the earliest birth certificate, it was possible to begin looking for the wedding of John Richardson and Elizabeth Pocock, Percy's parents. It took place on 26 June 1852, at St Nicholas parish church in Brighton. John was 21, and

Elizabeth seven years his senior. He was already a railway accountant; and his father, John Richardson, is described as a schoolmaster. Elizabeth's father, Thomas Pocock, is described as a general dealer. The two witnesses signing the marriage register were a Thomas P. and Charlotte Pocock, presumably relatives of the bride.

More information about the family can be discovered from the censuses of 1891, 1881 and 1861. When the 1891 census was taken, on 5 April, Percy G. Richardson was at 13 St Mary Magdalene Street, Brighton, where we know he remained until the next census, which was held on the night of 31 March 1901. There is a street index to the 1891 census of Brighton, so it was easy to locate the microfilm and folio reference for it. Percy, the head of household, was a journeyman baker and the father of two sons and a daughter, aged between one month and five years of age. He gave his own age as 21 and that of his wife, Alice, as 28. He had a widowed boarder, 65-year-old Phoebe Taylor, staying with him, who was in receipt of 'parish pay' (i.e. poor relief). From the 1901 census returns we know that she was his mother-in-law, but there is an age discrepancy of five years (she was 70 in 1901, which means she would have been 60 in 1891). Alice Taylor's birth certificate of 1863 revealed that Phoebe's maiden name was Goss. As with the 1901 census returns, Phoebe's birthplace was given as 'Rootham', Kent – probably a phonetic spelling of Wrotham.

The FRC's online personal-name index of the 1881 census of Sussex disclosed that Percy Richardson was then a young man of 17, and lodging with Francis Cowley in Brighton. Francis gave Percy's birthplace as Aldershot, in Hampshire, whereas when Percy completed the 1891 and 1901 household schedule he recorded himself, his wife and children as natives of Brighton. This inaccuracy may be explained by his landlord not knowing about Percy's background, and illustrates why it is always a good idea to obtain as much 10-yearly census information as possible as corroborative or alternative evidence. A look at the microfilm copy of the census enumerator's book showed that Mr Cowley ran a reasonably sized bakery, employing 10 resident assistants, bakers and house servants.

On 2 April 1871, the Richardson family was not listed in the census returns for Belmont Street, Brighton, where they resided when Percy was born in 1865. But in 1861 the census returns show that on the night of 7 April John Richardson was there with his wife Elizabeth and their five young offspring, the eldest of whom was eight. John gave his age as 30 and his birthplace as Middlesex, N.K. ('Not known'), and was working as a railway clerk. Elizabeth was engaged as a bonnet maker and, like their children, was born in Brighton. Sharing the same house, though in a separate apartment, was Mary Ann Levick, an unmarried schoolmistress, apparently born in Hanwell, Middlesex, 58 years before – which may be a clue to John's own birthplace, since his father was a teacher too. On 30 March 1851, 14 Richmond Street, Brighton, John's address in 1852 when he married, was described by the census enumerator as empty.

This is where the Brighton Line terminates. John Richardson travelled down there from Middlesex before 1852, probably as a recruit to work on the railways. His roots must be tracked in the London area around 1831, when he was born, before civil registration began.

2 The Pearces come to London

Annie Pearce was 24 when she became John William Richardson's wife in 1920. According to her marriage certificate, she was then working as a domestic nurse and her home was in St Michael's Place, Brighton. Her father, James Pearce, was a coal merchant, though when Annie was born in 1896 he was described as a general labourer, living in Old Oak Lane, East Acton, Middlesex, the address of her confinement. We do not know when Annie moved down to Sussex, but she may well have gone there in the course of her work. Annie's parents, James Pearce and Elizabeth Doe, got married at Christ Church, Chelsea, on 2 August 1891, as from 22 Flood Street. James was then 28, and his bride a year younger. Both fathers were labourers, like James himself.

As the 1891 census was taken four months earlier, on 5 April, Flood Street seemed a good place to begin to try and discover where James was born, because his name and that of his father are not uncommon and it might prove difficult to positively identify his birth entry in the quarterly GRO indexes. Alas, neither James nor Annie was found lodging anywhere in the street or its vicinity, so their given address at the time of marriage might simply have been one of accommodation and convenience while the banns were being read in the local church on the three Sundays preceding the ceremony. However, a William Bridwell was at this premises, the head of a household comprising himself, his wife Amelia and their daughter, and they occupied three

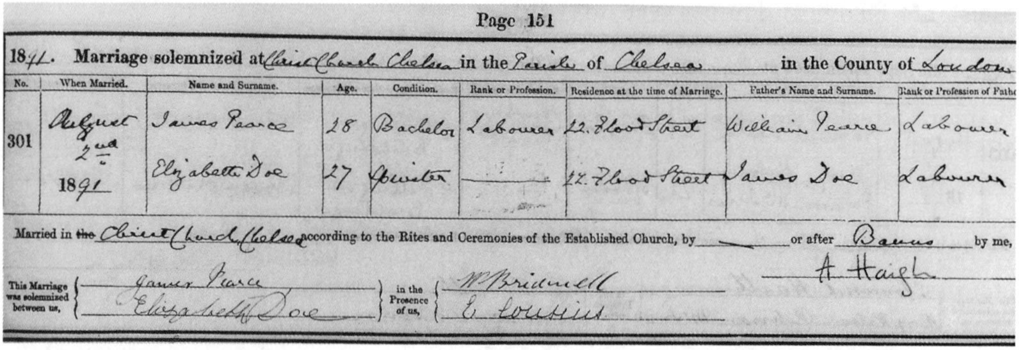

Page 151

1891. Marriage solemnized at Christ Church Chelsea in the Parish of Chelsea in the County of London

No.	When Married.	Name and Surname.	Age.	Condition.	Rank or Profession.	Residence at the time of Marriage.	Father's Name and Surname.	Rank or Profession of Father
301	August 2nd 1891	James Pearce	28	Bachelor	Labourer	22. Flood Street	William Pearce	Labourer
		Elizabeth Doe	27	Spinster	—	22. Flood Street	James Doe	Labourer

Married in the Christ Church Chelsea according to the Rites and Ceremonies of the Established Church, by ______ or after Banns by me, A. Haigh

This Marriage was solemnized between us, James Pearce, Elizabeth Doe — in the Presence of us, W Bridwell, E Cousins

Figure 35 Entry in the marriage register of Christ Church, Chelsea, recording the wedding of James Pearce and Elizabeth Doe, on 2 August 1891. Unlike a certificate from the GRO, this includes the actual signatures of the couple and the witnesses, W. Bridwell and E. Cousins. (London Metropolitan Archives, P74/CTC/7).

rooms in a building which was divided up into three apartments. William was a milkman, born 36 years previously in Potterne, in Wiltshire, like his wife. One of their two lodgers also came from Potterne, suggesting they had retained links with their home parish. As their daughter was born in London four years earlier, the family had been settled in the metropolis since 1887 or before.

The next tack was to consult the online personal-name index to the 1901 census returns. On the night of 31 March, James Pearce was sleeping with his family at his house in Old Oak Lane, Acton. He was the head of household, and by then he and Elizabeth (Eliza) had a brood of seven sons and daughters, the eldest of whom was eight and the youngest 10 months. James gave his age as 38 and his occupation as a coal dealer, working on his own account (self-employed). His birthplace was Potterne. It would seem that he came to stay with William Bridwell shortly before his wedding, as William's name appears as one of the signatories in the marriage register. A speculative search was made of the 1891 census returns of Potterne to see if James Pearce was there, but although there were nine separate households with Pearces recorded in them, he himself was absent.

Administrative County of London — The undermentioned Houses are situate within the Boundaries of the — Page 34

Civil Parish of Chelsea | ~~Municipal Borough~~ | ~~Municipal~~ Ward of Church | ~~Urban Sanitary District~~ | ~~Town or Village or Hamlet~~ | ~~Rural Sanitary District~~ | Parliamentary Borough ~~or Division~~ of Chelsea | Ecclesiastical Parish ~~or~~ District of Christchurch

1 No. of Schedule	2 ROAD, STREET, &c., and No. or NAME of HOUSE	3 HOUSES In-habited	4 HOUSES Uninhabited (U.), or Building (B.)	5 Number of rooms occupied if less than five	6 NAME and Surname of each Person	7 RELATION to Head of Family	8 CONDITION as to Marriage	9 AGE last Birthday of Males	10 AGE last Birthday of Females	11 PROFESSION or OCCUPATION	12 Employer	13 Employed	14 Neither Employer nor Employed	15 WHERE BORN	16 If (1) Deaf-and-Dumb (2) Blind (3) Lunatic, Imbecile or Idiot
312	20 Flood St	1		4	Richard J. Harrison	Head	M	64		Painter	X			London Pimlico	
					Eliza J. "	Wife	M		55					Berks Windsor	
					Herbert "	Son	S	22		Plumbers Labourer		X		London Chelsea	
					Charles "	"	S	20		Painter		X		" "	
					Willie "	"	S	16		Telegraph Messenger		X		" "	
					Edith F. "	Daur	S		13	Scholar				" "	
313	" "			1	Elizabeth Webber	Lodger	widow		32					Bristol	
311	" "				Priscilla A. Phelps	"	S		42	Cook & Housekeeper (Domestic)		X		Pembrokeshire S Wales	
314	22 "	1		3	William Bridwell	Head	M	36		Milk Man		X		Wilts Potterne	
					Amelia "	Wife	"		36					" Do	
					Amelia S. "	Daur	S		4					London Chelsea	
					Willie McDonald	Boarder	S	14		Baker		X		Essex Stratford	
					Robert Harris	"	S	24		Milkman		X		Wilts Potterne	
315	" "			1	Eliza Hopkins	Wife	M		47					London Shoreditch	
316	" "			2	Benjamin J. Martin	Head	M	30		Baker		X		Surrey Kennington	
					Lydia Do	Wife	M		25					Herts Barnet	
					Rose E. Do	Daur	—		4					Surrey Wandsworth	
					Phoebe E. Do	"	—		2					" Do	
					Amy Do	"			[illegible]					London Chelsea	
317	24 " "	1			George Wadle	Head	M	49		Builder	X			" "	
					Sarah Do	Wife			49					" Westminster	
					Elizabeth "	Daur			19					" Chelsea	
					William "	Son		14		Scholar				" Fulham	
					Fredrick "	"		13		"				" Chelsea	
					John "	"		11		"				" "	
					Emily "	Daur			5	"				" "	
					Henry "	Son		3						" "	
					Caroline "	Daur			[illegible]					" "	
318	26 " "	1			William Stevens	Head	M	50		Wood Dealer Timber				" Chelsea	
					Harriet "	Wife	M		39					" "	
					Christopher "	Son		8						" "	
8	Total of Houses and of Tenements with less than Five Rooms	4		5		Total of Males and Females		15	16						

NOTE.—*Draw the pen through such of the words of the headings as are inappropriate.*

Figure 36 The 1891 census return for 22 Flood Street, Chelsea, shows that William Bridwell, a milkman, and his family were there on census night – but not James Pearce and Elizabeth Doe, who gave this address as their place of residence at the time of their wedding four months later. (RG 12/63, f. 128, p. 34)

The Pearces of Potterne, Wiltshire, London and Brighton

Case study 2

= **Ann**
of Potterne, Wiltshire, pauper, formerly servant, 1851, bn. c. 1774, at Devizes, Wiltshire, aged 77 in 1851.

Mary Ann Hampton
bn. c. 1819, in Wiltshire, marr. 22 Sept 1834, at Potterne, aged 22 in 1841, dead by 30 March 1851.

= **William Pierce/Pearce**
of Potterne Wick, 1841, Butts, 1851, 1871, and Lower Street, 1861, all in Potterne, general labourer, 1841, thatcher 1851, bn. c. 1811 or 1813, at Potterne, aged 28 in 1841, 38 in 1851, 50 in 1861, 60 in 1871, died 30 Nov 1874, at Potterne, aged 61.

= **Ann Underwood**
of Lower Street, Potterne, 1881, 1891, agricultural labourer, 1861–81, bn. c. 1818–26, at Potterne, marr. 10 June 1851, at Potterne, aged 43 in 1861, 47 in 1871, 55 in 1881, 71 in 1891.

William Pearce
of Butts, Potterne, thatcher, 1851, bn. c. 1836/7, at Potterne, aged 4 in 1841, 15 in 1851.

Richard Pearce
of Lower Street, Potterne, argricultural labourer, 1861, bn. c. 1840, at Potterne, aged 10 months on 6 June 1841, 11 in 1851, 21 in 1861.

(Hester) Jane
bn. c. 1838, at Potterne, aged 3 in 1841, 13 in 1851.

Thomas Pearce
of Lower Street, Potterne, agricultural labourer, 1861, bn. c. 1842/3 at Potterne, aged 9 in 1851.

George Pearce
bn. c. 1853, at Potterne, aged 8 in 1861.

Sarah
of Lower Street, Potterne, agricultural labourer, 1881, bn. c. 1857, at Potterne, aged 4 in 1861, 14 in 1871, 24 in 1881.

Ann
bn. c. 1855, at Potterne, aged 6 in 1861.

Bertha
bn. c. 1893, at North Kensington, Middlesex, aged 8 in 1901.

Henry Pearce
bn. c. 1894, at Acton, aged 7 in 1901.

Ernest Pearce
bn. c. 1895, at Writtle, Essex, aged 6 in 1901.

Key:	bn	=	born
	c	=	circa (about)
	marr.	=	married
	.↓.	=	unnamed children
	QV	=	see RICHARDSON family tree

James Doe
labourer, 1891.

=

Frank Pearce
of Lower Street, Potterne, agricultural labourer, 1881–91, bn. c. 1860–1, at Potterne, aged 1 in 1861, 10 in 1871, 20 in 1881, 31 in 1891.

James Pearce
of Lower Street, Potterne, 1881, 22 Flood Street, Chelsea, Middlesex, 1891, and Old Oak Lane, East Acton, Middlesex, 1896, agricultural labourer, 1881, general labourer, 1896, coal dealer, 1901, bn. c. 1863, at Potterne, aged 8 in 1871, 18 in 1881, 28 in 1891, 38 in 1901.

=

Elizabeth
bn. c. 1864, at Writtle, Essex, marr. 2 Aug 1891, at Christ Church, Chelsea, after banns, aged 27 in 1891, aged 36 in 1901.

Fred Pearce
of Lower Street, Potterne, agricultural labourer, 1881–91, bn. c. 1859, at Potterne, aged 2 in 1861, 12 in 1871, 22 in 1881.

Charles Pearce
of Lower Street, Potterne, agricultural labourer, 1881, bn. c. 1865, at Potterne, aged 6 in 1871, 16 in 1881.

John William Richardson
QV

=

Annie
nurse (domestic), 1920, bn. 1 Feb 1896, at Old Oak Lane, East Acton, marr. 8 May 1920, at the Register Office, Brighton, aged 4 in 1901.

.↓.

Frank Pearce
bn. c. 1898, at Acton, aged 3 in 1901.

Rose
bn. c. 1899, at Acton, aged 2 in 1901.

William Pearce
bn. June/July 1900, aged 10 months on 31 March 1901.

The personal-name index to the 1881 census returns disclosed that James Pearce was then aged 18 and living in Wiltshire, where he had been born. He was an unmarried agricultural labourer, and was found in his widowed mother Ann Pearce's household in Potterne. On census night, 3 April 1881, Ann Pearce was living in Lower Street, and was an ag. lab. (agricultural labourer), aged 55. All of her four sons and her daughter were agricultural labourers, too, James being the youngest member of the family. They had spent all their lives in Potterne. On 5 April 1891, Ann was still there, occupying four rooms, but she now gave her age as 71 (according to the 1881 census it should have been 65, which serves to show how unreliable and uncertain people were about their ages), and only her son Frank and a granddaughter remained. Since Ann and her children were natives of Potterne, the next step was to trace them there again, in the 1871 census. On 2 April 1871, her husband, William, a 60-year-old general labourer, headed the Pearce household at Butts, Potterne. Ann's age was alleged to be 47 (not 45, as might be expected from the 1881 returns, when she herself had been the informant), and there were five children, the next to youngest being James, a schoolboy of eight. They all came from Potterne, so any surviving school admission registers there should note the various comings and goings of several generations of Pearces, including their dates of birth and paternity. *Kelly's Directory of Wiltshire* for 1903, in the General Reference area on the first floor of the FRC, mentions the endowment of the elementary school at Potterne in 1831 and its rebuilding and enlargement in 1865, so the family would have attended both establishments.

The 1863 quarterly birth indexes did not yield any James Pearce registered in Wiltshire, but there were five such entries in 1862 and 1864, the closest geographically being that of the James Pearce whose birth was registered at Devizes, 2 miles south of Potterne, between 1 July and 30 September 1862. However, this proved to relate to another James, also aged 18 at the time of the 1881 census (*see* Figure 38, on p. 155). From the 1871 and 1881 census returns, we know that James' father, William Pearce, died sometime between 3 April 1871 and 3 April 1881, the date of the latter enumeration, probably at Potterne, where he had apparently lived his entire life. By this period the quarterly death indexes report ages, so it was possible to trace him using his age in 1871, when he was 60, as a yardstick. His death took place on 30 November 1874, in Potterne, and his age was recorded as 61.

The 1861 census returns of Potterne, although obviously not recording James, showed William Pearce as a married man of 50, with a wife, Ann, aged 43, and seven older children, two of whom were agricultural labourers, like William and Ann, and three of whom were at school. The ages in the 1861 census enumerator's book have been crossed through by clerks in the Registrar General's Office in London, rendering them unreadable, so a search was made of the original document, at the PRO, Kew.

On the night of 30 March 1851, William was a widower, living at Butts, in Potterne village, with his four young children. He described himself as 'senr' (senior) and as

Administrative County Middlesex — The undermentioned Houses are situate within the boundaries of the — Page 24

Civil Parish	Ecclesiastical Parish	~~County Borough, Municipal Borough, or~~ Urban District	Ward of ~~Municipal Borough or~~ of Urban District	~~Rural District~~	Parliamentary ~~Borough~~ or Division	Town ~~or Village or Hamlet~~
of Acton	of E. Acton St. Dunstans	of Acton	of Acton North	of	of Ealing	of Acton.

1 No. of Schedule	2 ROAD, STREET, &c., and No. or NAME of HOUSE	3 HOUSES Inhabited	4 Uninhabited In Occupation	5 Uninhabited Not in Occupation	6 Building	7 Number of Rooms occupied if less than five	8 Name and Surname of each Person	9 RELATION to Head of Family	10 Condition as to Marriage	11 Age last Birthday of Males	12 Age last Birthday of Females	13 PROFESSION OR OCCUPATION	14 Employer, Worker, or Own account	15 If Working at Home	16 WHERE BORN	17 (1) Deaf and Dumb (2) Blind (3) Lunatic (4) Imbecile, feeble-minded
							Ethel Francis	Daur	S		7				Mid^x Acton	
							Fred Do	Son	S	6					Do	
							Alfred Do	Son	S	4					Do	
							James Do	Son	S	4					Do	
							Rose Do	Daur	S		1				Do	
155	3 Old Oak Lane	1				4	James Pearce	Head	M	38		Coal Dealer	Own acc.		Wilts. Potterne	
							Eliza Do	Wife	M		36				Essex Writtle	
							Bertha Do	Daur	S		8				North Kensington	
							Henry Do	Son	S	7					Mid^x Acton	
							Ernest Do	Son	S	6					Essex Writtle	
							Annie Do	Daur	S		4				Mid^x Acton	
							Frank Do	Son	S	3					Do	
							Rose Do	Daur	S		2				Do	
							William Do	Son	S	10 mo.					Do	
156	4 Do	1					Thomas Booker	Head	M	42		Pig Dealer (Cattle Dealer)	Own acc.	At home	London Kensington	
							Emma Do	Wife	M		34				London Hammersmith	
							Emma Do	Daur	S		21				Do. Kensington	
							Daniel Wakelin	Nephew	S	18					Do	
157	5 Do	1					William Baggs	Head	M	42		Farmer	Do	Do	London Notting Hill	
							Annie Do	Wife	M		40				Do	
							Alice Do	Daur	S		18				Do	
							Mary Do	Do	S		16				Do	
							Ernest Do	Son	S	12					Do	
							Alfred Do	Do	S	10					Mid^x Acton	
							George Do	Do	S	7					Do	
							David Do	Do	S	3					Do	
158	Wells Farm Old Oak Lane.	1					George Morris Jun	Head	M	32		Cattle Dealer	Employer		Putney Ldn	
							Maria Morris	Wife	M		38				London Fulham	
							George Do	Son	S	12					Mid^x Acton	
							Fanny Do	Daur	S		9				Do	
							Daniel Do	Son	S	8					Do	
4	Total of Schedules of Houses and of Tenements with less than Five Rooms	4				1	Total of Males and of Females...			18	13					

NOTE—Draw your pen through such words of the headings as are inapplicable.

Figure 37 The 1901 census return for 3 Old Oak Lane, Acton, home of James and Eliza Pearce and their young family since at least 1896. James's birthplace is clearly shown as Potterne, in Wiltshire, 38 years earlier. (RG 13/1201, f. 16, p. 24)

aged 38, a thatcher like his son William Pearce 'jnr' (junior), aged 15. His widowed mother, Ann Pearce, aged 77, made up a household spanning three generations, taking the family's history back to her approximate birth year of 1774, at nearby Devizes. Ann was a pauper by 1851 (she had once been a servant), so Potterne's churchwardens' accounts should reveal what support she was receiving. Her son and grandchildren were all natives of Potterne, and it may be that she came to care for the family or to be kept by them herself soon after William was widowed.

We thus know that William Pearce had fathered at least four children before 1851, by a wife as yet unknown, had remarried by 1853 when his son George was said to have been born, and had then produced another seven children after him, whose mother was Ann. George was at school in 1861, aged eight. Although there is a 10-year gap between Thomas and George (son of Ann), the 1861 census correctly described them both as the sons of the head of the household. On the face of it, they were the children of Ann too. It was only when the 1851 census was searched that the true situation emerged.

The censuses show that the Pearces moved around in Potterne, living at Butts in 1851, Lower Street by 1861, moving back to Butts by 1871, and returning to Lower Street by 1881, where Ann Pearce, the matriarch, was based in 1891. They were close neighbours of the Bridwells, though the Potterne Bridwell of Flood Street, Chelsea, in 1891, has not been traced back to his purported village home in any of the earlier census returns. *Kelly's Directory of Wiltshire*, 1903, reveals that Potterne then consisted of two streets, the main one running north to south on the road from Devizes to Market Lavington and Salisbury. Maps such as the 25-inch Ordnance Survey map of Potterne, compiled in the late nineteenth century, and the tithe map and apportionment of 1839 can be studied to show the proximity to each other of Butts and Lower Street and the changing landscape of the community. Copies of these are available at the Wiltshire Record Office, in Trowbridge, and at the PRO, Kew. The tithe apportionment may include William Pearce's name and that of his landlord, and reveal exactly where he lived. There may be photographic evidence, too; and the buildings and place names may still exist.

On 6 June 1841, William Pierce (note the different spelling) was at Potterne Wick, half a mile south of the village centre, on the road to Devizes. Although for the purposes of this census ages above 15 were supposed to be rounded down to the nearest five years, in this instance they were recorded precisely, so William's was given as 28 (placing his birth about 1813, in Wiltshire). The 1841 census did not record marital condition or relationship to the head of the household, nor exact birthplace beyond whether it was in the county where the person was enumerated that night. But on the face of it, it would seem that this was William, his wife, and young family, since the others in the household (Mary Ann, 22, Hester Jane, aged three, and Richard, six months old) would indicate a family unit.

1881 CENSUS-SURNAME INDEX, COUNTY: WILTSHIRE

PEARCE , Jacob PAGE: 03458

CENSUS DATA © BRITISH CROWN COPYRIGHT 1982.
MICROFICHE EDITION OF THE INDEXES © COPYRIGHT 1990, BY CORPORATION OF THE PRESIDENT OF THE CHURCH OF JESUS CHRIST OF LATTER-DAY SAINTS.

SURNAME	FORENAME	AGE	SEX	RELATIONSHIP TO HEAD	MARITAL CONDITION	CENSUS PLACE	OCCUPATION	NAME OF HEAD	WHERE BORN CO	WHERE BORN PARISH	NOTE	PUBLIC RECORD OFFICE PIECE ROLL/	FOLIO NO	PAGE NO	G.S.U. FILM NUMBER
PEARCE	Jacob	38	M	Head	M	Berwick Bassett	Ag Lab Shephe+	Self	WIL	Aldbourne		2037	32	1	1341491
PEARCE	James	88	M	Head	M	Melksham	Gen Lab	Self	WIL	Calne		2046	26	6	1341493
PEARCE	James	80	M	Head	M	Burbage	Annuitant	Self	WIL	Burbage		2061	34	8	1341497
PEARCE	James	80	M	Head	W	West Lavington	Occupant Of A+	Self	WIL	Market Lavington		2042	59	4	1341492
PEARCE	James	80	M	Head	W	Wilcott	Relief From T+	Self	WIL	Oare		2060	48	21	1341497
PEARCE	James	79	M	Fath	W	Sutton Veney	Formerly Shep+	PEARCE, Jos.	WIL	Imber	*	2057	90	13	1341496
PEARCE	James	77	M	Head	M	Bromham	Formerly Quar+	Self	WIL	Chittoe	*	2044	74	10	1341492
PEARCE	James	76	M	Head	M	Chittoe	Ag Lab	Self	WIL	Chittoe		2044	83	6	1341492
PEARCE	James	68	M	Head	M	Chippenham	Railway Labou+	Self	WIL	Chippenham		2033	57	11	1341490
PEARCE	James	57	M	Head	M	Figheldean	Farmer 1700 A+	Self	WIL	Haxon		2064	5	3	1341498
PEARCE	James	51	M	Ptnt	M	Devizes St Jam+	Coachman	I-"WILTS COUNTY LU+	WIL	Market Lavington	*	2041	90	7	1341492
PEARCE	James	50	M	Head	M	Maddington	Carter	Self	WIL	Imber		2063	46	2	1341497
PEARCE	James	48	M	Head	M	Warminster	Maltsters Lab+	Self	WIL	Warminster		2056	100	15	1341495
PEARCE	James	45	M	Head	M	Salisbury St M+	Plasterer	Self	WIL	Rembury		2072	95	6	1341500
PEARCE	James	45	M	Head	U	Trowbridge	Farm Servant	Self	WIL	Hilperton		2047	117	17	1341493
PEARCE	James	45	M	Head	M	Wilcott	Ag Lab	Self	WIL	Oare		2060	45	16	1341497
PEARCE	James	41	M	Head	M	West Wellow	Bricklayer	Self	WIL	W Wellow		1226	101	2	1341300
PEARCE	James	39	M	Head	M	Heytesbury	Ag Lab Shephe+	Self	WIL	Imber		2058	14	22	1341496
PEARCE	James	39	M	Head	M	Westbury	Ironwork Labo+	Self	WIL	Westbury Leigh		2054	51	7	1341495
PEARCE	James	38	M	Head	M	Westbury	Cloth Worker	Self	WIL	Westbury		2054	117	14	1341495
PEARCE	James	36	M	Head	M	Berwick St Jam+	Ag Lab	Self	WIL	Imber		2074	57	18	1341500
PEARCE	James	36	M	Head	M	Hindon	Shepherd	Self	WIL	Berwick St Leonard		2078	15	21	1341501
PEARCE	James	34	M	Head	M	Chippenham	Labourer Loca+	Self	WIL	Kington Langley		2033	7	7	1341490
PEARCE	James	33	M	Son	U	Chippenham	Masons Journe+	PEARCE, William	WIL	Chippenham		2032	83	37	1341489
PEARCE	James	33	M	Head	M	Salisbury St E+	Book Metropol+	Self	YKS	Rangeworthy		2071	67	11	1341499
PEARCE	James	27	M	Head	M	Poulshot	General Labou+	Self	WIL	Poulshot		2044	40	9	1341492
PEARCE	James	26	M	---	M	Devizes St Mary	Brewers Lab	CATLEY, Samuel	WIL	Stanton St Bernard		2039	87	29	1341491
PEARCE	James	26	M	Son	U	Imber	Agriculture L+	PEARCE, John	WIL	Imber		2058	48	2	1341496
PEARCE	James	24	M	Son	U	Potterne	Labourer (Agl)	PEARCE, Joseph	WIL	Worton		2043	19	1	1341492
PEARCE	James	23	M	Neph	U	Devizes St John	Late Errand B+	RUSS, John	MID	London	*	2039	35	18	1341491
PEARCE	James	19	M	Son	U	Chippenham	Carpenter	PEARCE, William	WIL	Chippenham		2033	30	9	1341490
PEARCE	James	19	M	Son	U	Wilcott	Ag Lab	PEARCE, Elizabeth	WIL	Wilcott		2060	42	9	1341497
PEARCE	James	18	M	Son	U	Melksham	Genl Lab	PEARCE, John	WIL	Bromham		2046	30	13	1341493
PEARCE	James	18	M	Son	U	Potterne	Ag Lab	PEARCE, Ann	WIL	Potterne		2043	20	4	1341492
PEARCE	James	17	M	Lodg	U	Aldbourn	Ag Lab Carter	BECKINGHAM, Richard	WIL	Pewsey		1276	37	15	1341311
PEARCE	James	15	M	Son	-	Chittoe	Ag Lab	PEARCE, George	WIL	Bromham		2044	84	7	1341492
PEARCE	James	14	M	Son	-	Bromham	Agricultural +	PEARCE, Thomas	WIL	Bromham		2044	74	9	1341492
PEARCE	James	13	M	Son	-	Melksham	Rope Factory +	PEARCE, Susan	WIL	Melksham		2045	66	26	1341492
PEARCE	James	9	M	GSon	U	Bremhill	---	PEARCE, Thomas	WIL	Calne		2035	16	5	1341490
PEARCE	James	7	M	Son	-	Rowde	Scholar	PEARCE, John	WIL	Rowde		2044	23	3	1341492
PEARCE	James	7	M	Son	U	West Dean	Scholar	PEARCE, David	WIL	West Dean		1227	58	8	1341300
PEARCE	James	5	M	Son	-	Hilperton	Scholar	PEARCE, Charles	WIL	Hilperton		2047	17	27	1341493
PEARCE	James	5	M	Son	-	West Wellow	Scholar	PEARCE, James	WIL	W Wellow		1226	101	2	1341300
PEARCE	James P.	13	M	Son	-	Fittleton	Ag Lab	PEARCE, John	---	Heckleston		2059	29	20	1341496
PEARCE	James W.	20	M	Son	U	Figheldean	---	PEARCE, James	WIL	Figheldean		2064	5	3	1341498
PEARCE	James W.	16	M	Son	U	Berwick Bassett	Ag Lab	PEARCE, Jacob	WIL	Broad Hinton		2037	32	1	1341491
PEARCE	Jamima	20	F	Wife	M	Imber	---	PEARCE, Edward	WIL	Tilshead		2058	51	7	1341496
PEARCE	Jane	77	F	Wife	M	Bromham	---	PEARCE, Joseph	WIL	Bromham		2044	50	9	1341492
PEARCE	Jane	75	F	Moth	W	Fyfield	Formerly Farm+	SPRULES, David	WIL	Overton		2038	113	5	1341491
PEARCE	Jane	67	F	Wife	M	Chippenham	---	PEARCE, James	WIL	Langley Chippenham		2033	57	11	1341490
PEARCE	Jane	62	F	Head	W	Aldbourn	Agrical Labor+	Self	WIL	Aldbourne		1276	23	40	1341311

+ = SEE ORIGINAL CENSUS FOR FULL DATA | m = MONTHS w = WEEKS d = DAYS | > = GREATER THAN < = LESS THAN | M = MARRIED U = UNMARRIED W = WIDOW(ER) D = DIVORCED O = OTHER | * = SEE MISCELLANEOUS NOTES

Figure 38 Page from the microfiche personal-name index to the 1881 census returns for Wiltshire. There are entries for two 18-year-olds named James Pearce, one the son of John Pearce and the other the son of Ann Pearce. Both of the given birthplaces lie within the registration district of Devizes, making it all the more important to supply the known parent's name as a checking point when applying for a copy of the relevant birth certificate.

The *International Genealogical Index* contains entries extracted from the Potterne parish registers of baptisms and marriages between 1653 and 1895, but these do not include the baptism of James Pierce (or Pearce) about 1862 or 1863, though William Pearce was found to have married Ann Underwood there on 10 June 1851 and Mary Ann Hampton on 22 September 1834. Because the *IGI* does not record everything that appears in the original registers and doesn't include burials at all, it would be important to check the registers for verification and further details about the family.

We already knew that by 1836 William was married to Mary Ann, who was the mother of his four children, William, Hester Jane, Richard and Thomas, all born before 1844. By 30 March 1851 he had been widowed, and around 1853 his son George was born to his wife Ann, who provided him with a further seven children, including James, who was born in 1862, making a grand total of 12 in all recorded in the census. Since the family was firmly entrenched in Potterne, the parish registers are the next source on the list to tap into – first finding out what period they cover, whether they have been microfilmed and made available for hire at an LDS Family History Centre, or if there is a transcript of them in the library of the Society of Genealogists, and, of course, the present whereabouts of the original records themselves.

CERTIFIED COPY OF AN ENTRY OF DEATH

GIVEN AT THE GENERAL REGISTER OFFICE

Application Number B010358/A

REGISTRATION DISTRICT Devizes, Wilts.

1874 DEATH in the Sub-district of Bromham in the County of Wilts

Columns:– 1		2	3	4	5	6	7	8	9
No.	When and where died	Name and surname	Sex	Age	Occupation	Cause of death	Signature, description and residence of informant	When registered	Signature of registrar
415	Thirtieth November 1874 Potterne	William Pearce	Male	61 years	Thatcher	Heart Disease	X The mark of Elizabeth Tilley In attendance Potterne	Second December 1874	George England Registrar

CERTIFIED to be a true copy of an entry in the certified copy of a Register of Deaths in the District above mentioned.

Given at the GENERAL REGISTER OFFICE, under the Seal of the said Office, the 2nd day of October 1997

DXZ 453918

See note overleaf

CAUTION:-It is an offence to falsify a certificate or to make or knowingly use a false certificate or a copy of a false certificate intending it to be accepted as genuine to the prejudice of any person or to possess a certificate knowing it to be false without lawful authority.

GENERAL REGISTER OFFICE ENGLAND

Figure 39 The certificate recording the death of William Pearce, on 30 November 1874, at Potterne, in Wiltshire. He was the father of James Pearce, born about 1862.

Research strategies

If you want to search parish records some distance from where you live and have friends or local family history society contacts in the area, you may prefer to arrange for this to be done for you, rather than make a long journey. You can request a search of your local registration-district indexes if your family came from the area where you now live. A visit to your local LDS Family History Centre could also prove extremely productive, since you can 'hire in' films of vital records indexes, census returns and parish registers from throughout the world – the only snag being that until you have searched a census return you won't know which one to look at next, and there may be a time lag before you can inspect another one specially hired in for you. If you live in London or need to research several branches of your family in various parts of the country, then the Family Records Centre is probably your best option, because it offers such a vast range of indexes and other resources under one roof.

The choice is yours. Perhaps you may opt to search centrally housed material first, and then examine local copies to tidy up any unfinished business and loose ends (though be prepared to find more!). You will certainly unearth all sorts of unexpected details about your family's past, and may wonder how some of them ever met each other, if they came from distant parts of the country or from abroad. This is what makes family history so absorbing. It also partly explains the lure of the Family Records Centre and suggests what can be achieved with patience, persistence and enthusiasm.

Everyone has their own research strategy, but here is a list of points to bear in mind as you embark on tracing your ancestors:

1. Plan ahead. Review your research plans regularly as you go along.
2. Make sure you are in the right place, at the right time. For example, the FRC doesn't hold wills after 1858; and if you visit on a Saturday, we can't redirect you to the Probate Searchroom, which is only open from Monday to Friday.
3. Don't try to take 'short cuts'. A registration district in the GRO indexes extends over an area of up to 11 different places, containing thousands of people, so don't attempt to rely on this to search the census returns.
4. Try the *IGI* to locate missing births and marriages, or to shorten the search period for siblings.

5. Use the National Probate Indexes to find out dates of death, and then apply for a death certificate to obtain more information.
6. Use the Death Duty register indexes to check dates of death, and to locate wills proved in courts other than the Prerogative Court of Canterbury before 1858.
7. Use the internet wisely. It is easy to lose your way and get diverted from one site to another. But initially it may be more cost effective than a journey to London, or elsewhere, and can help you plan where and what you want to search.
8. LDS Family History Centres may be a viable alternative to visiting London. Get addresses and contact details from **www.familysearch.org**.
9. Use your time effectively when in London. You might be able to combine a visit to the FRC with a trip to the Society of Genealogists or the London Metropolitan Archives (*see* map on p. xv, and pp. 4 and 17 for opening times), or even venture to the Guildhall Library (open Monday to Saturday, 9.30 a.m. to 4.45 p.m.) or the Hyde Park Family History Centre, which is open on Tuesdays and Thursdays up to 9 p.m., on Wednesdays and Fridays up to 7 p.m., and on Mondays and Saturdays until 5 p.m. (*see* pp. 165–7 for addresses).
10. Always check original sources when using compilations, indexes and transcripts, and read the introductions to such finding aids to learn how they work.
11. Always write down full references to your sources (including the title, author and publication details of books), particularly when making photocopies. Then you will be able to find them again, if you need to.
12. If in doubt, ask!

Tracing missing relatives

Sooner or later the scent may go cold – certain relatives seem to have disappeared without trace, and all your attempts to find their whereabouts or what happened to them have failed. What strategies can you employ to pick up the trail again?

It may be that the impasse lies beyond living memory, so the usual tack of asking other relatives will be useless, but you may decide you'd like to renew contact with their descendants. The advent of the internet has, literally, opened up the world to genealogists everywhere, enabling people to make contact with each other easily and to post notices and messages for others to read. Try **www.google.com** to see which websites might include references to the names of the relatives you are looking for, or place a query on **http://rootsweb.com** or **www.Ancestry.com**. This may do the trick, as there may be someone out there just waiting for your message! It also enables the finder to make contact with you.

If it's possible that your missing relatives are still alive, this is a much more sensitive issue – as they may have vanished for a good reason and don't want you or the family to find them. Be very careful in the way you handle your efforts to renew links, and bear in mind that your actions could stir up trouble. Cyndi's List (**www.cyndislist.com/finding.htm**) consists of hotlinks to national directories of many countries; and you can try **www.bt.com/index.jsp** to search for entries in UK phone books online.

The Office for National Statistics operates a paid search service called Traceline, PO Box 106, Southport PR8 2WA (telephone 0151 471 4811 or 4204, open Monday to Friday between 9 a.m. and 4.30 p.m.), using the National Health Service Central Register (NHSCR) to identify the current whereabouts of family or friends of the same sex with whom you have lost touch. Applicants must be aged 18 or over, and application forms can be obtained direct from Traceline. The initial search cost is £27.50. You will need to supply the missing person's surname, forename, and date of birth or approximate age now; if you can add the last known address, parents' names and any former name, that will be helpful. You should also state your relationship to the individual and how contact was lost.

If the search of the Register is successful, you will be notified whether the person is still living, in which case you will be invited to send a letter for forwarding to your relative, providing he or she consents. The cost of this further service is £22.50. To preserve the missing person's privacy, no information is ever disclosed to applicants about his/her address; and Traceline may refuse to deal with an application if it is felt to be against the interests of that party.

If the missing person has died in England or Wales, Traceline will give you enough information to enable you to buy a copy of the death certificate.

No forwarding service is offered in cases involving adoption (*see* pp. 48–9 for advice on what to do), or current or former spouses, or friends of the opposite sex – except that if an adopted person applies to locate a natural parent who is now dead, Traceline may release details of the year and registration district of death.

The Traceline service can be used by businesses seeking to pay out pensions to former employees or monies due under assurance policies; and it can also be used when the location of will beneficiaries is being sought.

Other approaches

- The FRC has produced a couple of fact sheets on Tracing Missing Persons, including useful addresses and phone numbers of agencies, organizations and charities who might be able to help. These can be downloaded from **www.familyrecords.gov.uk** and **www.pro.gov.uk**. A similar leaflet is available online on the British Library's website, **www.bl.uk**, though this is not designed specifically for family historians.

- Don't ignore family, known friends, neighbours and fellow residents who may have stayed in touch without your being aware. Think carefully about the implications of visiting or phoning a newly found relative without prior warning; a letter introducing yourself and inviting a reply would be more tactful, so that the initiative rests with them to respond.

- An advertisement or letter in the local newspaper or magazine of the area where your 'missing relatives' were last known to be can be productive, even if they do not respond to it. A neighbour or friend may give you vital information about them. 'Missing Persons' columns in the national press also reunite lost relatives and friends.

- Check marriage, birth, death and will indexes to see if you can discover what subsequently happened in their lives, and to obtain addresses at specific dates. Try overseas civil-registration indexes, too. A number of these are now available on the internet, such as those for New South Wales and Victoria, in Australia, and British Columbia, in Canada. An easy way of finding out if there are online birth, marriage and death indexes is to utilize **www.google.com** to make a search, using 'birth', 'marriage' and 'death' coupled with the relevant country, province or state as keywords. The indexes and/or registers of many countries have been microfilmed by the LDS, and you can hire them at a Family History Centre; for details, consult the *Family History Library Catalog* on **www.familysearch.org** or look at T. J. Kemp's *International Vital Records Handbook*.

- Armed with an address, you might want to tackle the annual Electoral Registers. Copies of local ones are usually held by reference libraries and county record offices. A complete set of those for the UK since 1947 is kept in the British Library, 96 Euston Road, London NW1 2DB (telephone 020 7412 7536). You will need a reader's ticket to search these (*see* p. 26); and for registers before 1984, you will have to give 48 hours' notice. Since the Registers are arranged by polling district and then by address, they will merely confirm a person's presence there in October of any year.

- Employers' records may also contain up-to-date details about former staff, and the firm or company may be willing to forward a letter from you to that person.

- Should you decide to leave the task to a specialist, you will have to pay a fee for this service. Finders Keepers, PO Box 229, Great Missenden, Bucks HP16 0YD, helps reunite children from National Children's Homes, Barnardo's, Church of England Homes, Catholic Homes, and so on; and the Salvation Army runs a Family Tracing Service, which offers a unique and confidential agency. The Association of British Investigators and the Institute of Professional Investigators will supply names and addresses of members in your area. You can find other tracing services by using an internet search engine such as **www.google.com**.

As another genealogist said, the surest way of finding your missing relatives is to win the Lottery – then they'll come looking for you!

Registration districts in England and Wales

The following are listed on **www.genuki.org.uk/big/eng/civreg/GROIndexes.html**.

1837–51

I, II, III	London and Middlesex
IV	London and Surrey
V	Kent
VI	Bedfordshire, Berkshire, Buckinghamshire and Hertfordshire
VII	Hampshire and Sussex
VIII	Dorset, Hampshire and Wiltshire
IX	Cornwall and Devon
X	Devon and Somerset
XI	Gloucestershire, Somerset and Warwickshire
XII	Essex and Suffolk
XIII	Norfolk and Suffolk
XIV	Cambridgeshire, Huntingdonshire, Lincolnshire and Suffolk
XV	Leicestershire, Northamptonshire, Nottinghamshire and Rutland
XVI	Oxfordshire, Staffordshire and Warwickshire
XVII	Staffordshire
XVIII	Gloucestershire, Shropshire, Staffordshire, Warwickshire and Worcestershire
XIX	Cheshire, Derbyshire and Flintshire
XX	Lancashire
XXI	Lancashire and Yorkshire
XXII, XXIII	Yorkshire
XXIV	Durham and Yorkshire
XXV	Cumberland, Westmorland, Lancashire and Northumberland
XXVI	Brecknockshire, Carmarthenshire, Glamorganshire, Herefordshire, Monmouthshire, Pembrokeshire, Radnorshire and Shropshire
XXVII	Anglesey, Caernarvonshire, Cardiganshire, Denbighshire, Flintshire, Merionethshire and Montgomeryshire

1852–1946

1a, 1b, 1c	London and Middlesex
1d	London, Kent and Surrey
2a	Kent and Surrey
2b	Hampshire and Sussex
2c	Berkshire and Hampshire
3a	Berkshire, Buckinghamshire, Hertfordshire, Middlesex and Oxfordshire
3b	Bedfordshire, Cambridgeshire, Huntingdonshire, Northamptonshire and Suffolk
4a	Essex and Suffolk
4b	Norfolk
5a	Dorset and Wiltshire
5b	Devon
5c	Cornwall and Somerset
6a	Gloucestershire, Herefordshire and Shropshire
6b	Staffordshire, Warwickshire and Worcestershire
6c	Warwickshire and Worcestershire
6d	Warwickshire
7a	Leicestershire, Lincolnshire and Rutland
7b	Derbyshire and Nottinghamshire
8a	Cheshire
8b, 8c, 8d, 8e	Lancashire
9a, 9b, 9c, 9d	Yorkshire
10a	Durham
10b	Cumberland, Northumberland and Westmorland
11a	Carmarthenshire, Glamorganshire, Monmouthshire and Pembrokeshire
11b	Anglesey, Brecknockshire, Caernarvonshire, Cardiganshire, Denbighshire, Flintshire, Merionethshire, Montgomeryshire and Radnorshire

For later registration districts (from June 1946 to March 1965, from 1965 to March 1974, and from June 1974 to 1993), see the lists at the Customer Services Desk on the ground floor of the FRC or consult J. A. Newport, comp., *An Index to Civil Registration Districts of England and Wales, 1837 to date.*

Details of current superintendent registrars' districts and sub-districts are to be found in R. Blatchford, *The Family and Local History Handbook.*

Abbreviations

AGRA	Association of Genealogists and Researchers in Archives
BIVRI	*British Isles Vital Records Index*
BL	British Library
CEB	Census enumerator's book
FFHS	Federation of Family History Societies
FHC	Family History Centre
FHLC	*Family History Library Catalog*
FRC	Family Records Centre
GOONS	Guild of One-Name Studies
GRO	General Register Office
GRO(S)	General Register Office for Scotland
GSU	Genealogical Society of Utah
HMC	Historical Manuscripts Commission
IGI	*International Genealogical Index*
LDS	Church of Jesus Christ of Latter-day Saints
LMA	London Metropolitan Archives
NAI	National Archives of Ireland
NAS	National Archives of Scotland
NBI	*National Burial Index*
NLW	National Library of Wales
NRA	National Register of Archives
ONS	Office for National Statistics
OS	Ordnance Survey
PCC	Prerogative Court of Canterbury
PCY	Prerogative Court of York
PRFD	Principal Registry of the Family Division
PRO	Public Record Office
PROCAT	Public Record Office Online Catalogue
PRONI	Public Record Office of Northern Ireland
SoG	Society of Genealogists

Useful addresses and websites

Association of Genealogists and Researchers in Archives (AGRA),
The Joint Secretaries, AGRA, 29 Badgers Close, Horsham, West Sussex RH12 5RU,
email **agra@agra.org.uk**, website **www.agra.org.uk**

Bank of England, Archive Section, Threadneedle Street, London EC2R 8AH,
telephone 020 7601 4889

Birth Link, Family Care, 21 Castle Street, Edinburgh EH2 3DN, Scotland

Borthwick Institute of Historical Research, St Anthony's Hall, Peasholme Green,
York YO1 2PW, telephone 01904 642315, website **www.york.ac.uk/inst/bihr**

British Isles Family History Service Centre, Genealogical Society of Utah,
185 Penns Lane, Sutton Coldfield, West Midlands B76 8JU, telephone 0121 384 2028

British Library, 96 Euston Road, St Pancras, London NW1 2DB, website **www.bl.uk**
Reader admissions office: 020 7412 7677
Enquiries regarding Electoral Registers: 020 7412 7536
General reader services enquiries: 020 7412 7676

British Library Oriental and India Office Collections, 96 Euston Road, St Pancras,
London NW1 2DB, telephone 020 7412 7873, fax 020 7412 7641,
email **oic-enquiries@bl.uk**, website **www.bl.uk/collections**

Capital Taxes Office, Ferrers House, PO Box 38, Castle Meadow Road, Nottingham
NG2 1BB, telephone 0115 874 0000

Census Help Desk, PO Box 1901, Malvern, Worcestershire WR14 3YB, telephone
01684 585298/585299, email **support@censushelpdesk.co.uk**, fax 01684 585372

Church of Jesus Christ of Latter-day Saints (LDS), website **www.familysearch.org**
see also British Isles Family History Service Centre, Hyde Park Family History
Centre, LDS Distribution Centre

Corporation of London Guildhall Library, Aldermanbury, London EC2P 2EJ,
telephone 020 7332 1862/3, email **Manuscripts.Guildhall@ms.corpoflondon.gov.uk**

Decree Absolute Search Section *see* Principal Registry of the Family Division

Family Records Centre, 1 Myddelton Street, London EC1R 1UW,
telephone 020 8392 5300, fax 020 8392 5307, email **enquiry@pro.gov.uk**,
website **www.familyrecords.gov.uk**
Certificate enquiries: telephone 0870 243 7788, fax 01704 550013,
email **certificate.services@ons.gov.uk**
Scottish Link: telephone 020 7533 6438
Group visits: telephone 020 8392 5300
Security/disabled parking: telephone 020 7533 6436

Federation of Family History Societies (FFHS), The Federation Administrator, PO Box 2425, Coventry CV5 6YX, email **info@ffhs.org.uk**, website **www.ffhs.org.uk** *see also* FFHS (Publications) Limited

FFHS (Publications) Limited, Units 15–16, Chesham Industrial Centre, Oram Street, Bury, Lancashire BL9 6EN, telephone 0161 797 3843, email **sales@ffhs.org.uk**, website **www.familyhistorybooks.co.uk**

Finders Keepers, PO Box 229, Great Missenden, Bucks HP16 0YD

General Register Office for England and Wales, PO Box 2, Southport, Merseyside PR8 2JD, telephone 0870 243 7788, email **certificate.services@ons.gov.uk**, fax 01704 560958, enquiries 01704 550013, website **www.statistics.gov.uk**
Adoptions Section: GRO, Smedley Hydro, Southport, Merseyside PR8 2HH, telephone 0151 471 4830
Overseas Section: GRO, PO Box 2, Southport, Merseyside PR8 2JD, telephone 0151 471 4801, email **overseas.gro@ons.gov.uk**

General Register Office for Scotland, New Register House, Edinburgh EH1 3YT, telephone 0131 334 0380, email **nrh.gros@gt.net.gov.uk**

General Register Office (Northern Ireland), Oxford House, 49–55 Chichester Street, Belfast BT1 4HL, telephone 028 9025 2000, website **www.groni.gov.uk**

General Register Office of Ireland, 8–11 Lombard Street East, Dublin 2, Ireland, telephone 003531 6354000, website **www.groireland.ie**

Genealogical Society of Utah (GSU), *see* British Isles Family History Service Centre

Genealogical Society of Victoria, Australia, website **www.gsv.org.au**

Guernsey Greffe, Royal Court House, St Peter Port, Guernsey GY1 2PB, telephone 01481 725277, fax 01481 715097, email **HM_Greffier@court1.guernsey.gov.uk**

Guild of One-Name Studies (GOONS), The Secretary, Box G, Society of Genealogists, 14 Charterhouse Buildings, Goswell Road, London EC1M 7BA, email **guild@one-name.org**, website **www.one-name.org**

Guildhall Library *see* Corporation of London Guildhall Library

House of Lords Record Office, House of Lords, London SW1A 0PW, telephone 020 7219 3074, email **hlro@parliament.uk**

Huguenot Society Library, University College London, Gower Street, London WC1E 6BT, telephone 020 7679 7094, email **ucylswm@ucl.ac.uk**, website **www.ucl.ac.uk/UCL-Info/Divisions/Library/huguenot.htm**

Hyde Park Family History Centre, 64–68 Exhibition Road, London SW7 2PA, telephone 020 7589 8561, fax 020 7823 8047, website **www.familysearch.org**

Isle of Man Civil Registry, Registries Building, Deemsters Walk, Bucks Road, Douglas, Isle of Man IM1 3AR, telephone 01624 687038, fax 01624 685296, website **www.gov.im/**

Jersey Judicial Greffe, States Building, 10 Royal Square, St Helier, Jersey, Channel Islands, telephone 01534 502335, email **jgreff@super.net.uk**, fax 01534 502399, website **www.jersey.gov.uk**

LDS Distribution Centre, 399 Garretts Lane, Sheldon, Birmingham B33 0UH, telephone 0121 785 2200 or 08700 102051

London Metropolitan Archives, 40 Northampton Road, London EC1R 0HB, telephone 020 7332 3820, email **ask.lma@corpoflondon.gov.uk**, website **www.cityoflondon.gov.uk**

Manchester District Probate Registry, 9th Floor, Astley House, 23 Quay Street, Manchester M3 4AT, telephone 0161 834 4319

National Archives, Ireland, Bishop Street, Dublin 8, Ireland, telephone 003531 4072300, email **mail@nationalarchives.ie**, website **www.nationalarchives.ie**

National Archives of Scotland, HM General Register House, Edinburgh EH1 3YY, telephone 0131 535 1314, email **research@nas.gov.uk**, website **www.nas.gov.uk**

National Library of Wales, Department of Manuscripts and Records, Aberystwyth SY23 3BU, telephone 01970 632800, email **ymh.lc@llgc.org.uk**, website **www.llgc.org.uk/**

National Organisation for Counselling Adoptees and their Parents (NORCAP), 112 Church Road, Wheatley, Oxfordshire OX33 1LU, telephone 01865 875000, email **enquiries@norcap.org**, fax 01865 875686, website **www.norcap.org.uk**

Personal Searches and Copies Department, York Probate Sub-Registry, Duncombe Place, York YO1 7EA, telephone 01904 624210, fax 01904 671782

Principal Registry of the Family Division, First Avenue House, 42–49 High Holborn, London WC1V 6NP
Probate Searchroom: telephone 020 7947 7022, website **www.courtservice.gov.uk/wills_probate/probate_famhist.htm**
Decree Absolute Search Section: telephone 020 7947 7017

Probate Searchroom *see* Principal Registry of the Family Division

Public Record Office, Ruskin Avenue, Kew, Richmond, Surrey TW9 4DU, telephone 020 8876 3444, website **www.pro.gov.uk**
Enquiries and advance ordering of documents (with exact references only): telephone 020 8392 5200, fax 020 8392 5286, email **enquiry@pro.gov.uk**
Special productions: 020 8392 5259
Census help desk: telephone 020 8392 5200, fax 020 8392 5286, email **1901census@pro.gov.uk**, website **www.census.pro.gov.uk**

Public Record Office of Northern Ireland, 66 Balmoral Avenue, Belfast BT9 6NY, Northern Ireland, telephone 028 9025 5905, fax 028 9025 5999, email **proni@dcalni.gov.uk**, website **http://proni.nics.gov.uk**

Religious Society of Friends Library, Friends House, 173–177 Euston Road, London NW1 2BJ, telephone 020 7663 1135, email **library@quaker.org.uk**, website **www.quaker.org.uk**

Royal Commission on Historical Manuscripts, Quality House, Quality Court, Chancery Lane, London WC2A 1HP, telephone 020 7242 1198, email **nra@hmc.gov.uk**, fax 020 7831 3550, website **www.hmc.gov.uk/archon**

Society of Genealogists, 14 Charterhouse Buildings, Goswell Road, London EC1M 7BA, telephone 020 7251 8799, fax 020 7250 1800, email **library@sog.org.uk**, website **www.sog.org.uk**

TALKadoption, freephone 0808 808 1234, website **www.talkadoption.org.uk**

Other useful websites featured in this book include:

Search engine
www.google.com

Portals
www.familia.org.uk
www.genuki.org.uk
 www.genuki.org.uk/indexes/SurnamesList.html
 www.genuki.org.uk/big/eng/RegOffice
www.cyndislist.com
www.Ancestry.com
http://rootsweb.com
 http://freebmd.rootsweb.com
 http://freecen.rootsweb.com
www.cwgc.org
www.englishorigins.com
www.scotsorigins.com
www.cheshirebmd.org.uk
www.archives.ca

UK telephone directory
www.bt.com/index.jsp

Maps
http://uk.multimap.com

National Gazetteer of Wales
www.gazetteer-wales.co.uk

Bibliography

Ancestors (PRO/Wharncliffe Publishing, bimonthly, April/May 2001–)

A–Z Geographers' London Atlas (Sevenoaks, 1995)

The A to Z of Georgian London (1747; Harry Margary, Lympne Castle, 1981)

The A to Z of Regency London (3rd edn 1813; Harry Margary, Lympne Castle, in association with the Guildhall Library, 1985)

The A to Z of Victorian London (1888; Harry Margary, Lympne Castle, and the London Topographical Society, 1987)

J. G. Bartholomew, *The Survey Gazetteer of the British Isles* (3 vols, London, 1904)

I. A. Baxter, *India Office Library and Records: A Brief Guide to Biographical Sources* (London, 2nd edn 1990)

A. Bevan, *Tracing Your Ancestors in the Public Record Office* (PRO, 6th edn 2002)

R. Blatchford, *The Family and Local History Handbook* (York, 6th edn 2002)

M. E. Bryant Rosier, comp., *Index to Parishes in Phillimore's Marriages* (Ramsey, Huntingdon, 4th edn 2000)

A. J. Camp, *Sources for Irish Genealogy in the Library of the Society of Genealogists* (SoG, 2nd edn 1998)

P. Christian, *The Genealogist's Internet* (PRO, 2001)

P. W. Coldham, *American Wills and Administrations in the Prerogative Court of Canterbury, 1610–1857* (Baltimore, 1989)

P. W. Coldham, *American Wills proved in London, 1611–1775* (Baltimore, 1992)

J. Cole and R. Church, *In and around record repositories in Great Britain and Ireland* (Ramsey, Huntingdon, 4th edn 1998)

S. Colwell, *Dictionary of Genealogical Sources in the Public Record Office* (London, 1992)

Computers in Genealogy (SoG, quarterly, 1982–)

The Dictionary of National Biography (Oxford, 1900–)

Family History Monthly (Sept/Oct 1995–)

Family History News and Digest (half-yearly, Sept 1977–)

The Family Record (quarterly, Jan 2001–), formerly *The Family Records Centre Newsletter* (Jan 1997 to Autumn 2000); to subscribe to the electronic version, email **FRC-Newsletter @pro.gov.uk**

Family Tree Magazine (monthly, 1984–, some early issues bimonthly)

S. Fowler and W. Spencer, *Army Records for Family Historians* (PRO, 2nd edn revised and updated by W. Spencer, 1998)

M. Gandy, *Catholic Missions and Registers, 1700–1880* (London, 1993), *Vol. 1: London and the Home Counties, Vol. 2: The Midlands and East Anglia, Vol. 3: Wales and the West of England, Vol. 4: North East England, Vol. 5: North West England, Vol. 6: Scotland*

M. Gandy, *Catholic Parishes in England, Wales and Scotland, An Atlas* (London, 1993)

Genealogists' Magazine (SoG, quarterly April 1925–)

J. Gibson, *Bishops' Transcripts and Marriage Licences: A Guide to their Location and Indexes* (FFHS, 4th edn 1997)
J. Gibson, *Probate Jurisdictions: Where to Look for Wills* (FFHS, 4th edn 1994, reprinted 1997)
J. Gibson and E. Hampson, *Census Returns, 1841–1891, on Microform: a directory to local holdings in Great Britain, Channel Islands, Isle of Man* (FFHS, 6th edn 1994, reprinted 1997)
J. Gibson and E. Hampson, *Marriage and Census Indexes for Family Historians* (FFHS, 8th edn 2000)
J. Gibson and M. Medlycott, *Local Census Listings, 1522–1930, Holdings in the British Isles* (FFHS, 3rd edn 1997)
J. Gibson and P. Peskett, *Record Offices: How to Find Them* (FFHS, 9th edn 2002)
J. Gibson and C. Rogers, *Poor Law Union Records*, Part 1 (with C. Webb): *South East and East Anglia* (FFHS, 2nd edn 1997), Part 2: *The Midlands and Northern England* (2nd edn 1997), Part 3: *South West England, The Marches and Wales* (2nd edn 2000), Part 4 (with F. A. Youngs): *Gazetteer of England and Wales* (2nd edn 1997)
J. Grenham, *Tracing your Irish Ancestors: The Complete Guide* (Dublin, 2nd edn 1999)
H. E. P. Grieve, *Examples of English Handwriting 1150–1750* (Essex Record Office Publications, 1954, 5th impression 1981)
Guildhall Library Research Guide 2: The British Overseas (Guildhall Library, 3rd revised edn 1994)
H. B. Guppy, *Home of Family Names in Great Britain* (London, 1890, reprinted 1968)
P. Hanks and F. Hodges, *A Dictionary of Surnames* (Oxford, 1988, reprinted with corrections, 1996)
D. T. Hawkings, *Index to Somerset Estate Duty Office Wills and Letters of Administration, 1805–1811* (Weston-super-Mare, 1995)
D. T. Hawkings, *Index to Somerset Estate Duty Office Wills, 1812–1857* (2 vols, Weston-super-Mare, 1995)
M. Herber, *Clandestine Marriages in the Chapel and Rules of the Fleet Prison, 1680–1754* (3 vols, London, 1998–2001)
J. Herlihy, *The Royal Irish Constabulary: A Complete Alphabetical List of Officers and Men, 1816–1922* (Dublin, 1999)
D. Hey, *Family Names and Family History* (London, 2000)
J. Houston, ed., *Index of cases in the records of the Court of Arches in Lambeth Palace Library, 1660–1913* (Chichester, 1972)
C. R. Humphery-Smith, ed., *The Phillimore Atlas and Index of Parish Registers* (Chichester, 2nd edn 1995)
K. A. Johnson and M. R. Sainty, eds, *Genealogical Research Directory, National and International* (Sydney, annual 1981–)
T. J. Kemp, *International Vital Records Handbook* (Baltimore, 4th edn 2000)
R. Kershaw, *Emigrants and Expats* (PRO, 2002)
R. Kershaw and M. Pearsall, *Immigrants and Aliens* (PRO, 2000)
S. Lewis, *Topographical Dictionary of Wales* (London, 3rd edn 1843)
S. Lumas, *Making Use of the Census* (PRO, 4th edn 2002)
O. Mason, comp., *Bartholomew Gazetteer of Places in Britain* (Edinburgh, 2nd edn 1986)
R. A. McKinley, *A History of British Surnames* (Harlow, 1990)
H. Meller, *London Cemeteries, An Illustrated Guide and Gazetteer* (Brookfield, Vermont, 3rd edn 1994)

T. J. Morgan and P. Morgan, *Welsh Surnames* (Cardiff, 1985, 1989)
L. Munby, *Reading Tudor and Stuart Handwriting* (Chichester, 1988)
N. J. N. Newington-Irving, *Will Indexes and Other Probate Material in the Library of the Society of Genealogists* (SoG, 1996)
J. A. Newport, comp., *An Index to Civil Registration Districts of England and Wales, 1837 to date* (Peter Pledger, Selsey, 1989)
Practical Family History (monthly, June/July 1997–)
Public Record Office, *Pocket Guides to Family History* series. Titles include *Getting Started in Family History, Tracing Catholic Ancestors, Tracing Irish Ancestors, Tracing Nonconformist Ancestors, Tracing Scottish Ancestors, Using Army Records, Using Birth, Marriage and Death Records, Using Census Returns, Using Criminal Records, Using Navy Records, Using Poor Law Records* and *Using Wills.*
S. A. Raymond, *British Family History on CD* (FFHS, 2001)
S. A. Raymond, *Family History on the Web, An Internet Directory for England and Wales* (FFHS, 2000)
S. A. Raymond, *Irish Family History on the Web, A Directory* (FFHS, 2001)
P. H. Reaney and R. M. Wilson, *A Dictionary of English Surnames* (London, 3rd corrected edn 1991)
Record Repositories in Great Britain (PRO, 11th edn 1999)
N. A. M. Rodger, *Naval Records for Genealogists* (PRO, 2nd edn 1998)
M. Scott, *Prerogative Court of Canterbury Wills and Other Probate Records* (PRO, 1997)
G. Shaw and A. Tipper, *British Directories, A Bibliography and Guide to Directories Published in England and Wales, 1850–1950, Scotland, 1773–1950* (London, 2nd edn 1997)
D. Shorney, *Protestant Nonconformity and Roman Catholicism, A guide to sources in the Public Record Office* (PRO, 1996)
K. Smith, C. T. Watts and M. J. Watts, *Records of Merchant Shipping and Seamen* (PRO, 1998)
Society of Genealogists, *Index to the Bank of England Will Extracts 1807–1845* (SoG, 1991)
Society of Genealogists, *A List of Parishes in Boyd's Marriage Index* (SoG, 1994)
Society of Genealogists, *Parish Register Copies in the Library of the Society of Genealogists* (SoG, 11th edn 1995)
W. Spencer, *Air Force Records for Family Historians* (PRO, 2000)
W. Spencer, *Army Service Records of the First World War* (PRO, 3rd expanded edn 2001)
D. J. Steel, *National Index of Parish Registers, Vol. 2: Sources for Nonconformist Genealogy and Family History* (Chichester, 1973, reprinted 1980)
D. J. Steel, *National Index of Parish Registers, Vol. 3: Sources for Roman Catholic and Jewish Genealogy and Family History* (Chichester, 1974). This also contains the Index to vols 1–3 (various editors for county vols, 1966–)
D. Stuart, *Latin for Local and Family Historians* (Chichester, 1995)
Sir Arthur Vicars, ed., *Index to the Prerogative Wills of Ireland, 1536–1810* (1897, reprinted Baltimore, 1967)
P. Wolfston, comp., revised by C. Webb, *Greater London Cemeteries and Crematoria* (London, 6th edn 1999)

Index